D1555604

*Freethought
in the
United Kingdom
and the
Commonwealth*

Freethought in the United Kingdom and the Commonwealth

A Descriptive Bibliography

GORDON STEIN

GREENWOOD PRESS

Westport, Connecticut • London, England

Library of Congress Cataloging in Publication Data

Stein, Gordon.
    Freethought in the United Kingdom and the Common-
wealth.

    Includes indexes.
    1.   Free thought--Commonwealth of Nations--
Bibliography.   I.   Title.
Z7765.S83   [BL2747.5]   016.211'0941   80-1792
ISBN 0-313-20869-7 (lib. bdg.)

Library of Congress Catalog Card Number: 80-1792
ISBN: 0-313-20869-7

First published in 1981

Greenwood Press
A division of Congressional Information Service, Inc.
88 Post Road West, Westport, Connecticut 06881

Printed in the United States of America

10 9 8 7 6 5 4 3 2 1

CONTENTS

PREFACE   vii
ACKNOWLEDGMENTS   xi
INTRODUCTION   xiii

1   The Rise and Decline of British Deism (1624-1760)   3
2   From Thomas Paine to the Start of the National Secular Society
    (1760-1860)   21
3   The Bradlaugh/Besant/Foote Era (1860-1915)   53
4   Freethought After Foote (1915-present)   99

APPENDICES   121
    I   Freethought in New Zealand   123
    II   Freethought in Australia   129
    III   Freethought in Canada   137
    IV   Freethought in India   143
    V   Freethought in Other Commonwealth Countries   153
    VI   Library Collections on British/Commonwealth Freethought   157
    VII   Theses/Dissertations and Works in Progress on British/
          Commonwealth Freethought   161

ADDENDA   165
GLOSSARY OF TERMS   167
AUTHOR AND PERSON INDEX   169
TITLE INDEX   177
SUBJECT INDEX   191

PREFACE

The term "freethought" is no longer one that has a clear meaning to most people. In this book the term is used in its narrow sense of thought that is free of the assumptions of religious dogma. It therefore includes atheism, rationalism, secularism, deism, agnosticism, and humanism. The freethought movement was organized mainly by people who felt that religion had done great harm in the world and that something ought to be done to fight its influence. The freethought movement, then, was a movement in opposition to organized religion. In the West (and especially in the United Kingdom and the British Commonwealth), freethought was primarily opposed to the leading religion of those areas, namely Christianity. It would follow, however, that freethought in India, for example, would be mainly opposed to Hinduism (which it is), while freethought in other areas would also have as its primary target whichever local religion was the most popular.

Freethinkers have always supported the concept of freedom of religion. This, however, also includes *their* personal right to have freedom *from* religion for themselves. Other ideas that freethinkers have historically supported have been freedom of the press, free speech, the separation of church and state, and a democratic form of government. The publications of the freethought movement have been among the first to advocate such ideas as birth control, the end of slavery, public education, and the idea of biological evolution. Individual freethinkers may have sometimes opposed one or more of these ideas (especially birth control), yet still remained within the good graces of the freethought movement.

The present book attempts to tell the history of the freethought movement in the United Kingdom and in the British Commonwealth largely through the publications of that movement. It is not simply a bibliography, however. The freethought movement had mainly a propaganda and educational function, and this was primarily done through its publishing activities. Therefore, it is possible to tell most of its history by discussing its publications. Personalities and events important in freethought history are also discussed.

The plan of this book is similar to that of its earlier companion volume, *Freethought in the United States* (Westport, Conn.: Greenwood Press, 1978). Although there is no definitive history of freethought in the United Kingdom, this book does not attempt to serve as one. Rather, it is a guidebook through the complex maze of a previously uncharted area of publishing. As such, it should prove interesting and useful to those future investigators who attempt to examine more fully an area of British history which is well worth further study. Only a small part of the workings of the movement have ever been examined in detail by historians. Perhaps this book will also increase interest in freethought as a legitimate subdivision of the fields of intellectual and social history.

The book is organized chronologically. The introduction discusses other reference works that cover the field of freethought to some extent. The first chapter then examines deism and its antecedents, covering roughly the period from 1624 to 1760. The second chapter discusses the period from 1760 to 1860, the time of Thomas Paine, Richard Carlile and George Jacob Holyoake. The third chapter covers the "Golden Age of Freethought," the Bradlaugh/Besant/Foote era from 1860 to 1915. The fourth chapter covers the period from 1915 until the present.

A series of appendices review the history of freethought in such Commonwealth countries as New Zealand, Australia, Canada and India. A guide to freethought collections in libraries is followed by a listing of unpublished theses and dissertations relating to freethought. A glossary and author, title, and subject indexes conclude the book.

In addition to identifying important works which deal with freethought, the book attempts to describe and evaluate them. The publications are placed within the context of the field of freethought as a whole. This book, however, is not designed to eliminate the need to consult the books described. Rather, it is a guide through the tangle of small, short-lived publishers, obscure authors, and scattered library holdings.

Within each chapter there are two distinct but interrelated sections: the narration and the bibliography. Hence, those who are interested solely in the bibliography need not plow through unneeded history, while those interested only in the descriptive aspects need not be distracted by complex citations. Of necessity, some titles do appear in the narrative. Titles are assigned a number alphabetically in each section, by the author's last name. The numbering is consecutive, starting with the introduction. In the bibliography section of each chapter, all the titles cited for the first time in that section appear in numerical sequence. Items cited earlier appear in the bibliography section of the chapter in which they were first cited, in their proper numerical order. Many entries are annotated.

A large number of the books listed in the bibliography have had more than one edition. To list all the editions for each entry would be beyond the scope of the bibliography. Therefore, in most cases only the first edition is listed. Occasionally, when it is felt that circumstances merit it, the first British and the first American edition are listed, or the first edition in English is added when the book was published initially in a foreign language.

This work is not intended to be an exhaustive listing of all the free-thought books, magazines and pamphlets ever published which relate to the United Kingdom or the Commonwealth (there were many thousands). Rather, it concentrates upon the important or "seminal" books. From that beginning, it should be fairly easy for anyone who wishes to do so to identify many of the other freethought publications not thought important enough to include in the present volume.

Some limitations have had to be made on the types of materials included or discussed. The definitions (see glossary) will indicate how the terms important in the field are being used. All publications whose primary aim was political, and not antireligious or freethought have been excluded. Many of these publications were socialist, anarchist, libertarian, or communist in orientation. Even though they were hostile towards religion (when they mentioned it), such books are already included in existing bibliographies. On the other hand, a number of titles have been included whose primary aim was historical or philo-sophical scholarship (and not the promulgation of freethought *per se*) on the grounds that they were not promoting another system of fixed beliefs (political, social or economic). Periodicals have not been included when their chief concern was the exposition of such political/economic systems as anarchism, libertarianism, socialism, or communism. In the case of some of the early New Zealand and Australian periodicals, however, this rule had to be bent since these periodicals were *both* freethought and spiritualist. In the case of India, almost all rules have had to be bent slightly. Indian freethought in the past 100 years has been intimately involved in the anticaste, nationalist and sociopolitical realms. The exact combinations involved have been specified whenever possible.

In a work involving as broad a historical and geographical scope as the present volume, mistakes are bound to escape unnoticed. Although each factual statement and date has been checked several times, errors are still possible. It would be greatly appreciated if any errors are brought to my attention.

Gordon Stein, Ph.D.

ACKNOWLEDGMENTS

Over the years, many people and institutions helped me in the preparation of this book. Although this list is not complete, I would like to thank the following institutions and people. First the institutions: The British Museum Library, Columbia University Library, Dr. Williams' Library, Harvard University Library, Henry Huntington Library, The Indian Rationalist Society, The Indian Secular Society, The Library of Congress, Lilly Library at Indiana University, The Manchester Cooperative Union Library, The National Secular Society, The New York Public Library, The New Zealand Rationalist Association, The Newberry Library, The Northwestern University Library, The Ohio State University Library, The Rationalist Press Association, The South Place Ethical Society, The Southern Illinois University Library, The University of Chicago Library, The University of Michigan Library, The University of Wisconsin Library, The Wesleyan University Library, and the Yale University Library.

Among the individuals, I would especially like to thank Jack Benjamin, David Berman, Bruce Breeze, Marshall Brown, M. S. Casie Chetty, David Collis, G. N. Deodekar, Constance Dowman, Gabriel Dubuisson, Eva Ebury, H. W. Edwards, John Gilmour, Jayagopal, J. F. C. Harrison, Jim Herrick, Michael Katanka, Bernard LaRiviere, Lavanam, Ralph McCoy, William McIlroy, Ian MacKinnon, Russell Maylone, Robert W. Morrell, Kit Mouat, Victor E. Neuburg, Harry H. Pearce, Edward Royle, A. B. Shah, Nathan Simons, Nigel Sinnott, George H. Smith, Barbara Smoker, A. Solomon, David Tribe, J. Trower, Nicolas Walter, Erwin Welsch, and Joel Wiener.

INTRODUCTION

The history of freethought in the United Kingdom includes the history of several separate movements, all working, at various periods of time, for the same general goals. These goals were freedom of thought in religious matters and a decrease in the amount of influence that organized religion had over the minds of men and the policies of government. Among the movements that participated in this common struggle were the deists, the secularists, the agnostics, the free-thinkers, the rationalists, the atheists, the positivists, the humanists, the Ethical Culturists, and, to an extent, the Unitarians.

There have been attempts to write histories of freethought in the United Kingdom. John M. Robertson's two two-volume works, *A History of Freethought, Ancient and Modern, to the Period of the French Revolution* (32) and *A History of Freethought in the Nineteenth Century* (33), contain detailed coverage of British freethought. While these two works are admirable, even amazing, in what they attempt and in what they actually do realize, they deal mostly with the development and maturation of a *thought process*, or mental outlook, which we can call "free thought." They do not deal much with the development of freethought organizations, publications, or personalities except as they reflect directly upon the development of that mental outlook. Robertson's books, although filled with footnotes citing authors and titles of sources, could not really be called "descriptive bibliographies," as the citations are both incomplete and secondary to the purpose of the works.

John Edwin McGee in his often overlooked *A History of the British Secular Movement* (21) comes closest to what the present work attempts to do. McGee gives a good summary of the history of the secular movement only in England from about 1850 to 1922 (with some coverage to 1945). There is an extensive list of books (a "bibliography" would not be an accurate term), at the end of the work, but the majority of these works are never cited in the text. Also, only the author, title and date of each publication is given. This makes the list (which McGee entitles "bibliography") virtually useless as a bibliography. McGee's work was printed as a large pamphlet on newsprint by E. Haldeman-Julius. True, this was Haldeman-Julius' normal printing style, but it has not helped increase the availability of copies of the work in library collections. Useful for dating events and as a supplement to other histories is G. H. Taylor's pamphlet *A Chronology of British Secularism* (41).

John M. Robertson's *Courses of Study* (30) went through three different editions. It is really a descriptive bibliography, although it is marred by incomplete citations and by an attempt to cover too large a field of knowledge. *Courses of Study* is not about freethought or its history. Rather, it attempts to give the reader a listing and evaluation of the most important books in various areas, such as the history of religion, philosophy, history, economics, and other fields. It really reflects Robertson's own wide reading and interests.

David Tribe's *100 Years of Freethought* (43) is a good general history of freethought from about 1850 to 1950. It emphasizes Britain but also covers several other countries briefly. It has two pages of "selected bibliography," that do not accurately reflect the numerous research sources used in the book. There are no footnotes or references, although the titles and dates of publications mentioned or quoted in the text are given in parentheses. The book is fine as far as it goes, but it is by no means a descriptive bibliography.

Susan Budd's *Varieties of Unbelief* (7) covers the part of the Victorian Age in which there was the greatest development of organized freethought in England. Although the book does have a few minor errors, it is well worth consulting. There are notes and references.

Edward Royle's *Victorian Infidels* (35) is very thorough and readable in its coverage of the 1840 to 1865 period of British freethought. Its limited coverage, as well as the fact that it is not a bibliography, makes it different from the present volume. Royle's book does have extensive notes and a good bibliography. A second volume, continuing the chronological coverage of the first book from the period 1866 to 1915, has also been published. It is entitled *Radicals, Secularists and Republicans* (34). Its format is similar to that of the first volume.

Charles Watts' *History of Freethought* (also published under the title *Freethought: Its Rise, Progress and Triumph*) (47) is a brief history, covering other countries in addition to England. It has no references or bibliography.

Fritz Mauthner's *Der Atheismus und seine Geschichte im Abendland* (22) is a massive four-volume work that covers the history of atheism in the West from ancient times. It is written in a typically prolix style and often wanders off the subject at hand. There is much on the deists, but little on the nineteenth-century British radical freethinkers, such as Bradlaugh. The work has never been translated into English.

Only Robertson's (32) and Mauthner's (22) works cover the deist movement at all. There are, however, several other books which concentrate solely on British deism. Among these are Robertson's *The Dynamics of Religion* (31), John Orr's *English Deism: Its Roots and Its Fruits* (25), and G. Lechler's *Geschichte der englischen Deismus* (16). There is also a long article by Friedrich Brie called "Deismus and Atheismus in der englischen Renaissance" (5) which covers the early period. Edouard Sayous' *Les Déistes Anglais* (36) also covers the period from 1696 to 1738.

There are a few biographies or autobiographies of leading free-thinkers which are written on such a scale that they provide an important insight into the entire freethought movement at the time at which their subject lived. Among these are David Tribe's *President Charles Bradlaugh, M. P.* (44), Arthur Nethercot's *The First Five Lives of Annie Besant* (24), Hypatia Bradlaugh Bonner and J. M. Robertson's *Charles Bradlaugh: A Record of His Life and Work* (4), Joseph McCabe's *Life and Letters of George Jacob Holyoake* (19), and Lee Grugel's *George Jacob Holyoake: A Study In the Evolution of a Victorian Radical* (15). Joseph McCabe also reveals much about the workings of the freethought movement in his autobiography, *Eighty Years a Rebel* (18).

There have been a number of bibliographies dealing with aspects of British freethought or with British freethinkers. For example, a published *Catalogue of the Library of the Rationalist Press Association* (27) has been issued. There was also a published *Catalogue of the Library of the Late Charles Bradlaugh* (3). It was really an auction catalog, as all the items were for sale. Another series of catalogs were the ten printed catalogs of the former freethought bookseller, David Collis (8), issued from 1969 to about 1971. These are valuable for the important bibliographical information they contain. J. M. Robertson's and G. W. Foote's extensive libraries were both sold at auction after they died. The printed catalogs issued were Hodgson's Number 14 (April 26, 1933) for Robertson's sale (29) and Dobell Number 251 (February 1916) for the Foote sale (10). There was also a *Catalogue of Books from the Library of the Late Edward Truelove* (46), produced in 1900 by the executors of his estate.

Several important author bibliographies of British freethinkers also exist. One is C. W. F. Goss' *A Descriptive Bibliography of George Jacob Holyoake, With a Brief Sketch of His Life* (13). Another is

Theodore Besterman's *A Bibliography of Annie Besant* (2), unfortunately not as thorough as one might wish. Gordon Stein's *Robert G. Ingersoll: A Checklist* (38) lists many British editions of the popular American freethinker's works. Thomas Paine can be considered a British free-thinker (although a good case can also be made for considering him an American). There is a published bibliography of the editions of his book *Common Sense* by Richard Gimbel, called *Thomas Paine: A Bibliographical Checklist of Common Sense* (12), as well as the catalog of *The Thomas Paine Collection of Richard Gimbel in the Library of the American Philosophical Society* (40). There is also a bibliography of Robert Owen (23).

There are two published catalogs of early deistic works, both of which include extensive coverage of British deism. These are J. A. Trinius' *Freydenker Lexicon* (45), which covers deistic works in all languages until 1765, and *The McAlpin Collection of British History and Theology* (11), compiled by Charles Ripley Gillett. It lists the books in the deism collection at the Union Theological Seminary of New York published until the year 1700.

There are two books which might be viewed as early attempts at a bibliography of the atheist (actually mostly *anti*-atheist) literature, and of the deist (actually mostly *anti*deist) literature. The anti-atheist and antideist literature is reviewed in John Albert Fabricius' *Delectus Argumentorum et Syllabus Scriptorum qui Veritatum Religionis Christianae Adversus Atheos, Epicureos Deistas seu Naturalistas, Idololatras, Judaeos et Muhammedanos Lucubrationibus suis Asseruerunt* (9). The deist literature of Anthony Collins, Matthew Tindal, and John Toland, along with all the responses to their writings, is discussed at great length in Urban G. Thorschmid's *Versuch einer vollständigen engelländischen Freydenker-Bibliothek* (42). Of course, the early date of this work (1765–67) limits its usefulness in many ways. It also has some advantages, in that many of the ephemeral answers to these deists are recorded here. Copies of many of these responses are no longer in existence.

Two general biographical dictionaries dealing only with freethinkers and rationalists should be mentioned. They are Joseph McCabe's *Biographical Dictionary of Modern Rationalists* (17), with many British entries, and Joseph Mazzini Wheeler's *A Biographical Dictionary of Freethinkers of All Ages and Nations* (48). Joseph McCabe also compiled the only encyclopedia of rationalism, entitled *A Rationalist Encyclopedia* (20).

Several books that treat the term "rationalism" in a restricted sense and attempt to cover only the more "respectable" aspects of the subject, also exist. The most important among these are Alfred W. Benn's *The History of English Rationalism in the Nineteenth Century*

(1) and Leslie Stephen's *History of English Thought in the Eighteenth Century* (39). Both of these do not even mention such important rationalist freethinkers as Charles Bradlaugh, George Jacob Holyoake, or their deist predecessors.

The very earliest period of "atheism" in England is covered in George Buckley's *Atheism in the English Renaissance* (6), and in John Redwood's *Reason, Ridicule and Religion: The Age of Enlightenment in England, 1660–1750* (28).

There are also a few important histories of particular freethought organizations. S. Ratcliffe's *The Story of South Place* (26) deals with the history of the major Ethical Culture society in England. The history of the Ethical Culture movement as a whole in England is dealt with in Gustav Spiller's *The Ethical Movement in Great Britain* (37). Adam Gowans Whyte's *Story of the R.P.A.* (49) gives the history of the Rationalist Press Association from its founding in 1899. F. J. Gould's *The Pioneers of Johnson's Court* (14) is a fuller study of the origins of the RPA and of the people who started it.

BIBLIOGRAPHY

1. Benn, Alfred W. *The History of English Rationalism in the Nineteenth Century*. London: Longmans, Green & Co., 1906. Reprint. New York: Russell & Russell, 1962.

2. Besterman, Theodore. *A Bibliography of Annie Besant*. London: The Theosophical Society in England, 1924. Useful as far as it goes, but Besterman missed many titles and editions, especially of Besant's freethought publications.

3. Bonner, Hypatia Bradlaugh, ed. *Catalogue of the Library of the Late Charles Bradlaugh*. London: H. Bradlaugh Bonner, 1891. After his death, Bradlaugh's large library was sold to pay his debts. Part of the library was political in content, but a large part consisted of freethought books.

4. Bonner, Hypatia Bradlaugh, and Robertson, John M. *Charles Bradlaugh: A Record of His Life and Work*. 2 vols. London: T. Fisher Unwin, 1894. Although a bit defensive about some of Bradlaugh's actions, this work is still important. It contains much first-hand evidence about Bradlaugh's life. Most of it was written by his daughter, with a section on Bradlaugh's political career by his friend, J. M. Robertson.

5. Brie, Friedrich. "Deismus und Atheismus in der Englischen Renaissance." *Anglia: Zeitschrift für englische Philologie* 48 (1924): 54–98, 105–68.

6. Buckley, George T. *Atheism in the English Renaissance*.

Chicago: The University of Chicago, 1932. Reprint. New York: Russell & Russell, 1965.

7. Budd, Susan. *Varieties of Unbelief*. London: Heinemann Publications, 1977. A good treatment of Victorian Age freethought in England, although there are a few minor errors. Good bibliography and notes.

8. Collis, David, comp. *Catalogues 1–10*. Corby, England: David Collis, 1969–1971. A series of ten catalogs offering scarce freethought material for sale. Many of the books came from the libraries of Ambrose Barker, Herbert Cutner and Charles Bradlaugh Bonner. There is much high quality bibliographic description by Collis.

9. Fabricius, John Albert. *Delectus Argumentorum et Syllabus Scriptorum qui Veritatum Religionis Christianae Adversos Atheos, Epicureos, Deistas seu Naturalistas, Idololatras, Judaeos et Muhammedamos Lucubrationibus suis Asseruerunt*. Hamburg, Germany: Theodori Christopheri Felginer, 1725. Contains a section on books written against (and for) atheism, and a similar section about books against deism. Because of the early publication date, there are very few books *for* atheism listed.

10. (Foote, G. W.). *Catalogue of the Library of G. W. Foote*. London: P. J. & A. E. Dobell, 1916. This is Dobell's Catalogue #251 (February 1916). Much of the library related to Foote's great interest in literature.

11. Gillett, Charles Ripley, comp. *The McAlpin Collection of British History and Theology*. 5 vols. New York: For the Union Theological Seminary, 1927–1930. Very valuable for early deistic work published before 1700.

12. Gimbel, Richard. *Thomas Paine: A Bibliographical Checklist of Common Sense, With an Account of Its Publication*. New Haven, Conn.: Yale University Press, 1956.

13. Goss. C. W. F. *A Descriptive Bibliography of George Jacob Holyoake, With a Brief Sketch of His Life*. London: Crowther & Goodman, 1908. The "sketch" is by Holyoake's daughter, Emilie Holyoake Marsh. Very valuable as a guide to Holyoake's enormous number of publications.

14. Gould, F. J. *The Pioneers of Johnson's Court*. London: Watts & Co., 1929. A history and capsule biographies of the founders of the Rationalist Press Association.

15. Grugel, Lee. *George Jacob Holyoake: A Study in the Evolution of a Victorian Radical*. Philadelphia: Porcupine Press, 1977. An abridgement of an excellent dissertation done at the University of Chicago.

16. Lechler, Gotthard V. *Geschichte des englischen Deismus*.

Stuttgart, Germany: Cotta'scher Verlag, 1841, Although it has never been translated into English, this work has been republished recently in Germany. It is well done, and still valuable as a study of the English deists.

17. McCabe, Joseph. *A Biographical Dictionary of Modern Rationalists*. London: Watts & Co., 1920. A very useful publication. An abridged and updated version was published by Haldeman-Julius Publications (Girard, Kansas, 1945) under the title *Biographical Dictionary of Ancient, Medieval and Modern Freethinkers* (see #490).

18. McCabe, Joseph. *Eighty Years a Rebel*. Girard, Kansas: Haldeman-Julius Publications, 1947. Virtually the only source to date about the life of this important freethinker and author.

19. McCabe, Joseph, *The Life and Letters of George Jacob Holyoake*. 2 vols. London: Watts & Co., 1908. Useful, although McCabe is sometimes too kind in his interpretations of Holyoake's motivations.

20. McCabe, Joseph. *A Rationalist Encyclopedia*. London: Watts & Co., 1950. Contains 1,800 articles on religion, history, etc.

21. McGee, John Edwin. *A History of the British Secular Movement*. Girard, Kansas: Haldeman-Julius Publications, 1948. Printed in the usual "Big Blue Book" format, including card covers and cheap newsprint paper, this work, though seriously flawed in several ways, is one of the best attempts at a readable yet well-researched history of British secularism. It covers the period from 1840 to 1922, with brief mention of events to 1945. An enormous list of authors and titles, masquerading as a "bibliography," follows the text. The work would have been better known and more appreciated had it not been printed in the format in which it was. Still, it is worth consulting.

22. Mauthner, Fritz. *Der Atheismus und seine Geschichte im Abendland*. 4 vols. Stuttgart & Berlin, Germany: Deutscher Verlags-Unstalt, 1922. Never translated into English, but recently reprinted. It is useful, although Mauthner is very verbose.

23. National Library of Wales. *A Bibliography of Robert Owen, the Socialist, 1771–1858*. Aberystwyth, Wales: National Library of Wales, 1925. This is the second edition, much enlarged. The first edition was published in 1914.

24. Nethercot, Arthur. *The First Five Lives of Annie Besant*. Chicago: The University of Chicago Press, 1960. This fine biography covers the first part of the life of the leading British women freethinker of the nineteenth century. It ends with her conversion to Theosophy. A second volume, *The Last Four Lives of Annie Besant* (same publisher, 1963) covers the rest of her life.

25. Orr, John. *English Deism: Its Roots and Its Fruits*. Grand

Rapids, Michigan: Wm. B. Eerdmans Publishing Co., 1934. Although written by a clergyman, this is a fair and even-handed treatment, probably the best existing introduction to English deism.

26. Ratcliffe, S. K. *The Story of South Place*. London: Watts & Co., 1955. A history of the most important British Ethical Culture Society.

27. Rationalist Press Association. *Catalogue of the Library of the Rationalist Press Association*. London: Watts & Co., 1937. There were earlier catalogs in mimeographed form. Many of the books listed were not freethought books, but rather on science, history and philosophy. Useful for identifying many of the RPA's own publications.

28. Redwood, John. *Reason, Ridicule and Religion: The Age of Enlightenment in England, 1660–1750*. London: Thames & Hudson, 1976.

29. (Robertson, John M.). *Catalogue of the Library of J. M. Robertson*. London: Hodgson's, 1933. Catalog #14 of the 1932–33 auction season. The sale occurred on April 26, 1933. Most of the books were sold very cheaply, even by the standards of that day. The catalog gives very little detail, often not even listing the titles of the freethought books, except as a lot.

30. Robertson, John Mackinnon. *Courses of Study*. London: Watts & Co., 1904 (first edition), 1908 (second edition), and 1932 (third edition). An impressive piece of work. Each "edition" is really an entirely different work; updated, rewritten and changed to reflect Robertson's increased knowledge as well as the needs and new publications of the times. The books are really Robertson's suggestions and comments upon the best books available in a number of fields of study, including religion (historical), philosophy, economics and history.

31. Robertson, John Mackinnon. *The Dynamics of Religion*. London: Watts & Co., 1926. This is the second edition. The first edition was published with the author using the pseudonym "M. W. Wiseman" (London: The University Press, 1897). Robertson admits the authorship in the second edition. The title is misleading, as the book is a history of deism in England.

32. Robertson, John Mackinnon. *A History of Freethought, Ancient and Modern, to the Period of the French Revolution*. 2 vols. London: Watts & Company, 1936. An absolutely essential book for the student of any area of freethought history, although Robertson's dense style takes time to read and appreciate. The book is fairly weak on U. S. freethought (there was little at this period about which to write), does not go into much detail about the organization of freethought, and neglects to mention freethought in India. Robertson takes the approach that "free thought" was a mental attitude. He traces the factors responsible for helping men achieve that state. The work is an

astounding piece of scholarship. It almost seems as if one man could not possibly have written it. The secret, if there is one, lies in the fact that these volumes are really the "fourth edition" of a work which was first published in 1899 as *A Short History of Freethought* (London: Swann, Sonnenschein). Reference (33) below is the other part of that "fourth edition."

33. Robertson, John Mackinnon. *A History of Freethought in the Nineteenth Century*. 2 vols. London: Watts & Company, 1929. The work was also issued as two volumes bound as one. It originally appeared as a series of separate pamphlets, each containing a section of the book. It was issued in such a way (probably for cost reasons) that if the covers of all the sections were removed and the contents bound together, a complete volume would result. The book is another essential reference for the student of freethought. Its faults are similar to the companion set above. In addition, it has weak sections on Canada, and nonexistent sections on India, Australia and New Zealand, and South Africa. Although this set was published seven years before reference (32), its coverage starts where that of reference (32) ends, permitting the two sets to be used as a single large reference history.

34. Royle, Edward. *Radicals, Secularists and Republicans: Popular Freethought in Britain, 1866–1915*. Manchester, England: Manchester University Press, 1980. A fine continuation of the author's *Victorian Infidels*, with much detail. Excellent bibliography and notes.

35. Royle, Edward. *Victorian Infidels*. Manchester, England: Manchester University Press, 1974. A very detailed and readable treatment of the 1840–1865 period in British freethought history. Excellent notes and bibliography.

36. Sayous, Edouard. *Les Déistes Anglais et le Christianisme Principalement depuis Toland jusqu'à Chubb (1696-1738)*. Paris: G. Fischbacher, 1882.

37. Spiller, Gustav. *The Ethical Movement in Great Britain: A Documentary History*. London: For the Author, [1934].

38. Stein, Gordon. *Robert G. Ingersoll: A Checklist*. Kent, Ohio: Kent State University Press, 1969. Lists many of the British editions of Ingersoll's works.

39. Stephen Leslie. *History of English Thought in the Eighteenth Century*. 2 vols. London: Smith, Elder & Co., 1876.

40. Stephans, Hildegard, comp. *The Thomas Paine Collection of Richard Gimbel in the Library of the American Philosophical Society*. Wilmington, Delaware: Scholarly Resources, 1976. A reproduction of the catalog cards of the largest Paine collection.

41. Taylor, G. H. *A Chronology of British Secularism*. London: The

National Secular Society, 1957. A pamphlet which is handy for checking the dates of various events important in freethought history or for seeing what happened in a given year. It covers the years 1840 to 1957.

42. Thorschmid, Urban Gottlob. *Versuch einer vollständigen engelländischen Freydenker-Bibliothek, in welcher den Schriften der englischen Freydenker die vortrefflichsten Schutzschriften für die christliche Religion und für die Geistlichen entgegengestellt werden.* Published in four volumes: Vol. 1: Halle, Germany: Verlegt von Carl Hermann Hemmerde, 1765. This entire volume is devoted to Anthony Collins' works and to responses to it. Vol. 2: Same publisher and place of publication, 1766. This entire volume is devoted to Matthew Tindal's works and to the responses to it. Vol. 3: Eassel, [Germany]: Verlegt von Carl Hermann Hemmerde, 1766. This entire volume is devoted to John Toland's works and to the responses to it. Vol. 4: Same publisher and place as volume 3, 1767. This volume deals mostly with John Toland also, although there are small sections on Samuel Parvish and Jacob Ilive.

43. Tribe, David. *100 Years of Freethought.* London: Elek Books, 1967. A well-done history of freethought in England, with brief mention of developments in other countries. It covers the period from about 1850 to 1950. There are many excursions into social issues, such as birth control history.

44. Tribe, David. *President Charles Bradlaugh, M. P.* London: Elek Books, 1971. Based upon the "Bradlaugh Papers," long thought lost, this biography sheds much new light upon the life of the most famous British freethinker of the nineteenth century.

45. Trinius, J. A. *Freydenker Lexicon.* 4 vols. Leipzig, Germany: Berglegts Christoph Gottfried Corner, 1759–1765. Reprinted in one folio volume by Bottega d'Erasmo, Turin, Italy in 1966.

46. (Truelove, Edward). *Catalogue of Books From the Library of the Late Edward Truelove.* [London]: Executors of the Estate of E. Truelove, [1900]. Sale catalog of a large and important freethought library. Truelove was a freethought bookseller.

47. Watts, Charles. *History of Freethought.* London: Watts & Company, n.d. [1885?]. Published also under the title *Freethought: Its Rise, Progress and Triumph* (same publisher). This was intended to be vol. 3 of *The Freethinker's Text Book* (277 & 288). Vol. 1 is by Charles Bradlaugh and vol. 2 by Annie Besant. It was issued in a binding to match these two earlier parts, but since it was published several years after them, it was usually not sold together with them. The contents tend to be too superficial to be really useful. There are also no notes or bibliography.

48. Wheeler, Joseph Mazzini. *A Biographical Dictionary of Free-thinkers of All Ages and Nations*. London: Progressive Publishing Co., 1889. Although this contains many typographical errors, it is a valuable piece of research, and often enables one to identify the author of anonymous freethought works.

49. Whyte, Adam Gowans. *The Story of the R.P.A. (1899–1949)*. London: Watts & Co., 1949. A history of the Rationalist Press Association.

Freethought
in the
United Kingdom
and the
Commonwealth

1
The Rise and Decline
of British Deism
(1624-1760)

We can best begin our study of freethought in the United Kingdom with the deist movement. This is not to say that there weren't atheists in England before the start of deism (there were), or that the first deistic book, Lord Herbert of Cherbury's *De Veritate* (89) was the first freethought work ever published in England (it probably wasn't). There were atheists and freethinkers and their publications before this time, but they were an isolated and rare phenomenon. However, Henry Smith's *God's Arrow Against Atheists* (113), which had its first edition in 1593, was an anti-atheistic work that must have been written in answer to some popular outpouring of atheistic sentiment. Smith's pamphlet is generally considered to be the first British work in English on atheism. It is, at least, the earliest to survive.

There were foreign books (usually in Latin) which dealt with atheism before this time. Bonnaventure DesPerriers' *Cymbalum Mundi* (77), although a work of fiction, was certainly atheistic in outlook. Its publication date (1537, for the first French edition published in Amsterdam) would make it virtually the first book of its type. The first English translation seems to have been published in 1723.

England in the seventeenth century, when deism first emerged, was in a time when the medieval period was still exerting an influence. Western man was emerging from his medieval past. Copernicus' idea that the sun was the center of the solar system was taking hold. The effect of this new idea upon the religious thought of the period was profound. No longer was the earth the center of the universe, as God's "special project."

Herbert of Cherbury (1583–1648) has aptly been called "the father of English deism". In his *De Veritate* (89), he takes most of the book to present his theory of knowledge, stating that there are some truths attainable through the use of reason, and some which are innate. Towards the end of the book, Herbert names five principles of natural religion. These are best stated in his *The Antient Religion of the Gentiles, and the Causes of Their Errors Considered* (88), published in 1663. The five principles are: 1) There is one supreme God, 2) He ought to be worshipped, 3) Virtue and piety are the chief parts of divine worship, 4) We ought to be sorry for our sins and repent of them, and 5) Divine goodness dispenses rewards and punishments both in this life and after it. *De Veritate* was not translated into English until 1937.

There are a number of critical and biographical works on Lord Herbert. The most important is his own *The Life of Edward, Lord Herbert of Cherbury* (87). There are also biographies by de Rémuset (78) and Gütter (86).

Even the beginning of deism, marked by the publication of *De Veritate*, was very slow to produce any similar publications. Between *De Veritate*, published in Paris in 1624, and the next important deistic work, Charles Blount's *Oracles of Reason* (64), in 1693, nearly seventy years passed. True, Thomas Hobbes published his *Leviathan* (90) in 1651, but this work is usually considered to be political in intent, and therefore outside the mainstream of deism, although Hobbes' method of applying reason to everything influenced the deists.

Another important influence was Benedict (or Baruch) Spinoza (1632–1677). His influence was considerably less than either Hobbes or Locke because Spinoza wrote in Latin—a language only the educated few could read well. Nevertheless, his *Theological-Political Treatise* (114) anticipated biblical higher criticism by 200 years and helped undermine the authority of the Bible for deists.

One notable work *against* atheism (not deism) was published during this period. It was Ralph Cudworth's *The True Intellectual System of the Universe* (73), published in 1678. This work is usually described as being responsible for the production of many atheists, since most who read it saw that Cudworth's arguments against atheism and for Christianity were weak and flawed. The statements he makes about atheism actually seem to be stronger than those about Christianity.

In 1679, Charles Blount (1654–1693) published the first of his works on religion. It was his *Anima Mundi* (61), containing only a mild amount of unbelief. The next year saw the publication of both Blount's *Great Is Diana of the Ephesians* (63), a strong attack upon the idea of revelation, and of his translation into English of Philostratus' . . . *Life of Apollonius of Tyana* (62).

Blount's life is not well covered in published works. There is a short biography of him by his friend Charles Glidon, included with Blount's *Miscellaneous Works* (64). Bonante's study of Blount (66), in Italian, is perhaps the most complete available. A bibliography of Blount's few writings has been published as an article by Gilmour (85). Two articles about Blount's influence are those of Villey (121) and Redwood (107).

Many antideistic and anti-atheistic works appeared in the closing years of the seventeenth century, but there really had not been much written yet by the deists. An exception was John Toland's *Christianity Not Mysterious* (117) that first appeared in 1696. Toland (1670–1722) leaned heavily upon ideas advanced by John Locke (1632–1704) in his *Essay Concerning Humane Understanding* (94) that was first published in 1690. Locke denied that man had *any* innate ideas. Even the idea of God, he said, was not an innate one. Man's idea of God came from the use of his reason, Locke said. God was spiritual, not material. These ideas were quickly adopted by the deists. They were glad to have reason as the method with which to establish the existence of God. However, Locke asserted the existence of revelation, and said that the major proof of revelation was the existence of miracles. This explains why so much of the later deistic attack on revelation was made against miracles. Locke also recognized the five articles of "natural religion," as listed by Herbert of Cherbury. This put natural religion on an empirical, rational basis.

John Toland followed Locke in the sense that Toland, who called himself a "Christian reformer," claimed that Christianity had been greatly corrupted from its original form, especially by priests. Genuine Christianity, he said, is free from both mystery and ceremony. Toland's stance against mystery in religion was based upon Locke's theory of knowledge, and the resultant idea that nothing can be true if it is contrary to reason or experience. Since mysteries (e.g., the Trinity) were contrary to reason, they must be rejected. Toland supported belief in God, the immortality of the soul, and the idea of future rewards and punishments (parts of Herbert's "natural religion"). He questioned the accuracy of the New Testament canon, holding that many of the apocryphal books were just as valid as the canonical books. Toland's book must be considered an important milestone in the history of deism. Many answers to it were published. None of Toland's shorter works (published later) had as much influence upon the direction and popularity of deism as did *Christianity Not Mysterious*.

There are several biographies of Toland. Among them are Lantoine's *Un Précurseur de la Francmaçonnerie: John Toland* (91), Twynam's *John Toland, Freethinker* (119), Desmaiseaux's *Some Memoirs of the Life and Writings of Mr. John Toland* (76), *An Abstract of the Life of the Author* [John Toland] (56). Mosheim's *De Vita, Fatis et Scriptis Joannis Tolandi* (102), and *An Historical Account of the Life and*

Writings of the Late Eminently Famous Mr. John Toland (74). There is also a chapter on Toland in *Half-Hours With the Freethinkers* (67). Toland's writings (and the answers to them) are discussed bibliographically in Thorschmid (42), volumes three and four.

The next important contribution to the deist cause was the Earl of Shaftesbury's (Anthony Ashley Cooper, 1671–1713) three-volume work, *Characteristics of Men, Manners, Opinions, Times* (109), published in 1711. There is some question in the minds of earlier writers about deism as to whether Shaftesbury should really be called a deist. Part of this doubt is due to the fact that he often criticized the deists in public, calling himself an orthodox Christian theist. At the same time, he wrote against the Bible and other orthodox issues. Obviously, the pretensions of orthodoxy were to protect himself. Another protective device used by Shaftesbury was the employment of dialogue as a format for his writing. In that way, it was difficult to tell which of the two positions expressed was really that of Shaftesbury. He also often used witty satire, irony, and ridicule. The most important of his ideas was that ethics and morality were above religion. He treated the subject of ethics extensively in some of his other writings. The use of ridicule and wit was picked up by some of the later deists, such as Thomas Woolston, often with devastating effect. Shaftesbury also clearly came out against emotion in religion (he called it "enthusiasm"), especially in his *Letter Concerning Enthusiasm* (110). The later deists echoed his sentiments.

Shaftesbury's life, letters, and some unpublished materials were brought together by Rand in *The Life, Unpublished Letters and Philosophical Regimen of Anthony, Earl of Shaftesbury* (106). The life is by Shaftesbury's son, the Fourth Earl. Other works which are important to an understanding of Shaftesbury are Schlegel's *Shaftesbury and the French Deists* (108) and Aldridge's *Shaftesbury and the Deist Manifesto* (50). Biographies include Brett's *The Third Earl of Shaftesbury* (68) and Fowler's *Shaftesbury and Hutcheson* (81).

Anthony Collins (1676–1729) gradually became a major writer for the deist cause. His first work, *A Discourse of Free-Thinking* (71), which appeared in 1713, brought forth numerous responses and had a wide circulation. It is primarily a plea for toleration of freethinkers and for the encouragement of freethinking itself. The last half of the book claims that many of the notable thinkers of the past were "free thinkers." However, Collins does not define this term to mean original and independent thinkers, but rather to mean those who rejected revelation and held deistic notions. This seems to be the first time the term was used in the way it is today. Collins also questioned the divine inspiration of the Bible, whether it was free of errors, and the lack of corruption from the Bible having been under the care of priests for so many years.

Collins wrote one other important work. This was his *A Discourse On the Grounds and Reasons of the Christian Religion* (72), published in 1724. The book was largely an attack upon the "argument from prophecy," namely that the New Testament (and thus Christianity) is true because many of the prophesies in the Old Testament are fulfilled by the occurrences told of in the New Testament. This attack upon the prophesies became an important deist weapon.

Collins argued his case as follows: 1) the New Testament depends for its truth upon its connection with the Old Testament, 2) that connection is the fulfillment of the Old Testament prophesies by Jesus, 3) it is therefore necessary that the prophesies relating to a messiah in the Old Testament were indeed fulfilled by Jesus, as described in the New Testament, 4) but there are serious difficulties in (3) above, namely that there are discrepancies between the quotations of the prophesies in the New Testament and the same prophesies in the Old Testament, 5) also, the prophesies in the New Testament cannot have been literally fulfilled by Jesus, because some of them had been literally fulfilled in the Old Testament already, while others refer to events which occurred many years before the birth of Jesus, 6) all that remains possible, therefore, is nonliteral fulfillment of the prophesies, 7) hence, the Old Testament prophesies were nonliterally fulfilled by Jesus, and so Christianity is true, 8) but nonliteral fulfillment is absurd, as almost anything could be called "fulfilled" by this means, 9) therefore, since the Old Testament prophesies have not been literally fulfilled by Jesus, there is no connection between the Old and the New Testaments. Therefore, this means that Christianity has no basis (see #1). Propositions 8) and 9) are not explicitly stated in Collins' book, but are strongly implied.

This example of Collins' reasoning has been given in detail to show that his writings were very carefully thought out analyses of the arguments given by the orthodox clergy. Voltaire was greatly influenced by reading Collins, at least according to Torrey's examination in his *Voltaire and the English Deists* (118).

There is one published biography of Anthony Collins. It is O'Higgins' *Anthony Collins—The Man and His Works* (103). O'Higgins paints Collins as almost a Christian, or as just outside the limits of Christianity. This view is challenged by Berman in his article "Anthony Collins and the Question of Atheism in the Early Part of the Eighteenth Century" (60). Berman argues that rather than being a "mere deist," Collins was a "speculative atheist." It should perhaps be noted that Collins himself never said that he was a deist. He always called himself a "free-thinker." Collins' life is also discussed at some length in the introduction to the German reprint of A Discourse of Free-Thinking (83). The introduction is by Gawlick. There is also a chapter on Collins in Half-Hours With the Freethinkers (67), First Series, #6. A Complete Catalogue of the Library of Anthony Collins, Esq., Deceased (59), compiled by Ballard, in two parts, also was published. It is an auction catalog, with Ballard being the auctioneer.

Thomas Woolston (1669–1733) was one of the most interesting and influential of the deists. He was trained as a clergyman, and spent many years as a teacher and scholar of religion at Cambridge. His earlier publications were slightly heretical, but mild enough in content to allow him to go unmolested. In 1720 he began a series of publications which became increasingly radical in content. His 1724 publication of The Moderator Between an Infidel and an Apostate (125) caused a considerable uproar. The work was an imaginary dialogue between Anthony Collins and the Church of England. Woolston was not punished for this writing, presumably because he had many years of orthodox teaching and scholarship behind him.

Eventually Woolston did leave his teaching post, and went to London. He continued to write unmolested there until 1728, when he was arrested and released on bail. Just at that time, the first of his series of six Discourses on the Miracles of Our Saviour (124) was published. These were his most famous works. The Discourses took up a large number of the New Testament miracles individually and discussed and ridiculed them. He tried to show that the early church fathers recognized that the "miracles" were allegories, and not literal events. The work was filled with wit and sarcasm, and was one of the few deistic works which was designed to appeal to the literate common man. For this reason, it was especially dangerous in the eyes of the clergy. The writing of the Discourses caused Woolston to be tried and imprisoned for blasphemy. He died while still officially in prison. He seems to have had the "freedom" of the prison, however, at the time of his death (something like being under "house arrest").

There is very little biographical material about Thomas Woolston which was published separately. There is an anonymous pamphlet called The Life of Mr. Woolston, With an Impartial Account of His Writings (58), thought to have been written by Stackhouse.

Peter Annet (1693–1769), a schoolmaster, nearly always wrote anonymously. He often signed his work as "By a Moral Philosopher." The most famous of the books associated with Annet is one which he may well not have written. This was The History of the Man After God's Own Heart (53), first published in 1761. The book is about the biblical David, and has been reprinted many times, enjoying quite a notorious reputation. Annet never admitted writing this book (although it *is* written in his style) and there are others to whom it has been attributed (John Noorthouck among them).

Annet's other publications include *The History and Character of St. Paul* (52). It pictures Paul as lazy, greedy, and dishonest. There is also what is probably Annet's most important work from the standpoint of theology, namely *The Resurrection of Jesus Considered: In Answer to the Tryal of the Witnesses* (55). It was written in response to Sherlock's *The Tryal of the Twelve Witnesses* (111), in which each of the witnesses to the Resurrection is given an imaginary cross-examination, and a "verdict" is reached. Sherlock's verdict was that Jesus *was* resurrected.

Annet is credited with having written the anonymous *Deism Fairly Stated and Fully Vindicated from the Gross Imputations and Groundless Calumnies of Modern Believers* (51), called by several experts perhaps the best defense of deism ever written by a deist.

Peter Annet signed his own name to only one of his publications, *Judging For Ourselves: Or, Free-Thinking the Great Duty of Religion* (54). This was the text of two lectures given in 1738–1739 at Plaisterer's Hall, London. They would seem to be the first public free-thought lectures ever given in English.

Works about Peter Annet are virtually nonexistent. About the longest, and most thorough, is a pamphlet by Twynam, called *Peter Annet (1693–1769)* (120). There were a large number of answers to Annet's writings published, as was the case with most of the controversial deistic writings.

Matthew Tindal (1656–1733) was a lawyer who spent most of his life in the association of Oxford University. His only deistic work was *Christianity as Old as the Creation* (116), published when Tindal was seventy-four years old. It was very popular, bringing forth over 100 replies. The book has been called "The Deistic Bible," because it brought together many of the arguments which had been used by other deists in their works.

Tindal's main thesis was that since God is perfect, the religion which he gave man at the Creation must also have been perfect. As the Old and New Testaments, as well as contemporary Christianity, were obviously not perfect, they must be corruptions of the original "perfect" Christianity given man at the Creation. Hence the title of the book. Tindal held that man's duty was to strip away the imperfections of Christianity and to get back to the original form, which he called "the religion of nature." The result was a critique of the Bible as a worthless and blameworthy book. Tindal's "natural religion" had the following articles: 1) belief in God, 2) doing what is for one's own happiness, and 3) promoting the common happiness.

The title page of *Christianity as Old as the Creation* bears the words "volume 1." Indeed, Tindal had actually completed the second volume of the work before he died in 1733. His will directed that the manuscript be published. His wife turned it over to the Bishop of London (for what purpose is unclear), and he, in turn, destroyed the manuscript in anger over its heterodox contents. Therefore, the second volume never appeared.

There are very few biographical sources for Tindal's life. The only separately published biography seems to be Curll's *Memoirs of the Life and Writings of Matthew Tindal* (75). There is a biographical sketch in the introduction to the German reprint edition of Tindal's book, written by Gawlick (116). There is also a chapter on Tindal in *Half-Hours With the Freethinkers* (67), First Series, #14. Tindal's writings are discussed bibliographically in volume 2 of Thorschmid's bibliography (42).

Thomas Chubb (1679–1747) was a working man (a candlemaker) who popularized the major arguments of deism for the masses. As such, he brought no new arguments to the public, but clarified those presented by other deistic writers. His most important work was *The True Gospel of Jesus Christ Asserted* (70). Chubb had been raised as a Christian, and his form of deism was what would today probably be called Unitarianism. He began to write for his own amusement. Eventually, one of his critiques of some of William Whiston's writings was sent by a friend to Whiston himself. Whiston published it, urging Chubb to become an author. Chubb came to London and wrote a number of commentaries upon religion, but none had the popularity or influence of *The True Gospel of Jesus Christ Asserted*. Some of his works were published posthumously. There seem to be no published biographies of Chubb.

Thomas Morgan (? – 1743) came from poor and obscure beginnings. He seems to have been been born in France, but his parents moved to the west of England when he was quite young. A minister recognized Morgan's ability while he was still a child. The minister saw to it that Morgan was prepared for the ministry and he was ordained in 1716. He served as a dissenting preacher for a few years, after which his views of the trinity caused him to be dismissed from his post. Morgan then began a career as a physician. He seems to have remained more interested in religious controversy than in medicine, however. His major work, a three-volume set, was called *The Moral Philosopher* (101). It was published from 1737 to 1740, with the first volume issued anonymously, and the second and third indicated as being by "Philalethes."

The Moral Philosopher's main value is in its first volume. The next two are mostly replies to critics, which caused him to restate his case. The work is not a presentation of new ideas, but rather a bringing together, with clarity, of the ideas of others.

Conyers Middleton (1863–1750) wrote his few deistic works toward the end of his life. In 1747 he published An Introductory Discourse to a Larger Work (100), in which he condemned many of the miracles claimed by the church. He came to the conclusion that there is no reason to believe that the miraculous powers which the church once had lasted past the time of the apostles. In 1749 Middleton published the "larger work" which had been promised. This was Free Inquiry Into the Miraculous Powers, Which are Supposed to Have Subsisted in the Christian Church (99). In the Free Inquiry, Middleton again rejected most of the early miracles of the church. He examined the reliability of the early church fathers and showed it quite low. Their testimony with regard to the miracles was unreliable, he said. Middleton gained a reputation as one of the most scholarly writers taking a deistic position. There are no biographies of Middleton, although there is an article about him, written anonymously, in the Westminster Review (57).

Henry St. John, Viscount Bolingbroke (1672–1751) would have made a much greater mark upon deistic thought had his works appeared earlier. They were all published posthumously, when deism had already begun its decline. His works are characterized by an extremely negative opinion of virtually everything, including the Bible, the church fathers, and the clergy. He did express a belief in God, but doubted a future life. He attacked the Christian religion both because it was based upon the fradulent Bible, and because it had been further corrupted by philosophers. His deistic works were published in his collected The Works of . . . Lord . . .Bolingbroke, With a Life (65). There are also lives of Bolingbroke by Macknight (95), Petrie (104), Sichel (112) and Dickinson (79). Bolingbroke's deism is the subject of a study by Merrill in From Statesman to Philosopher (98).

Bernard De Mandeville (1670–1733) was a physician who is best remembered for his book The Fable of the Bees (96). This work, which is mainly anticlerical, has often been viewed as a deistic work, since the fifth dialogue of the book argues for natural religion as opposed to revealed religion. Although the very next dialogue speaks of the necessity of revelation and for the belief in Christianity, most of Mandeville's readers took this as insincerity on his part. He also attacked the ethical teachings of Shaftesbury's Characteristics (109). Although

Mandeville's work is mostly negative, he does seem to merit the classification of deist. The F. B. Kaye edition of Mandeville's *Fable* (97), with extensive notes, is, by far, the best source for information about its author.

William Wollaston (1659–1724) is sometimes considered a deist and sometimes not. He was a retired clergyman when he published his book *The Religion of Nature Delineated* (123) in 1722. While the title makes it sound like a deistic work, the contents confuse the issue. The book contains almost no attack upon the Bible, the clergy, or Christianity. It is very "polite" and was quite popular, reaching a seventh edition by 1746. Wollaston attempts to build up a system of natural ethics, and winds up with something which is quite similar to Herbert of Cherbury's system of the previous century. He also believed in a future life. There is no biography of Wollaston, but there is a study of his ethical system by Thompson, called *The Ethics of William Wollaston* (115). There is also an article about Wollaston by Feinberg (80).

Several other British authors of note, such as David Hume and Edward Gibbon, have sometimes been proposed as deists. Although the result of their writing was to further deist ideas, their aim in writing does not seem to have been to do so. It seems, therefore, that to treat them as deists would be unfair.

Deism declined rapidly for many reasons. To attempt to spell each out is not easy. Suggestions can be made and lists given, but it was really a complex interplay of forces that was responsible. Here are some of the ingredients: 1) Most of the arguments for natural religion had already been given by 1740, 2) There was a religious revival, starting in 1736, led by the Wesleys and by George Whitefield, 3) There was a large body of antideistic literature published (some of which will be discussed below), 4) There were political developments (such as the American independence movement) brewing which diverted attention from religious controversy, 5) The divisions among the deists themselves seriously weakened their position, and, 6) The blaming of the deists for the moral corruption present around them also weakened their cause.

The antideists were a large and flourishing group of theologians who spent much of their time writing and preaching against what they perceived were the errors and evils of deism. Among the most important of these was John Leland. His *A View of the Principal Deistic Writers* (92) was an important source book for both sides in the controversy. Also important were Charles Leslie's *A Short and Easy Method With the Deists* (93) and Joseph Butler's famous *Analogy of Religion* (69).

There is a sketch of antideistic writings in Christian Pfaff's *Entwurff der Theologiae Anti-Deisticae* (105).

The original editions of the major deistic works have become extremely scarce today. Especially hard to find are the works of Peter Annet and Thomas Woolston, the most radical deists. Many of the primary works of the deists have been reprinted, however, with excellent new introductions (most by Günter Gawlick) by the Friedrich Frommann Verlag (Stuttgart-Bad Cannstatt, West Germany). This series was published in the late 1960s. Their re-publication helps greatly to solve the problems caused by the scarceness of the original works.

A number of deistic works have also been reprinted, starting in 1976, by Garland Publishing Co. (New York), as a part of their "British Philosophers and Theologians of the 17th and 18th Centuries" series. While the series is ongoing, the first group of titles reprinted includes many of the same ones that are in the German reprints. The Garland series also omits the same titles omitted by the Germans. This is to be regretted, as both Woolston and Annet are not included in either series.

Two other recent works contain selections from some of the more important deist works. The selections are fairly short, and they serve mainly to give a "flavor" of the original works. These anthologies are Peter Gay's *Deism: An Anthology* (84) and E. Graham Waring's *Deism and Natural Religion* (122).

There really were no deistic publishers as such. A few deist clubs, such as the Deistic Chapel founded in London in 1776 by David Williams, existed briefly. Deism remained almost entirely an unorganized, individualist movement in England. There were also very few periodical publications that could be called deist. The most important one was Peter Annet's *Free Enquirer* (82), lasting only nine issues.

To summarize the place of deism in history, we could do no better than to quote from Gay's *Deism: An Anthology* (84), p. 13:

Deism, we might say, is the product of the confluence of three strong emotions: hate, love and hope. The deists hated priests and priestcraft, mystery-mongering, and assaults on common sense. They loved the ethical teachings of the classical philosophers, and grand unalterable regularity of nature, the sense of freedom granted the man liberated from superstition. They hoped that the problems of life—of private conduct and public policy— could be solved by the application of unaided human reason, and that the mysteries of the universe could be, if not solved, at least defined and circumscribed by man's scientific inquiry. The deists were optimists about human nature: they rejected the Fall and thought that man could be at once good and wise. Had they only hated, they would have been cranks. Had they only loved, they would have been enthusiasts. Had they only hoped, they would have been visionaries. They were something more and something better as well. They were powerful agents of modernity.

BIBLIOGRAPHY

50. Aldridge, Alfred Owen. "Shaftesbury and the Deist Manifesto." *American Philosophical Society Transactions* 41 Part II (1951): 297–385.

51. [Annet, Peter]. *Deism Fairly Stated and Fully Vindicated From the Gross Imputations and Groundless Calumnies of Modern Believers.* London: W. Webb, 1746. Often called the best defense of deism ever written by a deist.

52. [Annet, Peter]. *The History and Character of St. Paul Examined: In a Letter to Theophilus, a Christian Friend.* London: F. Page, [1742?].

53. [Annet, Peter?]. *The History of the Man After God's Own Heart.* London: Printed for R. Freeman, 1761. This work as also been attributed to John Noorthouck, Archibald Campbell, David Mallet, George Pritchard and to a French citizen named "Huet." The issue of Noorthuck's authorship is treated in an article in *The Times Literary Supplement* of August 25, 1945 (p. 408), in which a good case is made for Noorthouck as the author. The work itself is a satirical life of the biblical David, and has been reprinted many times. See the next chapter for a further discussion of the authorship of this piece.

54. [Annet, Peter]. *Judging for Ourselves: Or Free-Thinking the Great Duty of Religion.* London: Printed for the Author, 1739.

55. [Annet, Peter]. *The Resurrection of Jesus Considered: In Answer to the Tryal of the Witnesses.* London: Printed for the Author, [1743].

56. Anonymous. *An Abstract of the Life of the Author* [John Toland]. In Toland's *Critical History of the Celtic Religion.* London: Lackington, Hughes, Harfing & Co., 1740.

57. Anonymous. "Conyers Middleton." *Westminster Review* 142 (July 1894): 68–80.

58. Anonymous [John Stackhouse?]. *The Life of Mr. Woolston, With an Impartial Account of His Writings.* London: J. Roberts, 1733.

59. Ballard, Thomas. *Bibliotheca Antonii Collins, Arm. Or, A Complete Catalogue of the Library of Anthony Collins, Esq., Deceased.* London: no publisher, 1730.

60. Berman, David. "Anthony Collins and the Question of Atheism in the Early Part of the Eighteenth Century." *Royal Irish Academy Proceedings* 75C (1975): 85–102. Collins is shown to be a "speculative atheist."

61. Blount, Charles. *Anima Mundi*. Amsterdam [i.e., London]: "Anno Mundi 00000" [i.e., 1678]. Second edition was London: Printed for Will. Cademan, 1679.

62. Blount, Charles, ed. *The First Two Books of Philostratus, Concerning the Life of Apolonius Tyaneus*. London: Printed for Nathaniel Thompson, 1680. Blount translated this work and also supplied the very anti-Christian critical notes. The rest of the work was never published.

63. Blount, Charles. *Great is Diana of the Ephesians*. London: no publisher, 1680.

64. Blount, Charles. *Oracles of Reason*. London: no publisher, 1693. Reprinted after Blount's death in the volume of most of his collected works, entitled *Miscellaneous Works of Charles Blount* (London: no publisher, 1695). This volume also contains a short biography of the author.

65. Bolingbroke, Viscount Henry St. John, Lord. *The Works of the Late Right Honorable Henry St. John, Lord Viscount Bolingbroke, With a Life*. 5 vols. London: David Mallet, 1754.

66. Bonante, Ugo. *Charles Blount: Libertinismo e Deismo nel Seicento Inglese*. Florence [Italy]: La Nuova Italia Editrice, 1972.

67. [Bradlaugh, Charles] as "Iconoclast," W. H. Johnson and Charles Watts. *Half-Hours With Freethinkers*. London: Austin & Co., 1865. Second Series. First series was published first by Austin & Co., London, 1857.

68. Brett, Richard L. *The Third Earl of Shaftesbury*. London: Hutchinson, 1951.

69. Butler, Joseph. *Analogy of Religion, Natural and Revealed, to the Constitution and Course of Nature*. London: Printed for J. & P. Knapton, 1736.

70. Chubb, Thomas. *The True Gospel of Jesus Christ Asserted*. London: Printed for T. Cox, 1738.

71. Collins, Anthony. *A Discourse of Free-Thinking*. London: no publisher, 1713. Issued initially without the author's name.

72. Collins, Anthony. *A Discourse on the Grounds and Reasons of the Christian Religion*. London: no publisher, 1723 [i.e., 1724].

73. Cudworth, Ralph. *The True Intellectual System of the Universe*. London: Printed for Richard Roystron, 1678. Anti-atheistic, but weak.

74. [Curll, Edmund]. *An Historical Account of the Life and Writings*

of the Eminently Famous Mr. John Toland. London: J. Roberts, 1722.

75. [Curll, Edmund]. *Memoirs of the Life and Writings of Matthew Tindal, LLD, With a History of the Controversies Wherein He Was Engaged.* London: E. Curll, 1733.

76. Desmaiseaux, Pierre. *Some Memoirs of the Life and Writings of Mr. John Toland.* In *A Collection of Several Pieces of Mr. John Toland.* London: J. Peele, 1726.

77. DesPerriers, Bonaventure. *Cymbalum Mundi, Ou Dialogues Satyriques sur Differens Sujects.* Amsterdam: Prosper Marchaud, 1537. The first English edition was London, 1712. A fictional work, which takes an atheistic position. Probably the first work of its kind. There were many editions.

78. deRémuset, Charles François Marie. *Lord Herbert de Cherbury, Sa Vie et ses Oeuvres.* Paris: Didier & Cie., 1874.

79. Dickinson, H. T. *Bolingbroke.* London: Constable, 1970.

80. Feinberg, Joel. "Wollaston and His Critics." *Journal of the History of Ideas* 38 (Apr/June 1977): 345–52.

81. Fowler, Thomas. *Shaftesbury and Hutcheson.* London: Sampson Low, Marston, Searle and Rivington, 1882.

82. *Free Enquirer.* A deistic magazine published in London by Peter Annet in 1761. It ran for nine issues. The entire run was reprinted by Richard Carlile in 1826.

83. Gawlick, Günter. *Introduction* (*"Einleitung"*) to the reprint edition of Anthony Collins' *A Discourse of Free-Thinking.* Stuttgart-Bad Cannstatt [W. Germany]: Friedrich Frommann Verlag, 1965. pp. 17–45.

84. Gay, Peter, ed. *Deism: An Anthology.* Princeton, N.J.: Van Nostrand Co., 1968.

85. Gilmour, J.S.L. "Some Uncollected Authors: XVII: Charles Blount." *Book Collector* (London) 7 (1958): 182–87.

86. Güttler, Karl. *Eduard, Lord Herberg von Cherbury.* Munich: C. H. Beck, 1897.

87. Herbert, Edward, Lord of Cherbury. *The Life of Edward, Lord Herbert of Cherbury.* Strawberry Hill [England]: Printed by Prat, 1764. Later editions were entitled *The Autobiography of Lord Herbert of Cherbury.*

88. Herbert, Edward, Lord of Cherbury. *The Antient Religion of the Gentiles and the Causes of Their Errors Considered.* Amsterdam: Typis Blaevorum, 1663. The first English Translation was London: John Nutt, 1705.

89. Herbert, Edward, Lord of Cherbury. *De Veritate.* [Paris]: no publisher, 1624. This edition was in Latin. Herbert had just returned to England after a post as British minister at Paris, hence the Paris

place of publication. The book was reprinted at London (again in Latin) in 1633. This latter edition would therefore be the first deistic book printed in England. A French translation was published in the 1600s, but the first English translation was not made until 1937 (Bristol, England: Arrow).

90. Hobbes, Thomas. *Leviathan*. London: Printed for Andrew Crooke, 1651. This work is really political in intent, but Hobbes' atheism shows through. In order to be logically consistent, Hobbes had to take the position that religion ought to be under the control of the monarchy. Many deists were influenced by Hobbes' work.

91. Lantoine, Albert. *Un Precurseur de la Francmaçonnerie: John Toland, 1670–1722*. Paris: E. Nourry, 1927.

92. Leland, John. *A View of the Principal Deistic Writers that Have Appeared in England in the Last and Present Century*. 2 vols. London: B. Dod, 1754–55.

93. Leslie, Charles. *A Short and Easy Method With the Deists*. London: Printed by W. Onley for H. Hindmarsh, 1698.

94. Locke, John. *Essay Concerning Humane Understanding*. London: Printed by Eliz. Holt for Thomas Basset, 1690.

95. Macknight, Thomas. *The Life of Henry St. John, Viscount Bolingbroke*. London: Chapman & Hall, 1863.

96. Mandeville, Bernard de. *The Fable of the Bees, Or Private Vices, Publick Benefits*. London: Printed for J. Roberts, 1714.

97. Mandeville, Bernard de. *The Fable of the Bees*. F. B. Kaye, ed. Oxford, [England]: 2 vols. The Clarendon Press of Oxford University, 1924. The best edition, with lengthy notes.

98. Merrill, Walter McIntoch. *From Statesman to Philosopher—A Study in Bolingbroke's Deism*. New York: Philosophical Library, 1949.

99. Middleton, Conyers. *Free Inquiry into the Miraculous Powers Which are Supposed to Have Subsisted in the Christian Church, From the Earliest Ages Through Several Successive Centuries*. Dublin: J. Smith, 1749.

100. Middleton, Conyers. *An Introductory Discourse to a Larger Work, Designed Hereafter to be Published, Concerning the Miraculous Powers Which are Supposed to Have Subsisted in the Christian Church*. London: R. Manby & H. Cox, 1747.

101. Morgan, Thomas. *The Moral Philosopher*. 3 vols. London: Printed for the Author, 1737–40.

102. Mosheim, Johann Lorenz. *De Vita, Fatis et Scriptis Joannis Tolandi*. In his *Vindiciae Antiquae Christianorum Disciplinae, Adversus Celeberioni viri Jo. Toland, Hiberni Nazarenum*. Hamburg, [Germany]: B. Schiller & J. C. Kisner, 1722.

103. O'Higgins, James. *Anthony Collins—The Man and His Works*.

The Hague: Martinus Nijhoff, 1970. O'Higgins' conclusions are challenged by David Berman (see #60).

104. Petrie, Charles Alexander. *Bolingbroke*. London: Collins, 1937.

105. Pfaff, Christoph M. *Entwurff der Theologiae Anti-Deisticae*. Giesen, [Germany]: Johann Jacob Braun, 1757.

106. Rand, Benjamin, ed. *The Life, Unpublished Letters and Philosophical Regimen of Anthony, Earl of Shaftesbury*. London: Swann Sonnenschein, 1900.

107. Redwood, John A. "Charles Blount (1654–93), Deism and English Free Thought." *Journal of the History of Ideas* 35 (1974): 490–98.

108. Schlegel, Dorothy B. *Shaftesbury and the French Deists*. Chapel Hill, N.C.: University of North Carolina Press, 1956.

109. Shaftesbury, Anthony Ashley Cooper, Third Earl. *Characteristics of Men, Manners, Opinions, Times*. 3 vols. [London]: no publisher, 1711.

110. Shaftesbury, Anthony Ashley Cooper, Third Earl. *Letter Concerning Enthusiasm and Reflections Upon a Letter Concerning Enthusiasm*. London: J. Morphew, 1708–1709.

111. Sherlock, Thomas. *The Tryal of the Twelve Witnesses*. London: T. Jones, 1734. A Mock trial in which the evidence of each of the biblical witnesses to the resurrection of Jesus "testifies" and a "verdict" is given in favor of the resurrection. The above work by Peter Annet (#58) was written to answer this.

112. Sichel, Walter Sidney. *Bolingbroke and His Times*. 2 vols. London: James Nisbet, 1901–1902. Greenwood Press reprint, 1968.

113. Smith, Henry. *God's Arrow Against Atheists*. London: John Danter, 1593. There was a second edition in 1611, and many later editions. This pamphlet must be given the credit for being the first entire work written against atheism in England.

114. Spinoza, Baruch. *Theological-Political Treatise*. "Hamburg" [Amsterdam]: "Apud Henricum Künraht" [J. Rieuwertsz or Christian Conrad], 1670.

115. Thompson, Clifford Griffeth. *The Ethics of William Wollaston*. Boston: R. G. Badger, [1922].

116. [Tindal, Matthew]. *Christianity as Old as the Creation: Or, the Gospel, a Republication of the Religion of Nature*. London: no publisher, 1730. Marked "Volume 1" on the titlepage, although no Volume 2 ever appeared. The manuscript of volume 2 was destroyed after Tindal's death. Reprinted by Friedrich Frommann Verlag in 1967.

117. Toland, John. *Christianity Not Mysterious, Or a Treatise Showing that There is Nothing in the Gospel Contrary to Reason, nor*

Above It, and that no Christian Doctrine Can Properly be Called a Mystery. London: S. Buckley, 1696. The first edition was issued without the author's name.

118. Torry, Norman L. *Voltaire and the English Deists*. New Haven, Conn.: Yale University Press, 1930. An important attempt to see how much influence the English deists had upon Voltaire by actually examining his library and his notes on his reading.

119. Twynam, Ella. *John Toland, Freethinker (1670–1722)*. London: [Pioneer Press], 1968.

120. Twynam, Ella. *Peter Annet (1693–1769)*. London: Pioneer Press [1938].

121. Villey, Pierre. "L'Influence de Montaigne sur Charles Blount et sur les Déistes Anglais." *Revue du Seizième Siècle* 1 (1913): 190–219; 392–443.

122. Waring, E. Graham, ed. *Deism and Natural Religion*. New York: Frederick Ungar Publishing Co., 1967.

123. Wollaston, William. *The Religion of Nature Delineated*. London: Privately printed, 1722. The edition of 1724 (2nd ed.) was printed by Samuel Palmer.

124. Woolston, Thomas. *Discourses on the Miracles of Our Saviour, In View of the Present Controversy Between Infidels and Apostates*. London: For the Author, 1727–1729. Six individual discourses were issued. In 1729, they were issued bound together, along with *Mr. Woolston's Defence of His Discourses*.

125. Woolston, Thomas. *The Moderator Between an Infidel and an Apostate*. London: Booksellers of London & Westminster, 1725. There were also two supplements to this published, namely *A Supplement to the Moderator Between an Infidel and an Apostate* London: Printed for the Author, 1725 and *A Second Supplement to the Moderator Between an Infidel and an Apostate; Or a Dissertation on Some Other Prophecies, Cited by the Bishop of Litchfield, Against the Author of the Grounds* [i.e., Anthony Collins]. London: Printed for the Author, 1725.

2

From Thomas Paine to
the Start of the
National Secular Society
———————— (1760-1860) ————————

With the decline of deism, a new era in British freethought history began. From about 1760 onwards, virtually no more strictly deistic works (except Paine's *The Age of Reason*, which will be discussed below) were published in England. There was a period of about thirty years (1760–1790) during which there was little freethought publishing, although many complaints from the clergy about the "infidelity" of the populace were heard.

A few notable works were exceptions to this lull in freethought publishing activity. The first of the "new" type of freethought literature to appear was an item which has already been briefly mentioned in connection with Peter Annet. This was *The History of the Man After God's Own Heart* (53), initially published anonymously in 1761. The work has been attributed to Annet, John Noorthouck, Archibald Campbell, David Mallet, and to a Frenchman named Huet. It was popular and was reprinted a number of times.

In 1781, William Nicholson's *The Doubts of Infidels* (209) first appeared, again anonymously. It also ran to a number of editions. The year 1782 saw the pseudonymous printing (with "William Hammon" claiming to be the author) of *Answer to Dr. Priestley's Letters to a Philosophical Unbeliever* (254), now thought to be by Matthew Turner. The book is, according to David Berman (139), the first book published in English claiming to have been written by an admitted atheist.

The forces of Christianity were dealt a severe blow by the publication of Edward Gibbon's *The Decline and Fall of the Roman Empire* (166), the fifteenth and sixteenth chapters of which carefully documented that much of what had been taught as the history of early Christianity was badly in need of a revision. The work first appeared in 1776, with the last volume of the first edition being published in 1788.

The 1790s saw the publication of the first freethought work that really reached the working man as its audience. The book was *The Age of Reason* (215) by Thomas Paine. Paine (1737–1809) had a varied and interesting career, much of which had nothing to do with freethought, and therefore need concern us only briefly. In fact, Paine never actually belonged to the freethought movement or to deist circles. He did not write his deistic work, *The Age of Reason*, until 1794–1795, a period when deism in England was all but extinct. The late date also explains why Paine was not considered a deist when the movement was popular. Nevertheless, *The Age of Reason* has been perhaps the most popular and influential freethought book ever written.

Thomas Paine was born in Thetford, England. After trying his hand at several occupations with little success, he met Benjamin Franklin (then in England). This meeting produced a letter of introduction from Franklin to Franklin's son-in-law in Philadelphia, along with the suggestion that Paine seek his fortune in America. Paine arrived in Philadelphia in 1775, becoming the editor of the *Pennsylvania Magazine* (228). He soon published *Common Sense* (217), which ignited popular sentiment for independence from England. Paine returned to England in 1787. There he read Edmund Burke's book *Reflections on the French Revolution* (141), and responded with a work of his own, *Rights of Man* (221). This work brought him the admiration of the French revolutionary regime and an invitation to become a member of the new legislature. Paine left for France, just ahead of an English arrest warrant. He was charged in England with having published a "false wicked and seditious libel" in *Rights of Man*. Paine was tried and convicted in absentia, then declared an outlaw in England.

While in France, Paine fell into disfavor with the powers leading the Revolution when he pleaded that the life of the deposed monarch be spared. He hid from the authorities, in fear of his life, while writing his thoughts upon religion in the form of the first part of *The Age of Reason*. The manuscript of the first part was translated into French by François Lanthenas. It appeared as *La Siècle de la Raison* (219), with the author given as "F. Lanthenas," and no mention of Paine.

The official French censors were not pleased with the work, although they took no action to stop it. After an initial period of discouragement with the book, Paine saw that the "de-Christianization" spirit was again strong in France. This prompted him to completely rewrite the first part of *The Age of Reason* in English. The rewritten version differs considerably from the earlier French draft. He completed the new draft just six hours before he was arrested and put in prison. He thought that his stay in prison would be brief, as he was an "honorary" American citizen. A number of complications prevented his release until he had spent over ten months in jail. He was then offered refuge in the home of the American ambassador to France, James Madison. Paine stayed with Madison for a year and a half, writing the second part of *The Age of Reason*, published in 1795. Both parts of the book continued to sell well in France, England, and the United States. Paine could not return to England, so he returned to the United States in 1802.

The hatred stirred up by the publication of *The Age of Reason* turned many people against Paine, who was accused of having written an atheistic book. It is quite plain from an examination of the book itself that it is a purely deistic work since Paine says that he believes in God. His aim in writing the book was to expose the errors of the Bible in order to improve man's relationship with God. Strangely enough, the book was published over forty years after British deism died. In the United States, the book caused a late flowering of deism (see *Freethought in the United States* [140]). In England, the book was very popular with the working classes.

Paine wrote one other major work attacking the Bible (in this case the Old Testament prophecies of the coming of the Messiah). The book was called *Examination of the Passages in the New Testament, Quoted from the Old, and Called Prophecies Concerning Jesus Christ* (218), first published separately in 1806. This may have been a draft for Part 3 of *The Age of Reason* that Paine had said he would eventually write. The *"Examination"* has often been republished as Part 3 of *The Age of Reason*, although Paine himself never called it that. His promised "Part 3" simply never appeared.

It has been mentioned that *The Age of Reason* was the most popular freethought book ever published. It has remained in print for over 175 years and has gone through hundreds of editions and many translations. The book has been temporarily suppressed, caused many people to be jailed for publishing it, and credited with making more people into freethinkers than any other book, with the possible exception of the Bible itself. Over 100 answers to the book were written, and all but one are now forgotten. The exception was Richard Watson's (The Bishop of Llandaff) *An Apology for the Bible* (259). It was the only answer to which Paine himself responded. Paine wrote a response called *Reply to the Bishop of Llandaff* (220), published posthumously.

There have been many biographies of Thomas Paine. The first few painted quite an unfavorable picture of him, charging, among other things, that he was unkempt and a drunkard. One of these biographies was judged libelous (151) and publication was discontinued. The first favorable biography was one by his friend Rickman (235). Other early biographies included those by Carlile (147), Vale (255), Sherwin (238), and Linton (198).

The first full biography, using original source materials, was Conway's *Life of Thomas Paine* (157), published in 1896. This book has been accused of glorifying Paine, but it is still worth consulting. Modern biographies of Paine include those by Hawke (171), Van der Weyde (256), Williamson (262), Aldridge (128), Cohen (154), Gould (168), and Edwards (162). The collected works of Paine were first published in a four-volume edition (158) edited by Conway. Since that time, a number of minor works by Paine have been identified and added to the most complete edition yet published, *The Complete Writings of Thomas Paine* (163), edited by Foner.

One person who suffered imprisonment for publishing Paine's works was Richard Carlile (1790–1843). He was born in Ashburton, England, and was apprenticed to learn the tinsmith's trade as a child. After several years in that trade, he came to London in 1811. By 1817 he had married and become politically radicalized by the publications of Paine, William Cobbett and William Hone. He borrowed money from his employer in order to buy copies of the various radical periodicals to sell around London. Carlile also started selling Sherwin's magazine *The Republican*, which was later called *Sherwin's Political Register* (239). Sherwin turned over his periodical to Carlile, along with his printing press and bookshop. Carlile soon issued a pirated edition of William Hone's parodies of the Church of England creed and other items. Hone had withdrawn these publications from circulation upon being threatened with prosecution for them. Carlile was arrested and charged with "blasphemous libel." He was held in prison for eighteen weeks, but was released without trial when Hone was acquitted of the same charges. Carlile immediately began issuing editions of Thomas Paine's works, beginning with *Rights of Man* (222). In early 1819, he issued an edition of Paine's *Theological Works* (223) that included *The Age of Reason* (216).

The forces of law were swift in coming. Carlile was arrested and tried for having published a blasphemous libel. After his trial, which included Carlile's reading of the entire text of *The Age of Reason* to the jury, he was convicted and sentenced to one and a half years in jail for publishing *The Age of Reason*. In addition, one and a half years were added for having published Palmer's *Principles of Nature* (224), and an additional three years for failing to pay the 1500 pound fine levied upon him. The entire stock of his bookshop had been seized by the police, supposedly to meet his fine, but it was claimed that the stock (worth several thousand pounds at retail) was inadequate to meet any of the fine. The net effect was that Carlile received six years in jail.

In jail, those prisoners who had enough money could arrange to have some degree of comfort. Carlile continued to edit *The Republican* (239) and to write. His mail was looked at, but not censored. In fact, Carlile seems to have enjoyed the relative calm of the jail enough to have willingly repeated the experience several more times in the future. Carlile even had some company in his cell for a part of his sentence: his wife and sister joined him as fellow prisoners. This came about because of the tactics which Carlile adopted after his jailing. A call was issued for volunteers to work in the bookshop, and risk arrest for selling the prosecuted publications. Dozens of people responded to the advertisements. A continuous stream of people were arrested and jailed for selling Carlile's publications from his shop. Eventually, the government capitulated and the arrests stopped.

It had been mentioned that one of the publications for which Carlile was tried was Palmer's *Principles of Nature* (224). This book had been issued as one of a series of freethought tracts (mostly translations from the French, or the first British edition of American works, as the Palmer item was). The series was at times bound up with a title page and issued as *The Deist, or Moral Philosopher* (143). It was not really a magazine (as has been occasionally stated). Three "volumes" of *The Deist* were issued over a ten-year period (1819–29), but a comparison of several copies of the same volume number shows that they contain many different tracts (although some tracts are the same). Among the authors whose works appear in *The Deist* are D'Holbach, Palmer, Voltaire, Carlile, and Annet.

Carlile was responsible for the publication of a number of periodicals in addition to *The Republican* (which ran from 1819 to 1826, with the exception of a brief period in 1822). Among his other publications were *The Moralist* (205), *The Newgate Monthly Magazine* (208), *The Lion* (199), *The Prompter* (233), *The Gauntlet* (165), *The Scourge* (237), *The Church* (153), *The Christian Warrior* (152) and *Isis* (193).

Carlile's own writings were usually reprints of his articles in his own periodicals. They include *The Life of Thomas Paine* (147), *An Address to the Men of Science* (148), *The Gospel According to Richard Carlile* (146), *An Exposure of Freemasonry* (145), and *Every Woman's Book* (144). The last of these has the distinction of being the first book in English which gave specific information on birth control. It should also be added that Carlile published accounts of both his own trial (*The Mock Trial of Richard Carlile* [150]) and of those of his wife and shopmen (149).

No full biography of Richard Carlile exists at present, although one is currently being written (see Appendix VII). Several attempts at a partial biography have been made. Holyoake wrote *The Life and*

Character of Richard Carlile (184). Campbell's *The Battle of the Press as Told in the Story of Richard Carlile* (142) provides a collection of Carlile's letters, strung together with narrative. Aldred's *Richard Carlile, Agitator* (127) and Cole's *Richard Carlile* (155) can also be mentioned. A long chapter on Carlile also appears in Wickwar's *The Struggle for Freedom of the Press, 1819–1832* (260).

Robert Taylor (1784–1844) was a remarkable man. The son of fairly well-to-do parents, his high intelligence and good memory were soon apparent. Taylor was sent to train as a surgeon, and later became a member of the Royal College of Surgeons. He practiced medicine for a short while before becoming interested in being a clergyman. He then attended Cambridge, receiving his B.A. in 1813. For a while he was a curate at Midhurst (after becoming ordained in the Church of England), but long discussions with a skeptical local resident shook his beliefs. A period of extensive reading and thought followed, prompting him to publically declare himself a deist. As a result, he lost his curacy, and became an outcast.

Taylor wandered to London and Dublin, not managing to find steady employment. In November 1824, he held the first meeting (in London) of a group he called "The Christian Evidence Society." Taylor had formed this group for the purpose of examining the worth of the evidences for Christianity. He soon found that his lectures and discussion groups were gaining in popularity. Nearly one-hundred lectures were given before their great popularity so alarmed the authorities that a charge of blasphemy was brought against him.

Taylor's blasphemy trial was held on October 24, 1827. A published report of the trial exists (253). He was convicted and sentenced to a year in jail. While there, he wrote two of his three major works, *Syntagma of the Evidences of the Christian Religion* (252), and *The Diegesis* (250). He also contributed articles to Richard Carlile's magazine *The Lion* (199). After his release from jail, Taylor and Carlile embarked upon an "infidel mission" in the north of England, lecturing and debating with the clergymen (when their challenge to debate was taken up). After returning to London, Taylor lectured at a hall called The Rotunda. His lectures on the astronomical basis of Christianity were later published as *The Devil's Pulpit* (249). A second charge of blasphemy was brought against Taylor for one of his lectures. This time he was convicted and sentenced to two years in jail. He had a difficult time in this jail, and emerged a broken man. Taylor married a wealthy widow and retired to France, where he practiced as a surgeon until his death.

There has never been a full biography of Taylor, although a pamphlet covering his life was written by Cutner (161). Another, even shorter, pamphlet on Taylor was written by Aldred (126). There is a chapter on Taylor in *Half-Hours with the Freethinkers* (67), First Series, #23. Taylor started his autobiography in his journal *The Philalethean* (251), although that journal ceased publication after only eight issues.

Julian Hibbert (1800–1834) made an important contribution to the British freethought movement, despite his short life. He was the son of wealthy West Indian plantation owners, and he used his money to further freethought activities and radical politics. He contributed a few anonymous articles to Richard Carlile's *The Republican* (239). When Carlile was being prosecuted for blasphemy, Hibbert contributed several thousand pounds to help pay his expenses. He also aided Robert Taylor. Hibbert spoke a few times at Carlile's Rotunda, and employed James Watson as a compositor after Watson was released from jail for selling Carlile's publications. When Watson went into business later as an independent freethought book publisher, Hibbert gave him a press, type, and money.

Hibbert published four separate items of his own. Two were reprints of Greek works, which Hibbert printed in his own Greek typeface. The other two were more strictly freethought works, and deserve further mention. The first was *A Brief Sketch of the Life and Writings of the Baron D'Holbach* (174), while the second was the first section of *A Dictionary of Modern Anti-Superstitionists* (175). This was an ambitious project for a complete biographical dictionary of freethinkers. Unfortunately, it never got past the name Annet. The section "A – Annet," which was published, did reach 128 pages in length, and showed vast scholarship.

Hibbert's early death (at age thirty-four) has been attributed to the shock he received at being denounced publicly (in court) by a magistrate for refusing to take the oath on a Bible. Hibbert's death followed shortly thereafter, although he had been in delicate health for most of his life.

There are no full biographies of Hibbert. There is a bio-bibliographical article by Gilmour (167), an article by Wiener in *The Biographical Dictionary of Modern British Radicals* (261), and an article by Holyoake in *The Reasoner* (181). Hibbert remains important as a behind-the-scenes financier who helped play an important role in the freethought movement.

Godfrey Higgins (1772–1833) was the only son of wealthy parents. He went to Cambridge, but did not graduate. Higgins then studied law, but did not practice. When his father died and left him a large sum of money, he became a "country squire." He served several years in the volunteer militia, retiring as a major. He also was a justice of the peace and a magistrate. Higgins used his position as a magistrate to start the first reform of the British mental hospitals. He then devoted himself to the study of the origins of religions. It is said that he spent ten hours a day for more than twenty years in this activity.

Higgins' first publication as a result of this study was *Horae Sabbaticae* (179), in 1826. He then produced *The Celtic Druids* (178) and *An Apology for the Life of Mohammed* (177). These served as preludes for his greatest work, *Anacalypsis* (176), published in two large volumes (the second one posthumously). Although Higgins died when his major work was almost complete, the reception it received would have totally discouraged him. It was more or less ignored. The book did, gradually, become a standard reference work for freethinkers for the next seventy-five years. It contains a treasure house of obscure information on the early origins of Christianity and the eastern religions. Much of the scholarship in it is now outdated, but the book remains a monument to the industriousness of a single scholar.

There has never been a biography of Godfrey Higgins. Perhaps the best account of his life (with a bibliography of his works) is the chapter by Shepard (called "Postface") which is found at the end of the University Books edition of *Anacalypsis*. Although *Anacalypsis* has been reprinted several times, it is still a rather difficult book to obtain.

Charles Southwell (1814–1860) began life with several strikes against him. He was the youngest of thirty-three children, and the only child of his father's last marriage. He grew up in poverty in London, leaving school at the age of twelve. Part of the reason was financial, but Charles was also a discipline problem at school. He became interested in religion through reading a volume of sermons forced upon him by a religious fellow worker. In 1830 he left his factory job and became a radical bookseller in London. Southwell joined a lecturing society, and was soon called upon to give lectures, when it was discovered that he had a natural talent for public speaking. After a short term of service in the Spanish Legion fighting in Spain, he returned to London and became a "missionary" for Robert Owen. A personality clash with someone in the movement caused Southwell to leave. We next find him in Bristol, where he opened a bookshop and publishing office with a printer named William Chilton in 1841. In November of that year, the partners issued the first number of a magazine called *The Oracle of Reason* (210). This has been called the first openly atheistic magazine ever published in England.

Southwell was soon in trouble over *The Oracle of Reason*. A blasphemy charge was placed against him. Southwell spent some time in jail before the authorities would accept his bail. Nevertheless, *The Oracle* continued to appear. At his trial for blasphemy in 1842, Southwell defended himself but was convicted. A published report of *The Trial of Charles Southwell for Blasphemy* (247) exists. Southwell received a sentence of twelve months in jail and a 100 pound fine. While he was in jail, George Jacob Holyoake was one of the editors of *The Oracle*.

After Southwell's release from jail, he resumed lecturing. He also appeared in a number of Shakespearean plays, but never really made a success of either venture. Southwell did publish a number of pamphlets, including a now very rare autobiography entitled *Confessions of a Freethinker* (242). He also founded a magazine called *The Investigator* (192). Southwell left rather suddenly for Australia in 1855.

Upon his arrival in Australia, Charles Southwell tried to earn his living as a public lecturer. Since he was not known to be a freethinker at that point, his historical lectures were well attended. It was only after he announced his candidacy for the Legislative Council of Victoria that his freethought reputation caught up with him. He lost the election. Another round of Shakespearean performances took Southwell to Auckland, New Zealand on tour, where he remained. The last few years of his life were spent in Auckland. He started a newspaper, called *The Auckland Examiner* (129), which was a one-man muckraking operation. He kept it going for over three years. The paper expired just two weeks before Southwell himself died of what appears to have been tuberculosis. Southwell was buried in Auckland.

Charles Southwell's publications are all pamphlets or journal articles. Among his most important writings can be included *Review of a Controversy Between the Rev. Brewin Grant and G. J. Holyoake* (245), which made Holyoake his enemy, *An Apology for Atheism* (240) and its abridgement, called *Superstition Unveiled* (246), *I Am An Infidel. Why Are You a Christian?* (243), *Christianity Proved Idolatry* (241), and *The Impossibility of Atheism Demonstrated* (244).

Other than the rare autobiography, there is no published biography of Southwell. His autobiography covers only the early part of his life. There is a chapter on Southwell in the second series of *Half-Hours With the Freethinkers* (67). An article about him by Standring (248) gives a good sketch of his early life. The mistaken idea that Southwell converted to Christianity late in life and edited a Methodist newspaper seems to have creeped into the literature. The fallacy of this idea, and a good picture of Southwell's last years are provided in the series of articles entitled *Charles Southwell in Australia and N.Z.* (227) by Pearce.

George Jacob Holyoake (1817–1906) is the first person to be discussed in this book whose life greatly overlapped two major periods of freethought history. Holyoake, born in Birmingham, was an important "radical" freethinker during the 1840s, and remained an active free-thought leader (although of a more conservative kind) until his death at the age of eighty-eight in 1906. Thus, he was also a leading figure of the "Bradlaugh Era." In order to fit Holyoake neatly into this history, therefore, his life and career will be divided into two sections, with the year 1860 as the midpoint. This chapter will deal only with the earlier part of his career.

Holyoake came from a poor family with a large number of children. His early education was obtained at the Birmingham Mechanic's Institute, where he excelled in mathematics. He soon became a teacher there, and then superintendent of the educational classes. In 1840, Holyoake left the Institute to become a "socialist missionary" for Robert Owen. Owen's movement was then very strong among the working classes. Holyoake's job was to lecture about Owenism in the Worcester area, and then in the Sheffield area. When his fellow "missionary," Charles Southwell, was prosecuted for blasphemy (after Southwell had left Owen's service), Holyoake was outraged. Although he was not an atheist himself at that time, he volunteered to take over the editorship of *The Oracle of Reason* (210). Holyoake was on his way by foot to visit Southwell in jail when he stopped at Cheltenham to give a scheduled lecture on "Home Colonisation." After the talk, a minister in the audience asked him about man's duty to God. Holyoake, evidently trying to be a bit sarcastic, replied that the people were obviously too poor to have a deity, and that God ought to, therefore, "be put upon half-pay." Holyoake proceded to Bristol, but saw in the Cheltenham newspaper of the next day that he ought to be prosecuted for blasphemy for his comments. He returned to Cheltenham to clear his name, but was arrested and charged with blasphemy. At his trial, Holyoake was counselled by the heroic Richard Carlile, but Holyoake was nevertheless convicted and sentenced to six months in jail.

While in jail, we wrote two of his better-known pamphlets, *A Short and Easy Method With the Saints* (190) and *Paley Refuted in His Own Words* (187). Upon his release, he started a magazine called *The Movement* (206), which lasted two years. He also wrote his *Practical Grammar* (188).

Holyoake was involved for short periods with other journals, none of which was very successful. In 1849, he published *The Life and Character of Richard Carlile* (184), the first separate biography of Carlile. The year before this, he published *A Logic of Facts* (186) and the year after this, *The Logic of Death* (185), both of which went through many editions. The year 1850 also saw the publication of Holyoake's account of his trial for blasphemy, which he entitled *The History of the Last Trial by Jury for Atheism in England* (182).

Holyoake had begun the publication of his most important and longest lasting journal, *The Reasoner* (234) in 1846. It ran, in one form or another, until 1872. During this time, Holyoake also held a number of public debates about "secularism," a term which he invented in 1851. Several of these debates were subsequently published. In 1857, Holyoake's investigation of the trial and imprisonment of Thomas Pooley for blasphemy in Cornwall eventually led to Pooley's release. His *The Trial of Theism* (191) followed in 1858.

Holyoake had long been involved in the Co-operative Movement. He can be considered the historian of that movement in many ways. His first history was *Self Help by the People: History of Co-operation in Rochdale* (189), published in 1858 and going through many editions and translations.

In 1853, Holyoake was presented with a "testimonial," including 250 pounds in cash. With this money he bought the printing business of James Watson, an important freethought publisher. He renamed the company "Holyoake & Co." His brother Austin was also involved in the printing business. The company continued as such until 1863.

At about this time, Holyoake became involved with Charles Bradlaugh. We must therefore leave the rest of his story to the chapter on Bradlaugh. The additional works by Holyoake and the biographies and bibliographies of him will be discussed there.

Henry Hetherington was born in London, learned the printing trade, in fighting the tax on periodicals and for helping to obtain freedom of the press in England. However, Hetherington was also an important figure in freethought publishing, as well as a convicted blasphemer. The blasphemy charge was a result of having sold C. J. Haslam's *Letters to the Clergy* (170), and cost Hetherington four months in jail in 1841.

Henry Hetherington was born in London, learned the printing trade, and became involved with the Trades Unions in London. His interest in the working man soon involved him in the Chartist movement, and then into open defiance of the laws about licensed printing. His major publication was *The Poor Man's Guardian* (232), published without the required tax stamp on it. For so doing, Hetherington received two six-month jail terms. The paper continued to be published by his friends.

Hetherington's untimely death was due in large measure to his refusal to admit that he needed help. He caught a case of cholera, and it was too late to save him by the time he admitted that he was ill. George Jacob Holyoake gave the address at Hetherington's funeral, attended by more than 2,000 people.

As a freethought publisher, Henry Hetherington produced some important works. Most of his freethought publishing activity occurred in the early 1840s. It was a period when there were few freethought publishers. Among his publications were *The Library of Reason* (196), a collection of freethought essays, Cooper's *The Infidel's Text-Book* (160), the report of his own blasphemy trial (173), his own pamphlet *Cheap Salvation* (172), and *A Few Hundred Bible Contradictions* (195). This last title belonged to a most unusual book, written by Peter Lecount (using the pseudonym "John P.Y., M.D."). It was a three-volume work, running to 1,180 pages, and remains to this day the longest single work ever published by the freethought press. It is also now one of the rarest, probably because it originally sold for twenty-seven shillings, an enormous price for a book in those days. Hetherington was also the editor of the periodical *The Freethinker's Information for the People* (164).

The only real biographies of Henry Hetherington are two pamphlets. One is Barker's *Henry Hetherington (1792—1849)* (130). The other is Holyoake's *The Life and Character of Henry Hetherington* (183), which is based upon Holyoake's funeral oration.

Robert Cooper (1819-1868) was a socialist, Owenite and free-thought leader who is little know today, even by historians of these three movements. He was born near Manchester. Referred to as a "socialist prodigy," he was teaching school at the age of fourteen, a lecturer at fifteen, and held his first debate at seventeen. By the time he was eighteen years old, his printed lectures on original sin (161) had already sold 12,000 copies. In 1840-1841, he became a full-time socialist lecturer for Robert Owen at Hull, Newcastle, and Sunderland. After this, Cooper lectured at Edinburgh and Glasgow. In 1842, he led meetings against unemployment. Remaining loyal to Owen, he was sent to London by Robert Owen himself in 1845 to serve as a lecturer and organizer there. Cooper stayed in London until 1858, after which his health became poor. This illness forced him to retire to Manchester.

Robert Cooper started a monthly periodical in London called *The London Investigator* (200) in 1854. Its main claim to fame was that Charles Bradlaugh became its editor in 1858 (when its name had been shortened to *The Investigator*). It was Bradlaugh's first magazine editorship, and it lasted until 1860, when he founded *The National Reformer* (207). This is discussed in the next chapter. Cooper is best known for his two books *The Infidel's Text-book* (160) and *The Immor-*

tality of the Soul (159). Both of these were reprinted in the United States.

There has never been a separately printed biography of Robert Cooper. He did write a short autobiography in *The National Reformer* (June 14 - July 26, 1868). This autobiography is found attached to a few editions of his *The Infidel's [or Inquirer's] Text-Book*.

Thomas Paterson (c. 1801–?) sprang into the spotlight to become one of the most outspoken freethinkers of the 1840s, then vanished into obscurity almost as quickly. No death date is available for Paterson because he emigrated to the United States in the late 1840s (probably in 1848), and never took a public position about anything in the United States. He seems to have left absolutely no trace of himself after leaving Scotland.

Paterson was born in the vicinity of Lanark, Scotland. Little is known about his early life. He does not seem to have been involved in the freethought movement until May 1841, when he was living at Brighton. At that time George Jacob Holyoake, then the lecturer at the Sheffield Hall of Science, asked Paterson to become the "curate" of the Hall. After Holyoake was imprisoned for blasphemy, his job as editor of *The Oracle of Reason* (210) was taken over by Paterson (August 1842). In the Christmas season of 1842, Paterson placarded windows in his bookshop with posters advertising "The Existence of Christ Disproved." He was arrested and tried the following January for "displaying obscene literature in a public thoroughfare." Paterson was convicted and spent one month in Toothills prison.

When two Scottish booksellers (Finlay and Robinson) were arrested for selling blasphemous publications in Edinburgh, Paterson went to Edinburgh and set up a "Blasphemy Depot," as he called it, which sold all of the prosecuted works. He was arrested in August 1843, tried, convicted, and sentenced to fifteen months' felon's treatment in Perth jail. After his release, he travelled about Britain, and shortly thereafter left for America.

Paterson's publications are few. He wrote a number of articles in *The Oracle of Reason* and his trial for blasphemy was published (226). His first trial for displaying obscene placards was also published as *God Versus Paterson* (225). There are no published biographies of any sort. Paterson remains a mysterious figure who was involved in the freethought movement for only a short time.

Matilda Roalfe (1813–1880) wrote virtually nothing. She was active in the freethought movement for only a few years. Roalfe was primarily a bookseller and publisher who served a term in jail for "blasphemy." She was made a freethinker by questions asked her by her Sunday school class. One of Roalfe's friends was William Chilton, who followed Thomas Paterson as the editor of *The Oracle of Reason* (210). When Chilton needed a replacement for Paterson (who was going on trial for blasphemy) to run the Edinburgh bookstore, he asked Matilda Roalfe to do so. She ran the store during part of 1843, and then opened her own "atheistical depot" in Edinburgh to sell free-thought publications. Roalfe was arrested for selling blasphemous publications and, after conviction, received sixty days in jail with felon's treatment. Upon her release she published a pamphlet entitled *Law Breaking Justified* (236), in which she announced her intention to go on selling freethought publications.

Matilda Roalfe began a magazine in 1844 called *The Plebeian* (229), with William Baker. While publishing this in Edinburgh, she sold books and published a number of freethought tracts for others, including some of the tracts of "The Infidel Tract Society." She married Walter Sanderson and settled at Galashiels, her further involvement with the freethought movement being minimal.

There is almost no published biographical information on Matilda Roalfe. Her trial for blasphemy forms a section of the pamphlet on *The Trial of Thomas Paterson for Blasphemy* (226).

James Watson (1799–1874) was born at Malton in Yorkshire. He came to London in 1822 in response to an appeal from Richard Carlile for people who would volunteer to work in the Carlile bookshop to carry on the fight for a free press. Carlile, his wife, and his sister were all in jail (or standing trial) for publishing and selling blasphemous publications. To volunteer, therefore, was not without its risks. In fact, James Watson *was* arrested in February 1823 for selling a copy of Palmer's *Principles of Nature* (224). After conviction, Watson received a twelve-month sentence.

Upon his release from prison, Watson became a compositor on Carlile's *The Republican* (239). He was really an apprentice, learning the art of composition. Julian Hibbert then hired him to set the type for a number of books he was printing privately. When Watson became ill, Hibbert nursed him back to health. Julian Hibbert gave Watson his printing press and type, also leaving him 450 guineas in his will (Hibbert died in 1834). These gifts enabled Watson to set up his own print shop and publication office. With the money from Hibbert, Watson printed an edition of D'Holbach's *The System of Nature* (180), another of Volney's *Ruins of Empires* (257), and several other works.

Watson became the major freethought publisher during the period from 1835 to 1853. In 1853, a legacy left to George Jacob Holyoake enabled him to buy Watson's press and business. Watson's major publications are discussed later in this chapter.

James Watson served three prison terms. In addition to the term for selling Palmer's book, he served six months for selling *The Poor Man's Guardian* (232), a Hetherington publication, in 1833. In 1834, he again served six months in jail for participating in a political rally.

Watson never wrote anything that was separately published. He did lecture to workingman's groups. There is a short biography of Watson by Linton, called *James Watson: A Memoir* (197).

The title of the most switchable freethinker belongs to Joseph Barker (1806–1875). He was alternately a Methodist minister and a freethought leader. Barker was born near Leeds. He became a Methodist New Connection minister. In 1845, he became a Unitarian. In 1848, he became a deist. In 1851, he went to the United States and became converted to freethought by the influence of the radical abolitionists. In 1854, Joseph Barker was elected president of the Hartford Bible Convention, a freethought meeting. He returned to England in 1855, where he held a long public debate in 1855 with Brewin Grant at Halifax. Barker returned to the U. S., where he became a freethought lecturer at Philadelphia in 1857. In 1860 he returned to England and held a public debate with Thomas Cooper. He was then associated with Charles Bradlaugh in the formation and editing of *The National Reformer* (207) in 1860–1861. Barker finally broke with Bradlaugh over the issue of birth control (Bradlaugh favored it, Barker opposed it). In 1863, he reconverted to Christianity, becoming a Primitive Methodist minister. He returned to the United States as a Methodist minister in 1868, but seems to have done nothing notable.

Barker published a large number of pamphlets of his own, reflecting his position on both sides of the religious spectrum. Some of his more important freethought writings include *How Did You Become an Infidel?* (131), *Confessions of Joseph Barker, a Convert from Christianity* (133), and *An Essay on the "Essays and Reviews"* (134). Also of importance is his *The Bible: Its Worth, Origin and How to Read It* (132). Besides editing *The National Reformer* with Bradlaugh in 1860–61, Barker had his own magazines during his Christian phases. He also wrote an autobiography, *The Life of Joseph Barker* (135), which was edited by his nephew (J. T. Barker), and published posthumously. There is a chapter on Barker in *Half-Hours With the Freethinkers* (67), First Series, #23.

Robert Owen (1771–1858) is well known as a socialist leader and utopian. He was opposed to organized religion for economic reasons. He thought that it helped hold the working class in poverty and ignorance. Owen's stance on religion made some of his economic doctrines difficult for some to accept. Owen's connection to freethought lies in those writings, which included *The Advantages and Disadvantages of Religion* (211) and sections of *A New View of*

Society (214). There was also his debate with Alexander Campbell (212). His son, Robert Dale Owen, was associated with Frances Wright D'Arusmont in some of his utopian schemes. Although born in Scotland, Frances Wright spent most of her life in the United States. She has therefore been discussed in the *Freethought in the United States* (140) volume.

There are two bibliographies of Robert Owen's writings and of works about him. One is by The National Library of Wales, and is called *A Bibliography of Robert Owen, The Socialist, 1771-1858* (23). The other makes up a large part of the book *Quest For The New Moral World* (169), by Harrison. The bibliography occupies slightly over 100 pages of the book. There is an autobiography of Robert Owen (213), and a large number of biographies, chief among them those by Podmore (230), Cole (156), Jones (194) and, Pollard and Salt (231).

Jeremy Bentham (1748–1832) was noted primarily for his social and economic reforms and writings. He was a freethinker, and was responsible for several freethought publications. Two of them were Thomas Scott pamphlets called *The Church of England Catechism Examined* (137) and *A Few Self-Contradictions of the Bible* (138). Bentham was also the author (and George Grote the editor) of a powerful book called *Analysis of the Influence of Natural Religion on the Temporal Happiness of Mankind* (136), issued under the pseudonym "Philip Beauchamp."

Francis Place (1771–1854) was a London tailor who held an important place in the reform movements of the workingman. He was also important as an innovator of birth control. Place was a friend of Richard Carlile's and often supported him. He was an atheist, but wrote little for publication on any subject (other than flyers). There is a good biography of him by Wallas called *The Life of Francis Place* (258).

Emma Martin (1812–1851) was born in Bristol. She was raised as a strict Baptist. In 1839, she heard a lecture by Alexander Campbell which made her a religious doubter. After leaving her husband around 1840, she became a freethought lecturer. Emma Martin was quite popular during the 1840s. In 1845, she was scheduled to debate about Christianity with Robert Lowery in Scotland, when she was arrested. She subsequently posted placards all around Glasgow announcing that the sermon at a large church there would be attended by her, and the contents publicly criticised. For doing this, she was fined three pounds for causing a disturbance. Her popularity as a lecturer was such that she left from Leicester on an extended lecture tour in 1844. Mrs. Martin suffered from "consumption" (i.e., tubercu-

Iosis), which was responsible for her early death in 1851. George Jacob Holyoake performed the funeral service at her burial in Highgate Cemetery.

Emma Martin was the author of a number of freethought pamphlets. Among them were *A Few Reasons for Renouncing Christianity and Professing and Disseminating Infidel Opinions* (203), *Baptism a Pagan Rite* (201), *A Funeral Service, Occasioned by the Death of Richard Carlile* (204), and *The Bible No Revelation* (202). The only "biographical" writing about Mrs. Martin is the rather uninformative chapter about her which appeared in the Second Series of *Half-Hours With the Freethinkers* (67). Her main contribution was as a highly respected and effective public lecturer for freethought.

There were only a few freethought organizations which existed during this period. The Anti-Persecution Union was formed during the time at which George Jacob Holyoake was being tried for blasphemy (i.e., 1842–1843). It raised money and issued publications to help fight or prevent blasphemy prosecutions. Many speeches and meetings were held to protest the prosecutions of Holyoake, Southwell, Paterson, Finlay, Roalfe, and others. One of the major organizers of the Union was Maltus Q. Ryall.

The London Secular Society was formed in 1853 by James Watson, George Jacob Holyoake and others. It hired Samuel Pooley as a full-time missionary. Holyoake and others went on lecturing tours for the Society. Its activities declined after 1855.

The London Atheistical Society, formed in 1843, had the purpose of establishing the right of free discussion on all religious subjects and of obtaining the repeal of all laws interfering with the right of conscience. Thomas Powell was an early secretary.

Fleet Street House in London was formed by George Jacob Holyoake as a headquarters for freethought activities. Watson's publishing business was moved here in 1853, when the House began its major period of activity. In addition to publishing, freethought leaders were trained, and the building served as a meeting house. It lasted until 1862.

The Halls of Science were an outgrowth of the Owenist movement. They were set up all over England. The freethinkers often used these facilities when the Owenites ran them, and they took them over for various periods after Owenism declined as a movement. The major London facility of this type was the City Road Hall of Science. Holyoake lectured here, and much later, it was to be one of Charles Bradlaugh's major speaking platforms. The John Street Institution in London was similarly used for freethought lectures for many years.

The first freethought organizations were the Zetetic Societies, the first being formed at Edinburgh in 1821 to support the ideas of Richard Carlile. Other minor "organizations" were the meeting houses run by Carlile himself (The Rotunda), Robert Taylor (The Aeropagus), and Charles Southwell (Paragon Hall).

There was a proliferation in the number of freethought periodicals published during this period. Richard Carlile led the way with his publications, including *The Republican* (239), *The Lion* (199), *The Gauntlet* (165), *Isis* (193), *The Prompter* (233), and the others which have been mentioned. There was also Taylor's *Philalethean* (251), Southwell's *Oracle of Reason* (210) and *Investigator* (192), Holyoake's *The Reasoner* (234) and *The Movement* (205), the first few years of Bradlaugh's *The National Reformer* (207), and rather obscure *Freethinker's Information for the People* (164).

A number of freethought publishers made their first appearance during this period. Again, Richard Carlile was among the pioneers. His publications included most of Thomas Paine's works, many of the first translations into English of D'Holbach's and Voltaire's works (many of these included in *The Deist* [143]), Volney's *Ruins* (257), Robert Taylor's works (249, 250, 252), Palmer's *Principles of Nature* (224), Carlile's own pamphlet writings, and reports of the various blasphemy trials with which he was involved (149).

James Watson obtained the press which originally belonged to Julian Hibbert and set himself up as a printer and publisher of freethought books in 1843. He published some of Charles Southwell's pamphlets, some of Robert Taylor's pamphlets, some of D'Holbach's works, and many Robert Owen items (and Robert Dale Owen as well), many Thomas Paine works, many of George Jacob Holyoake's early writings, and some of Emma Martin's pamphlets. He stopped publishing under his own imprint in 1854.

Holyoake and Company (started in 1854) published many of the works of Joseph Barker, many Robert Cooper pamphlets, most of George Jacob Holyoake's own writings, many of Robert Owen and Robert Dale Owen's writings, Thomas Paine's works, and some Voltaire and Volney. Holyoake and Company (consisting of Austin and George Jacob Holyoake) was succeeded by Austin and Company in 1864. They published many of the same items as Holyoake and Company, plus pamphlets of John Watts, Austin Holyoake, Charles Bradlaugh's early works, and, of course, George Jacob Holyoake's writings. The company ceased publishing with Austin Holyoake's death in 1874.

Matilda Roalfe published freethought works and had a freethought bookstore for a short time in the 1842–1844 period in Edinburgh.

She published some of Charles Southwell's pamphlets, along with a few items relating to blasphemy trials.

Henry Hetherington published a number of blasphemy trial reports, his own pamphlet writings, the *Library of Reason* (196) series, and Peter Lecount's three-volume work, *A Few Hundred Bible Contradictions* (195), called the longest freethought book ever published.

There were several other freethought publishers who could be lumped together as rather less important. These include Abel Heywood of Manchester (whose sons continued the company from its 1835 founding until well into the 1880s), B. D. Cousins of London, and Frederick Farrah, whose publishing activities were at their peak during the next major period of freethought activity. Daniel Isaac Eaton also published a number of Thomas Paine items, some of which caused him to be imprisoned.

Between the years 1760 and 1860, a great change had come over the British freethought movement. First of all, it became a movement, with periodicals, publishers, and organizations of its own. Secondly, it changed from a form which accepted the existence of a God while criticizing the rest of orthodox Christianity (i.e., deism), into a frank form of atheism, in which even the existence of God was questioned. The large number of blasphemy prosecutions which occurred during this period made freethinkers unite and agree that something had to be done to oppose the laws against blasphemy. We can justifiably say that the birth of British freethought, as we know it later, occurred during the first half of the nineteenth century. By 1860, the next phase was primed to begin.

BIBLIOGRAPHY

126. Aldred, Guy A. *The Devil's Chaplain: The Story of the Rev. Robert Taylor, M.A. [sic], M. R. C. S. (1784–1834)* [sic]. Glasgow, Scotland: Strickland Press, n.d. [c. 1945]. If the mistakes in the title are any indication (and they are), this work is not very trustworthy.

127. Aldred, Guy A. *Richard Carlile, Agitator*. Glasgow, Scotland: Strickland Press, 1923. Another version was published in 1941, along with an earlier pamphlet of the same title in 1912.

128. Aldridge, Alfred Owen. *Man of Reason: The Life of Thomas Paine*. London: Crescent Press, 1960.

129. *Auckland Examiner, The*. An iconoclastic, muckraking newspaper, edited and published at Auckland, New Zealand by Charles Southwell, from December 1856 to July 1860.

130. Barker, Ambrose. *Henry Hetherington (1792–1849)*. London: Pioneer Press, [1938].

131. Barker, Joseph. *An Answer to the Question, How Did You Become an Infidel? With Some Account of My Religious Experience*. London: Holyoake & Co., n.d. [c. 1859].

132. Barker, Joseph. *The Bible: Its Worth, Origin and How to Read It*. London: Beveridge & Barker, n.d. [c. 1859].

133. Barker, Joseph. *Confessions of Joseph Barker, A Convert From Christianity*. London: Holyoake & Co., 1858. Reprinted from *The Reasoner*.

134. Barker, Joseph. *An Essay on the "Essays and Reviews."* London: Barker & Co., n.d. [c. 1861].

135. Barker, John Thomas, ed. *The Life of Joseph Barker, Written by His Nephew, John Thomas Barker*. London: Hodder & Stoughton, 1880. Barker also wrote two earlier versions of his autobiography. One was called *Teachings of Experience; Or, Lessons I Have Learned on My Way Through Life* (London: James Beveridge, 1869). The other, substantially the same in content, although rewritten, was *Modern Skepticism: A Journey Through the Land of Doubt and Back Again. A Life Story*. (Philadelphia: Smith, English & Co., 1874).

136. Bentham, Jeremy and Grote, George, ed. [as "Philip Beauchamp"]. *Analysis of the Influence of Natural Religion on the Temporal Happiness of Mankind*. London: Richard Carlile, 1822.

137. Bentham, Jeremy. *The Church of England Catechism Examined*. Ramsgate, England: Thomas Scott, 1868.

138. Bentham, Jeremy. *A Few Self-Contradictions of the Bible*. London [Ramsgak]: Thomas Scott, n.d. (c. 1868].

139. Berman, David. "The Genesis of Avowed Atheism in Britain." *Question* 11 (1978): 44–55. Published by Rationalist Press Association, London.

140. Brown, Marshall G. and Stein, Gordon. *Freethought in the United States: A Descriptive Bibliography*. Westport, Conn.: Greenwood Press, 1978.

141. Burke, Edmund. *Reflections on the French Revolution*. London: Printed for L. Dodsley, 1790.

142. Campbell, Theophilia Carlile. *The Battle of the Press as Told in the Story of Richard Carlile*. London: A. & H. B. Bonner, 1899.

143. Carlile, Richard, ed. *The Deist; or Moral Philosopher. Being an Impartial Inquiry After Moral and Theological Truths: Selected from the Writings of the Most Celebrated Authors in Ancient and Modern Times*. London: R. Carlile. Issued as three bound volumes (as well as available by each title separately). Bound volume title pages were dated: Vol. 1: 1819, Vol. 2: 1819, Vol. 3: 1826. Some

of the individual titles in the 1819 volumes bear publishing dates as late as 1826. Among the titles included are: *Letters to Eugenia* (Baron D'Holbach), *A Letter from Thrasybulus to Leucippe* (usually attributed to Freret), *Church Reform* (Richard Carlile), *The Important Examination of the Holy Scriptures* (Voltaire), *A Letter to the Rev. Dr. S. Chandler, From the Writer of The Man After God's Own Heart* [Peter Annet?], *Answer to Dr. Priestley's Letters to a Philosophical Unbeliever* (M. Turner), *Watson Refuted* (Samuel Francis), *A Letter to Sir Samuel Shepherd, Knt.* (Richard Carlile), *Principles of Nature* (Elihu Palmer), *The God of the Jews; or Jehovah Unveiled* (Voltaire), *The Doubts of Infidels* (W. Nicholson), *Christianity Unveiled* (Baron D'Holbach), *The Life of David; Or The History of the Man After God's Own Heart* (Peter Annet?), *Good Sense* (Baron D'Holbach), *The Free Enquirer* (edited by Peter Annet), *Lectures* (Peter Annet) and *Lord Chesterfield's Ears* (Voltaire). The titles seem to have been fairly indiscriminately bundled together for binding in each volume, since there is some wide variation in the contents of individual copies of Vol. 1 and Vol. 2 examined.

144. Carlile, Richard. *Every Women's Book.* London: R. Carlile, 1826. The first book of practical birth control advice in English.

145. Carlile, Richard. *An Exposure of Freemasonry.* London: R. Carlile, 1831. Later rewritten and issued as *A Manual of Freemasonry.* London: William Reeves, [1853].

146. Carlile, Richard. *The Gospel According to Richard Carlile.* London: R. Carlile, 1827.

147. Carlile, Richard. *The Life of Thomas Paine, Written Purposely to Bind With His Writings.* London: M. A. Carlile, 1820.

148. Carlile, Richard, *An Address to the Men of Science, Calling upon Them to Stand Forward and Vindicate the Truth . . . London: R.* Carlile, 1821.

149. Carlile, Richard, ed. The published trials included *Report of the Trial of Mrs. Carlile* [Jane Carlile]. London: J. Carlile, 1821; *Report of the Trial of Mary-Anne Carlile for Publishing A New Year's Address to the Reformers of Great Britain.* London: R. Carlile, 1821; *Report of the Trial of Humphrey Boyle . . . as "A Man With Name Unknown," for Publishing a Blasphemous and Seditious Libel. . . .* London: R. Carlile. 1822; *Report of the Trial of Mrs. Suzannah Wright for Publishing, in His Shop, the Writings and Correspondence of R. Carlile.* London: R. Carlile, 1822.

150. Carlile, Richard, ed. *Reports of the Proceedings of the Court of King's Bench . . . Being the Mock Trials of Richard Carlile for Alleged Blasphemous Libel.* London: R. Carlile, 1822. Parts of this were issued in 1819 and 1820.

151. Cheetham, James. *The Life of Thomas Paine, Author of Common Sense, Rights of Man, etc., etc., etc.,* New York: Southwick and Pelsue, 1809. Another hostile biography was by "Francis Oldys" [George Chalmers?], called *The Life of Thomas Paine, the Author of Rights of Man, Age of Reason &c. With a Defence of His Writings.* London: Printed for I. Stockdale, 1792.

152. *Christian Warrior, The.* Periodical published by Richard Carlile, in London, from 1842–1843.

153. *Church, The.* A periodical published by Richard Carlile in London, in about 1838. No copies are known to have survived.

154. Cohen, Chapman. *Thomas Paine: Pioneer of Two Worlds.* London: National Secular Society, n.d. [c. 1950].

155. Cole, G. D. H. *Richard Carlile.* London: Victor Gollancz for the Fabian Society, 1943. Fabian Tract Series, #13.

156. Cole, G. D. H. *Robert Owen.* London: E. Benn, 1925.

157. Conway, Moncure D. *The Life of Thomas Paine.* 2 vols. New York: G. P. Putnam's Sons, 1892.

158. Conway, Moncure D., ed. *Writings of Thomas Paine.* 4 vols. New York: G. P. Putnam's Sons, 1894–1896.

159. Cooper, Robert. *The Immortality of the Soul, Religiously and Philosophically Considered: A Series of Lectures.* London: James Watson, 1852. Also published in the United States by J. P. Mendum, (Boston, 1882).

160. Cooper, Robert. *The Infidel's Text-Book, Being the Substance of Thirteen Lectures on the Bible.* Hull, England: R. Johnson, 1846. Reprinted in the United States by J. P. Mendum (Boston, 1858) and also issued by Mendum under the title of *The Inquirer's Text-Book.*

161. Cooper, Robert. *A Lecture on Original Sin, Delivered in the Social Institution, Great George Street, Salford.* Manchester, England: A. Heywood, 1838.

161a. Cutner, Herbert. *Robert Taylor.* London: Pioneer Press, [1954]. This pamphlet is the best biographical study of Taylor.

162. Edwards, Samuel. *Rebel: A Biography of Tom Paine.* New York: Praeger Publishers, 1974.

163. Foner, Philip, ed. *The Complete Writings of Thomas Paine.* 2 vols. New York: Citadel Press, 1945. The most complete edition of Paine's writings so far published.

164. *Freethinker's Information for the People, The.* A freethought periodical, edited by Henry Hetherington, and published by Paton and Love in Glasgow, 1842–1843. It ran for two volumes.

165. *Gauntlet, The.* A freethought periodical published in London by Richard Carlile, in 1833.

166. Gibbon, Edward. *The History of the Decline and Fall of the Roman Empire*. London: 6 vols. Printed for W. Strahan & T. Cadell. Published between 1776 (vol. 1) and 1788 (vol. 6).

167. Gilmour, J. S. L. "Some Uncollected Authors: XXVI: Julian Hibbert, 1800–1834." *The Book Collector* (London) 9 (1960): 446–51.

168. Gould, F. J. *Thomas Paine (1737–1809)*. London: Leonard Parsons, 1925.

169. Harrison, John F. C. *Quest for the New Moral World*. New York: Charles Scribner's Sons, 1969. British edition published by Routledge & Kegan Paul (London, 1969), under the title *Robert Owen and the Owenites in Britain and America: The Quest for a New Moral World*.

170. Haslam, Charles Junius. *Letters to the Clergy of All Denominations, Showing the Errors, Absurdities and Irrationalities of Their Doctrines*. Manchester, England: Abel Heywood, 1838. Originally published as a series of pamphlets. The book is basically a critique of those portions of the Old Testament which Haslam felt contained immoralities.

171. Hawke, David Freeman. *Paine*. New York: Harper & Row, 1974.

172. Hetherington, Henry. *Cheap Salvation; Or, An Antidote to Priestcraft: Being a Succinct, Practical, Essential and Rational Religion, Deduced from the New Testament, the General Adoption of Which Would Supersede the Necessity for a Hireling Priesthood, and Save this Over-Taxed Nation Fifteen Millions Per Annum!!!* London: Published by the Author [1832].

173. Hetherington, Henry. *A Full Report of the Trial of Henry Hetherington, on an Indictment for Blasphemy, Before Lord Denman and a Special Jury, at the Court of Queen's Bench, Westminster, on Tuesday, December 8, 1840; For Selling Haslam's Letters to the Clergy of All Denominations: With the Whole of the Authorities Cited in the Defence, at Full Length*. London: Henry Hetherington, 1840.

174. [Hibbert, Julian]. *A Brief Sketch of the Life and Writings of the Baron D'Holbach*. London: James Watson, 1834. This pamphlet was also included (repaginated) as the Introduction to Watson's edition of Holbach's *The System of Nature* (#179). This edition was retitled *Nature and Her Laws*.

175. [Hibbert, Julian]. *A Dictionary of Modern Anti-Superstitionists: Or, An Account, Arranged Alphabetically, of Those, Who, Whether Called Atheists, Sceptics, Deists, Latitudinarians, Religious Reformers, or &C. Have, During the Last ten Centuries, Contributed Towards*

the *Diminution of Superstition*. London: R. Carlile, 1826. Only the first two parts, reaching the name of Peter Annet and comprising 128 pages, were ever published. The reason given for stopping publication was "for want of purchasers."

176. Higgins, Godfrey. *Anacalypsis, an Attempt to Draw Aside the Veil of the Saitic Isis; or an Inquiry Into the Origin of Languages, Nations and Religions*. 2 vols. London: Longman, Rees, Orme, Brown, Green and Longman, 1836. Volume one was published in 1833, and volume two issued posthumously in 1836 (edited by George Smallfield). A partial reprint (volume one only) was issued in 1878 by J. W. Bouton (New York). A full reprint was issued by Macy-Masius (New York) in 1927, with another reprint by University Books (New Hyde Park, N.Y.) in 1965.

177. Higgins, Godfrey. *An Apology for the Life and Character of the Celebrated Prophet of Arabia Called Mohammed or the Illustrious*. London: R. Hunter, 1829.

178. Higgins, Godfrey. *The Celtic Druids, or an Attempt to Shew that the Druids Were Priests of Oriental Colonies Who Emigrated from India, and Were the Introducers of the First or Cadmean System of Letters, and the Builders of Stonhenge, of Carnac and of Other Cyclopean Works in Asia and Europe*. London: R. Hunter, 1827.

179. Higgins, Godfrey. *Horae Sabbaticae: or an Attempt to Correct Certain Superstitions and Vulgar Errors Respecting the Sabbath*. London: A. J. Valpy, 1826. Two later British editions and one American one (Peter Eckler) were done.

180. Holbach, P. H. T. Baron D'. *The System of Nature*. (Watson's edition was retitled *Nature and Her Laws*) 2 vols. in one. London: J. Watson, 1834.

181. Holyoake, George Jacob. "Julian Hibbert." *The Reasoner* 29 (1855): 105-6.

182. Holyoake, George Jacob. *The History of the Last Trial by Jury for Atheism in England: A Fragment of an Autobiography*. London: J. Watson, 1850. A detailed report of Holyoake's blasphemy trial in 1842.

183. Holyoake, George Jacob. *The Life and Character of Henry Hetherington*. London: J. Watson, 1849. Adapted from Holyoake's oration at Hetherington's funeral.

184. Holyoake, George Jacob. *The Life and Character of Richard Carlile*. London: J. Watson, 1849. The first biography of Carlile.

185. Holyoake, George Jacob. *The Logic of Death; Or, Why Should the Atheist Fear to Die?* London: J. Watson, 1850.

186. Holyoake, George Jacob. *A Logic of Facts; Or Plain Hints on Reasoning*. London: J. Watson, 1848.

187. Holyoake, George Jacob. *Paley Refuted in His Own Words*. London: Hetherington, [1843]. Written while Holyoake was in jail.

188. Holyoake, George Jacob. *Practical Grammar; Or, Composition Divested of Difficulties; With Select Examples from the Writings of Elegant Authors, Containing All that is Necessary for Ordinary Purposes and no More; and Intended for the Use of Those Who Have Little Time to Study*. London: J. Watson, 1844.

189. Holyoake, George Jacob. *Self Help by the People: History of Co-operation in Rochdale. Part I, 1844–1857*. London: Holyoake & Co., 1858.

190. Holyoake, George Jacob. *A Short and Easy Method With the Saints*. London: Hetherington, [1843]. Written while in jail.

191. Holyoake, George Jacob. *The Trial of Theism*. London: Holyoake & Co., [1858].

192. *Investigator, The*. (London). A freethought journal, edited by Charles Southwell, and published in 1843. It lasted twenty-eight issues.

193. *Isis*. (London). A journal published by Richard Carlile in 1832, and containing mostly the speeches and writings of "Isis," the stage name of Eliza Sharples Carlile, later Richard's common law wife. Isis' lectures were delivered at The Rotunda, and were probably written for her by Robert Taylor.

194. Jones, Lloyd. *The Life, Times and Labours of Robert Owen*. 2 vols. London: S. Sonnenschein, 1889–1890.

195. [Lecount, Peter] as "John P. Y., M.D.". *A Few Hundred Bible Contradictions, A Hunt After the Devil, and Other Odd Matters*. 3 vols. London: [Henry Hetherington], 1843.

196. *Library of Reason, The*. London: Hetherington, n.d. [c. 1843]. A series of twenty-three short freethought pamphlets, most of them reprints or translations of earlier works, which were published as a single volume, with the above title.

197. Linton, W. J. *James Watson: A Memoir*. Manchester, [England]: Abel Heywood & Son, 1880.

198. Linton, W. J. *The Life of Paine*. "By the Editor of *The National*." London: J. Watson, 1839. Later editions were called *The Life of Thomas Paine*.

199. *Lion, The*. A freethought periodical, published in London in 1828–29 by Richard Carlile. It was almost entirely devoted to the career, ideas and problems of the Rev. Robert Taylor.

200. *London Investigator, The*. A periodical published in London, with Robert Cooper as the first editor. It was freethought in nature, and ran from April 1854 as a monthly. Later, Cooper retired in 1857, and Edward Truelove became publisher, with W. H. Johnson as

editor. The word *"London"* was dropped from the title in 1857. Charles Bradlaugh took over as editor in 1858. *The Investigator* stopped publishing in 1859.

201. Martin, Emma. *Baptism a Pagan Rite*, London: [James] Watson, 1844.

202. Martin, Emma. *The Bible No Revelation, Or the Inadequacy of Language to Convey a Message from God to Man*. London: Hetherington, 1844.

203. Martin, Emma. *A Few Reasons for Renouncing Christianity and Professing and Disseminating Infidel Opinions*. London: [James] Watson, n.d. [c. 1844].

204. Martin, Emma. *A Funeral Sermon, Occasioned by the Death of Richard Carlile, Preached at the Hall of Science, City Road, London*. London: Printed and Published for the Author, [1843].

205. *Moralist, The*. A periodical published in London by Richard Carlile in 1823. Only a few issues were published.

206. *Movement, Anti-Persecution Gazette and Register of Progress, The*. A magazine edited by George Jacob Holyoake. It was published weekly in London from December 1843 until mid-1845. M. Q. Ryall was the editor towards the end of its life.

207. *National Reformer, The*. A weekly freethought magazine, started by Charles Bradlaugh and Joseph Barker in April 1860. By mid-1861, Barker had left after a dispute, and George Jacob Holyoake replaced him, with John Watts as subeditor, Bradlaugh relinquishing the magazine for a while. Holyoake and Bradlaugh quarreled, and Holyoake left the editorship to John Watts in 1863. In 1866, John Watts suddenly died. Bradlaugh resumed the editorship, with Charles Watts as subeditor. Watts left after a fight in 1877. *The National Reformer* became the organ of the National Secular Society, when it was formed by Bradlaugh in 1866. Annie Besant became coeditor with Bradlaugh in 1877, and remained until her depature to Theosophy in 1889. Bradlaugh carried on the editorship alone until his death in January of 1891. After that time, John M. Robertson became the editor until the magazine finally went out of business in 1893.

208. *Newgate Monthly Magazine, The*. Issued from within the walls of Newgate prison (London) but not printed there, by the shopmen who had been imprisoned there for selling publications in Richard Carlile's shop. It was published in 1824–1825, reaching two volumes.

209. [Nicholson, William]. *The Doubts of Infidels*. London: Printed for the Author, 1781. Reprinted in London in 1819 by Richard Carlile. It also appeared in *The Deist* (#143).

210. *Oracle of Reason, The*. The first openly atheistic magazine in England, it was published at Bristol from November 1841 until

1843. It was a weekly, and completed its second volume (104 issues) before closing. The first editor was Charles Southwell. After his imprisonment, George Jacob Holyoake, William Chilton, and Thomas Paterson took over. Each was jailed in turn (although not for material which had appeared in *The Oracle*).

211. Owen, Robert. *The Advantages and Disadvantages of Religion*. Glasgow: Printed by Robert Harriston, 1829.

212. Owen, Robert and Campbell, Alexander. *Debate on the Evidences of Christianity* . . . Bethany, Virginia: A. Campbell, 1829.

213. Owen, Robert. *Life of Robert Owen. Written By Himself. With Selections From His Writings and Correspondence*. 2 vols. London: E. Wilson, 1857–58.

214. Owen, Robert. *A New View of Society; Or Essays on the Principle of the Formation of Human Character*. London: Printed for Cadell and Davies by R. Taylor & Co., 1813.

215. Paine, Thomas. *The Age of Reason; Being an Investigation of True and Fabulous Theology*. Paris: Printed for Barrois Sr., 1794. Part I. First edition of Part II is [Paris]: Printed for the Author, 1795. The H. D. Symonds (London, 1795) edition was an unauthorized one.

216. Paine, Thomas. *The Age of Reason*. London: R. Carlile, 1819.

217. Paine, Thomas. *Common Sense*. Philadelphia: R. Bell, 1776.

218. Paine, Thomas. *Examination of the Passages in the New Testament, Quoted from the Old and Called Prophecies Concerning Jesus Christ*. New York: Printed for the Author [1807]. This was first called "*The Age of Reason, Part III*" in the edition published in London by Daniel Isaac Eaton in 1811.

219. [Paine, Thomas]. *La Siècle de la Raison; ou le Sens Common des Droits de l'Homme*. "Par P. Lanthenas" [Paris: no publisher, 1793], 80p.

220. Paine, Thomas. *Reply to the Bishop of Llandaff*. London: R. Carlile, 1819. First separate edition. First published as an article in *The Theophilanthropist* (New York), 1810.

221. Paine, Thomas. *Rights of Man*. London: L. Jordan, 1791. Part II: London: L. Jordan, 1792.

222. Paine, Thomas. *Rights of Man*. London: R. Carlile, 1818.

223. Paine, Thomas. *Theological Works of Thomas Paine*. London: R. Carlile, 1819. Contains *The Age of Reason*, Parts I, II and "III," *Letter to the Hon. Thomas Erskine, Discourse Delivered to the Society of Theophilanthropists, Essay on the Origin of Free-Masonry*, and *Reply to the Bishop of Llandaff*.

224. Palmer, Elihu. *Principles of Nature; or, A Development of the Moral Causes of Happiness and Misery Among the Human Species*. London: R. Carlile, 1819. First published in New York in 1801.

225. Paterson, Thomas. *God Versus Paterson. The Extraordinary Bow-Street Police Report.* London: George Clarke, [1843].

226. Paterson, Thomas. *The Trial of Thomas Paterson for Blasphemy, Before the High Court of Justiciary, Edinburgh, With the Whole of His Bold and Effective Defence.* London: Published for the Anti-Persecution Union by H. Hetherington, 1844.

227. Pearce, Harry Hastings. "Charles Southwell in Australia and N.Z." *New Zealand Rationalist* 18 (#8) through 19 (#12). May 1957 through September 1958 issues. A monthly series of articles which helps to fill in the last years of Southwell's life and clear up several errors about him.

228. *Pennsylvania Magazine, or American Monthly Museum.* Philadelphia: Jan, 1775–July 1776. Edited by Thomas Paine.

229. *Plebian, or Poor Man's Advocate and Journal of Progress, The.* A magazine published by Matilda Roalfe and William Baker from Edinburgh in 1844. No copies known.

230. Podmore, Frank. *Robert Owen: A Biography.* 2 vols. London: George Allen & Unwin, 1906.

231. Pollard, Sidney and John Salt, eds. *Robert Owen: Prophet of the Poor.* Lewisburg, Pennsylvania: Bucknell University Press, 1971. British edition: London: Macmillan, & Co. 1971.

232. *Poor Man's Guardian, The.* Henry Hetherington's best known periodical publication, which was published in London from 1831 to 1835.

233. *Prompter, The.* Magazine published in London by Richard Carlile from 1830 to 1831.

234. *Reasoner, The.* A weekly periodical published by George Jacob Holyoake. It began in London on June 3, 1846, continuing until June 30, 1861 (nos. 1–789). It then became a monthly with the subtitle *The Counsellor* until December 1861 (nos. 790–94). It then adopted the subtitle *Secular World*, and ran from May 10, 1862 to June 1, 1864 (nos. 795–827) as a weekly. Its subtitle was then changed to *The English Leader* on June 4, 1864, and continued thus, as a weekly until October 15, 1864 (nos. 828–47). On the one issue of December 1, 1864 it takes the subtitle *Secular World* again (no. 848) and is a monthly. It becomes just *The Reasoner* for the monthly issues of 1865 (nos. 849–59, although misnumbered on the issues as "828–839"). On January 6, 1866, it became subtitled *The English Leader* again, and was again a weekly. It ran thus (with interruptions) until July 14, 1866 (nos. 860–87). After a period of nonpublication, it resumed as *The Reasoner: Review Series* (a monthly) in November and December 1868 (nos. 888-89). It lapsed again, and resumed in April and May 1870 as *The Reasoner: Review Series* (nos. 890-91).

Another lapse followed and its final issues, as simply *The Reasoner*, were as a monthly from January 1871 to July 1872 (nos. 892–910).

235. Rickman, Thomas Clio. *The Life of Thomas Paine*. London: Thomas Clio Rickman, 1819.

236. Roalfe, Matilda. *Law Breaking Justified*. Edinburgh: Matilda Roalfe & Co., 1844.

237. *Scourge, The*. A periodical published in London by Richard Carlile, in 1834.

238. Sherwin, W. T. *Memoirs of the Life of Thomas Paine, With Observations on His Writings, Critical and Explanatory*. London: R. Carlile, 1819.

239. *Sherwin's Political Register* (later called *The Republican*). The first periodical with which Richard Carlile was associated. It was started by W. T. Sherwin in 1817 in London. Carlile became an agent selling it until 1819, when he was asked by Sherwin to take it over. He renamed it *The Republican*, and continued the magazine as a freethought publication until the end of 1820, when it stopped for a year. It was resumed early in 1822, and lasted until the end of 1826, reaching fourteen volumes.

240. [Southwell, Charles]. *An Apology for Atheism: Addressed to Religious Investigators of Every Denomination, by One of its Apostles*. London: J. Watson, 1846.

241. [Southwell, Charles]. *Christianity Proved Idolatry; Or, A Short and Easy Method With the Christians*. Glasgow: Paton & Love, 1844.

242. Southwell, Charles. *Confessions of a Freethinker*. [London?]: no publisher, n.d. [c. 1845].

244. Southwell, Charles. *The Impossibility of Atheism Demonstrated: With Hints to Nominal Atheists: In a Letter to the Freethinkers of Great Britain*. London: J. Watson, n.d. [c. 1850].

245. Southwell, Charles. *Review of a Controversy Between the Rev. Brewin Grant and G. J. Holyoake, In the Cowper Street School Room, City Road, On the Question "What Advantages Would Accrue to Mankind Generally, and to the Working Classes in Particular, by the Removal of Christianity and the Substitution of Secularism in its Place?"* London: James Watson, 1853.

246. Southwell, Charles. *Superstition Unveiled*. London: E. Truelove, 1854. An abridgement of his *Apology for Atheism*.

247. Southwell, Charles. *The Trial of Charles Southwell for Blasphemy*. London: Hetherington, 1842. Reported by William Carpenter.

248. Standring, George. "Charles Southwell." *Our Corner* (London) 11 (1888): 155–67, 315–16.

249. Taylor, Robert. *The Devil's Pulpit*. London: R. Carlile, 1829–30 (weekly numbers). This work was not published as a com-

plete volume for many years. When it was, the work was often called "*Astronomico-Theological Lectures.*" There was an American edition.

250. Taylor, Robert. *The Diegesis*. London: R. Carlile, 1829. An investigation into the origins of Christianity before the year 200 A.D. This work was written in prison, and many of the necessary reference sources were not available to Taylor. Many of the quotations are reproduced *from memory*. There were several American editions.

251. Taylor, Robert, ed. *The Philalethean*, London: [Robert Taylor], 1823. A short-lived periodical, important mostly because it contains a portion of Taylor's autobiography (called "The Life and Opinions of Talasiphron").

252. Taylor, Robert. *Syntagma of the Evidences of the Christian Religion*. London: R. Carlile, 1829. A defence of the Manifesto of the Christian Evidence Society, which Taylor had founded to investigate the value of the "evidences" for Christianity. There was an American edition.

253. Taylor, Robert. *Trial of the Reverend Robert Taylor A. B. M. R. C. S. Upon a Charge of Blasphemy, With His Defence, as Delivered by Himself, Before the Lord Chief Justice and a Special Jury, on Wednesday, October 24, 1827. To Which is now Added the Judgement of the Court of the King's Bench, and the Reverend Defendant's Address to the Court, on Receiving its Judgement. With the Whole of the Proceedings in this Case, on the 7th of February, 1828*. London: R. Carlile, 1828.

254. [Turner, Matthew?] as "William Hammon." *Answer to Dr. Priestley's Letters to a Philosophical Unbeliever*. London: no publisher, 1782. Reprinted in 1826 by Richard Carlile in London.

255. Vale, Gilbert. *The Life of Thomas Paine*. New York: G. Vale, 1841.

256. Van der Weyde, William M. *Life of Thomas Paine*. New Rochelle, New York: Thomas Paine National Historical Association, 1925. Published as the first volume in the "Patriot's Edition" of Paine's collected works.

257. Volney, Constantine Chassboeuf, Count de. *Ruins of Empires*. London: J. Watson, 1834.

258. Wallas, Graham. *The Life of Francis Place*. London: Longmans, Green & Co., 1908.

259. Watson, Richard [The Bishop of Llandaff]. *An Apology for the Bible; In a Series of Letters, Addressed to Thomas Paine, Author of a Book Entitled, The Age of Reason, Part the Second*. Lancaster, England: W. Hamilton & W. & R. Dickson, 1796. Many other editions this same year.

260. Wickwar, William H. *The Struggle for Freedom of the Press, 1819–1832*. London: Geo. Allen and Unwin, 1928. Contains a long chapter on Richard Carlile.

261. Wiener, Joel H. "Julian Hibbert" article in *The Biographical Dictionary of Modern British Radicals. Volume 1: 1770–1830*. Edited by Joseph Baylen & Norbert J. Gossman. Hassocks, Sussex, England: Harvester Press, 1979, pages 221–22. See also the articles on Richard Carlile (p. 79–82) and Robert Taylor (By Edward Royle, p. 467–470).

262. Williamson, Audrey. *Thomas Paine: His Life, Work and Times*. London: George Allen & Unwin, 1973.

3
The Bradlaugh/Besant/ Foote Era
───── (1860-1915) ─────

The period from 1860 to 1866 marks an important transition time in the British freethought movement. The ascendency of Charles Bradlaugh as a freethought leader was beginning, and it was the start of the most prolific phase of British freethought. It was also a time of quarreling among emerging freethought leaders. Some of the quarrels were portents of troubled relationships that would re-emerge during the next fifty years.

Charles Bradlaugh tried to cooperate with Joseph Barker in the coeditorship of *The National Reformer* (207). They soon fought and dissolved the partnership. Bradlaugh and Holyoake tried to work together, but also disagreed and went their separate ways. G. W. Foote and Holyoake clashed over the editorship of *The Secularist* (416). Bradlaugh and Charles Watts clashed over the issue of birth control. Watts finally left Bradlaugh and Annie Besant, and went his own way. Bradlaugh and W. Stewart Ross ("Saladin") had a long fight over birth control that ended in the courts.

People appeared and disappeared from the leadership ranks of freethought. Charles Southwell died in New Zealand; John Watts appeared and died young; G. W. Foote appeared and stayed to become the eventual unchallenged leader; Annie Besant appeared, rose to the top, and then disappeared quickly; Charles Watts became a success both in England and in Canada. Holyoake endured. At the top of the leadership pack was Charles Bradlaugh, who remained unsurpassed, until his death, as the leader of British freethought during this period. We start our examination of this epoch of freethought history with a look at the life of Charles Bradlaugh.

Charles Bradlaugh (1833-1891) was probably the greatest single figure in British freethought in any period. Certainly no other individual was more responsible for the growth of the British freethought/atheist/ secularist movement in the latter part of the nineteenth century than he.

Bradlaugh was born in Hoxton (North London), the son of a poor lawyer's clerk. His great intelligence was apparent early. Charles was made a Sunday School teacher, and in the course of his studies, came upon what he viewed as contradictions and discrepancies among the four Gospels. When he brought his questions to the pastor's attention, he was told that he was suspended from the Sunday School, while his parents were told that he had atheistic tendencies. Bradlaugh's parents forced him out of the house, and the sixteen-year-old Bradlaugh was left to fend for himself.

At first he earned a meager living as a coal merchant, but news of his so-called atheistic tendencies soon lost him most of his customers. At the same time, Bradlaugh attended the open-air lectures held at Bonner's Fields. During his period he lived with the widow of Richard Carlile and her children, who welcomed him as a boarder. Bradlaugh continued his readings in theology, becoming more skeptical as he read. When his money was finally exhausted, Bradlaugh enlisted in the army in order to obtain the enlistment bonus. He was sent to Ireland as a member of the Dragoon Guards. There he met and became friendly with James Thomson, later to be renowned as the author of *The City of Dreadful Night* (429), one of the most atheistic poems in the English language. Eventually, a small legacy from his aunt enabled Bradlaugh to purchase his own discharge from the army in 1853.

Back in London, Bradlaugh obtained a position as a solicitor's clerk. He also married at this time. In order to shield his employer from any scandal, Bradlaugh adopted the name "Iconoclast" for all his speaking and writing activities. He was now making a name for himself as a freethought lecturer, and was learning the law. In November 1858 he took over as the editor of *The Investigator* (200). The magazine lasted only until August 1859. At that time Bradlaugh was asked to help start a new freethought magazine, to be called *The National Reformer* (207). He became coeditor with Joseph Barker, and the first issue came out in April 1860. Bradlaugh and Barker soon quarreled over the appropriateness of birth control propaganda in the magazine. Barker left his editorial post, and was replaced by George Jacob Holyoake. This arrangement lasted only three months. At that time, the two men disagreed over a legal matter. Bradlaugh took full control of *The National Reformer*. As his duties for freethought increased, he turned over the editorship to John Watts (February 1863). Unfortunately, John Watts died in 1866, leaving Bradlaugh to again assume the full editorial responsibility.

In 1866, Charles Bradlaugh decided to improve the organization of freethought in England. He and Charles Watts formed the National

Secular Society. This organization brought together as many of the various isolated freethought organizations as it was possible to do. The NSS still exists.

Bradlaugh was a powerful speaker and debater, perhaps the best that the British freethought movement has ever produced. He went on rather unsuccessful lecture tours to the United States in 1873 and 1875. One time the weather failed to cooperate and undermined his health. The other time he had to rush back to England to enter an election for parliament, occasioned by the death of the incumbent. Bradlaugh did not win.

Charles Bradlaugh ran for parliament from Northampton six times before he was elected. When he finally did receive a majority, in 1880, the House of Commons refused to allow him to affirm instead of taking the oath of office. When Bradlaugh agreed to take the oath, the House refused to allow him to do so. The case was fought for several years, and sapped a great deal of Bradlaugh's strength. He finally was seated in 1885, after being re-elected by Northampton each time the House declared his seat vacant. Once he was seated, Bradlaugh became an influential member of the parliament until his death. He became known as the unofficial "member for India."

In 1877, Charles Bradlaugh and his new partner, Annie Besant, were involved in a legal prosecution over the birth control book *The Fruits of Philosophy* (354). This case is discussed fully elsewhere in this book. In both this case and in his parliamentary struggle, his vast knowledge of the law eventually brought him victory. In 1877, Bradlaugh and Besant formed the Freethought Publishing Company. This is discussed more fully later in this section. In 1882 an attempt was made to implicate Bradlaugh in the blasphemy prosecution brought against G. W. Foote for material in *The Freethinker* (325). As Bradlaugh was not involved in this publication, his indictment was eventually dropped.

In 1888 the libelous biography of Bradlaugh (*Life of Charles Bradlaugh, M.P.* [367]) appeared. William Stewart Ross ("Saladin") was involved, and the subject is discussed in the part about him. This legal process took a great toll on Bradlaugh's health. His daughter Alice also died in 1888, and the additional defection of Annie Besant to Theosophy in 1889 didn't help matters either. Charles Bradlaugh's health had been deteriorating for some time under his tremendous workolad. In January 1891, he finally succumbed to kidney disease.

Charles Bradlaugh's writings are voluminous. In addition to editing the magazines already mentioned, many of his magazine articles were reprinted as pamphlets. He also wrote a number of books which did not first appear as magazine articles. Among his most notable books were *The Freethinker's Text-Book* (288), *Humanity's Gain From Unbelief* (290), *A Plea For Atheism* (293), *The Autobiography of Charles Bradlaugh* (286), *Speeches* (295), *Labour and Law* (292), *The Impeachment of the House of Brunswick* (291), and *Genesis* (289).

Bradlaugh's pamphlets were issued over the years, but occasionally were collected into single volumes. Among these pamphlet volumes were *Debates in Theology* (287), *Theological Essays* (296), and the collected reprint entitled *The Political Pamphlets of Charles Bradlaugh* (294). Charles Bradlaugh also participated in many debates, some of which were published. A number were collected in the work *Debates in Theology*, mentioned above. Others are available only as separate pamphlets.

There have been a number of biographies of Charles Bradlaugh. The first was his early *Autobiography* (286). Shortly after his death, his daughter and his friend Robertson collaborated to produce *Charles Bradlaugh: A Record of His Life and Work* (4). Robertson expanded his section into a separate work later (389). During Bradlaugh's life, an attempt at a biography was made by Smith, called *The Biography of Charles Bradlaugh* (419). Perhaps the best biography of Bradlaugh is the fairly recent *President Charles Bradlaugh, M.P.* (44) by Tribe. Bradlaugh's papers have been made available on commercial microfilm, with an Index by Royle (411). There have also been a number of magazine articles about Bradlaugh, including one by Micklewright (368). The political fight which Bradlaugh had to endure before taking his seat in the House of Commons is discussed in Arnstein's *The Bradlaugh Case* (269). Because Bradlaugh's life was so closely intertwined with that of Annie Besant for twelve years, much information about Bradlaugh can also be found in a number of biographies of Annie Besant, especially Nethercot's *The First Five Lives of Annie Besant* (24).

Annie Wood Besant (1847-1933) was born in London. Her father had been trained as a physician, but had obtained a good position with the City of London, and had never practiced medicine. When Annie's father died, she was only five. His death caused a financial crisis in the Wood household. Annie was finally sent to be a live-in pupil of Miss Maryat, who taught a few lucky young ladies the basics of a good education. Annie was a good pupil, mastering French, German, and literature. She married the Rev. Frank Besant, an Anglican clergyman and the brother of the author Walter Besant, in 1867. They went to live in Cheltenham. Annie Besant wrote a number of short pieces of fiction while she was there, including several which were published in magazines. She also had two children and looked forward to a quiet life as a clergyman's wife.

While reading works on theology, she began to doubt the truth of Christianity. In an attempt to resolve her doubts, which she hid from her husband, she read additional books on the subject. They only increased her doubts. Mrs. Besant finally went to see a fairly liberal clergyman, and discussed her feelings with him. He tried to have her convert her feelings into a sort of Christ-based humanism, but Mrs. Besant was still torn by doubts. She finally went to see the famous theologian Dr. Pusey at Oxford. He was of little help, merely telling her that her doubts were blasphemous, and to have faith. Mrs. Besant then made the acquaintance of Charles Voysey, a liberal clergyman, and through him met Thomas Scott. Scott was a wealthy man who had devoted his last years to the publishing and free distribution of a series of heretical tracts. Annie Besant wrote a number of tracts for his series, but insisted that they all be published anonymously to avoid her husband any embarrassment.

When Mrs. Besant was asked to take communion with her husband, she could not bring herself to do so, and they separated. Annie Besant retained custody of her daughter. In 1874, she moved to London to try to support herself with her pen. She soon met Edward Truelove, who suggested that she hear Charles Bradlaugh speak. She did so, and was soon writing for *The National Reformer* (207). For some reason, Bradlaugh sensed that Mrs. Besant was a valuable addition to the freethought ranks. She was a naturally gifted orator, utilizing this talent very frequently upon the freethought platform. Her husband used her atheism as an excuse to obtain the custody of her daughter, an act for which she never forgave him. In 1877, Annie Besant was involved with Charles Bradlaugh in the trial which resulted from the publication of Knowlton's *The Fruits of Philosophy* (354). This is discussed in more detail in the section under Charles Watts. After the trial, Besant felt that Knowlton's work was too dated and incomplete, so she wrote her own pamphlet advocating birth control, called *The Law of Population* (279). She also made a large contribution to *The National Reformer* in the form of articles, many of which were issued later as pamphlets. Some of her lectures were also later issued in this form. The number of her published pamphlets is quite large. All of these (except the early anonymous ones published by Thomas Scott) were published by Bradlaugh and Besant, or by their Freethought Publishing Company in London. A number of Annie Besant's pamphlets also appear in *The Atheistic Platform* (275), a series of pamphlets by different authors issued together. Her book-length publications include *The Freethinker's Text-Book, Part II* (227), *My Path to Atheism*

(280), a collection of her early Thomas Scott pamphlets, and her collected *Theological Essays and Debates* (282). She also write *The History of the Great French Revolution* (278), and edited her own magazine, called *Our Corner* (378). Her political pamphlets (twenty-seven of them) have been reprinted as *A Selection of the Social and Political Pamphlets of Annie Besant* (281).

One of the jobs that Annie Besant had for *The National Reformer* was the occasional reviewing of books. One book which she was sent for review in 1889 was *The Secret Doctrine* (285) by Helena Blavatsky. For some unaccountable reason, Annie Besant was very impressed with this mixture of scholarship, mysticism, and incomprehensibility; so much that she sought an appointment to see Mrs. Blavatsky. Helena Blavatsky was noted for her magnetic personality, which duly impressed Annie Besant. Eventually, she left the freethought movement and joined Mrs. Blavatsky's Theosophical movement, where she remained for the rest of her long life. Mrs. Besant became the leader of Theosophy, and resided in Madras, India (headquarters of Theosophy) for many years.

The loss of Annie Besant to the freethought movement was a great shock to Charles Bradlaugh and to others. Numerous articles about Theosophy and about Mrs. Blavatsky's frauds were published in the freethought press, but nothing could change Mrs. Besant's mind. She occasionally appeared on the freethought platform until late 1890, when the severing of her relationship to freethought was complete.

There have been many books written about Annie Besant. She wrote her own *Annie Besant: An Autobiography* (274), but it covers only the period of her life until 1893 in the first edition, and until 1908 in the second edition. Earlier, she had written what she called *Autobiographical Sketches* (276), containing good coverage of her career in the freethought movement. Of the many biographies, the best by far is Nethercot's two-volume work, *The First Five Lives of Annie Besant* (24) and *The Last Four Lives of Annie Besant* (376). Other biographies include Besterman's *Mrs. Annie Besant* (283), Williams' *The Passionate Pilgrim* (445) and "Geoffrey West's" (really Welles) *Mrs. Annie Besant* (438). Besterman also produced *A Bibliography of Annie Besant* (2), not one of his best bibliographies. There are also a number of biographical pamphlets and articles that appeared in the Theosophical press, and concentrated upon that phase of her life.

Charles Watts (1836-1906) was a prolific pamphleteer and one of the best platform speakers that the freethought movement produced. He was also the founder of the family of Wattses that dominated British freethought publishing for over one-hundred years. Charles Watts was born in Bristol, England. He came from a religious family. At an early age, he became a debater, but not, at first, on freethought subjects. His early religious doubts were ended by the "conversion" to freethought that occurred when he was fifteen, as a result of hearing George Jacob Holyoake lecture. Charles' brother John also joined the secular movement at this time.

At the age of sixteen, Charles Watts went to London, where he met many of the freethought leaders of the day. In 1864, he joined his brother John in a printing business. John Watts was then the temporary proprietor of *The National Reformer* (207). Charles Watts became the subeditor of this publication in 1864, and the subeditor under Bradlaugh when the latter retook control of the magazine upon the death of John Watts in 1866. He remained as subeditor unil 1877.

In 1877, a serious division occurred within the freethought movement. A prosecution had been launched by the government against a book called *The Fruits of Philosophy* (354) by Charles Knowlton. This was an early birth control item which had originally been published in the United States over forty years previously. The Freethought Publishing Company (with Bradlaugh, Besant and Watts as partners) had issued an edition of Knowlton's book in 1877. An outside printer had (unknown to the partners) added some obscene illustrations to a number of the copies. Watts decided to plead guilty to the charge of having published an obscene libel, while Bradlaugh and Besant decided to plead innocent for freedom of speech reasons. This difference caused Watts to withdraw from the Freethought Publishing Company and to found his own company, known at first simply as "C. Watts," but later as "Watts & Co." It should be added that the printing equipment used by the Freethought Publishing Company had been that of Austin Holyoake (who died in 1874). It was bought from his estate by Charles Watts, who then printed much of the Freethought Publishing Company's publications.

Watts' publishing company survived the last two decades of the nineteenth century by allying itself with "Saladin" (W. S. Ross) in the printing of magazines and pamphlets. Watts and Saladin were partners in the publishing of *The Secular Review* (414), which Watts had originally purchased from its founder, George Jacob Holyoake. In 1878, Watts established the British Secular Union, mainly as an alternative to the National Secular Society headed by Charles Bradlaugh. The British Secular Union published an annual, called *The British Secular Almanac* (297), a rival of the *National Secular Society Almanac* (375).

Watts continued to be a popular debater and lecturer. Many of his publications were published by his own Watts & Co. They were often originally debates, lectures, or magazine articles. Because of his skill as a lecturer, the Toronto [Canada] Secular Society asked him to become their permanent leader. Watts agreed and returned to England to make the arrangements. He arrived in Toronto with his family in 1884. Charles Watts founded the magazine *Secular Thought* (415) in 1885. It ran under Watts' supervision until 1891, at which time he returned to England (in response to the death of Charles Bradlaugh). *Secular Thought* continued to be published until 1911. It ran under Watts' supervision until 1891, at which time he returned to England (in response to the death of Charles Bradlaugh). *Secular Thought* continued to be published until 1911. There is more about this phase of Charles Watts' career in the appendix on Canadian freethought.

After Charles Watts returned to England, he was given the leadership of the Birmingham Secular Society, which used a building called Baskerville Hall as its meeting place. The group was not on a firm financial footing, and the venture did not last long. Watts returned to London and continued his printing and publishing businesses (They had been run during his absences by his son, Charles A. Watts). In 1896, when the Rationalist Press Association was being formed, Watts & Company (primarily under the leadership of Charles A. Watts) became the official printers and publishers to the R.P.A. Over the next sixty years, Watts & Co. published hundreds of books, selling millions of copies. We will discuss this publishing company in more detail later. Charles Watts lived only long enough to see the beginnings of this publishing success.

Charles Watts' own writings are almost impossible to find in library collections today. This is because they were nearly all pamphlets. The few books that Watts wrote include *The Meaning of Rationalism* (435), *The History of Freethought* (47), and the *Debate on Christianity* (434). There is no bibliography of Watts' writings, and the fact that his total output of pamphlets is unclear, makes exact knowledge of his writings vague. He did write at least forty-five pamphlets.

There are also no real biographies of Charles Watts. A short pamphlet called *Sketch of the Life and Character of C. Watts* (408) by Saladin (Ross) does exist, but it covers Watts' life only up until the publication date of 1878. There were a few articles about his early career in the periodicals of the time (e.g., the one by Law in 1878 [355]), and a memorial tribute by J. P. Gilmour, which appeared in 1935 (326).

George William Foote (1850–1915) was one of the most important freethought leaders. He was born in Plymouth, England. At the
age of eighteen he came to London and was soon involved in the
freethought movement. Bradlaugh spotted him as a young man of
exceptional ability, and encouraged him to participate in freethought
activities. By 1874, Foote was already the author of a number of
articles and had developed a reputation as a lecturer. He began his
first publication on his own early in 1876. It was called *The Secularist*
(416). The magazine was started in coeditorship with George Jacob
Holyoake, who soon withdrew as the result of a quarrel. There was
some bitterness which remained between Foote and Holyoake for
the rest of their lives. Foote continued to publish *The Secularist* for
a few more months, until June of 1876, when it was merged with
Charles Watts' *Secular Review* (414). Foote then tried another magazine, *the Liberal* (358). It lasted the year 1879 only.

In 1881, G. W. Foote launched his most successful publishing
venture, *The Freethinker* (325). It has lasted until the present day,
despite many problems. In 1882, a blasphemy prosecution was
launched against Foote, printer Whittle, and proprietor Ramsey.
Foote defended himself, and the jury was unable to agree on a verdict.
The case was retried in 1883, with the new printer, Kemp, among
the indicted. The second jury also was hung, but the third trial brought
convictions. Foote received twelve months in jail, Ramsey nine and
Kemp three. While he was in prison, Foote was tried again, but this
time the judge (Coleridge) reinterpreted the law against blasphemy,
and found him innocent. After serving his term, Foote resumed the
Bible cartoons which had been the source of his first indictment. He
was not prosecuted again.

Foote began a high-class literary magazine, called *Progress* (383)
in 1883. It ran until 1887. Foote was also an inveterate pamphleteer.
Many of his pamphlets consisted of articles reprinted from one of his
various magazines. There were also books compiled from a series
of his journal articles. Among books of this type can be counted *Bible
Romances* (311), *Bible Heroes* (310), *Arrows of Freethought* (308),
Crimes of Christianity (314), *Letters to the Clergy* (320), and *The
Grand Old Book* (317). Foote also wrote *Infidel Deathbeds* (318),
and *The Bible Handbook* (309), both of which went through many
editions. He also wrote *Flowers of Freethought* (316).

One of G. W. Foote's major accomplishments was his working
out of the strategy by which bequests to freethought organizations
could be found to be legal. Prior to this time, most such bequests
were held to be illegal because they were to be used to oppose Chris-

tianity, which was considered to be a part of the law of England. This issue (in England) was settled by the so-called Bowman Case. Bowman had left a large sum of money to the Secular Society, Ltd. (this was Foote's creation, designed to receive legal bequests). Bowman's relatives contested his will, and the case was carried all the way to the House of Lords, which found the bequest legal. Until then, a bequest left for anti-Christian purposes had been held to be void.

George William Foote was a masterful speaker and debater. He was very skillful in the use of satire and wit. Several of his debates with Christians were published, including ones with McCann (312), Lee (322) and Woffendale (313). He was also a great lover of literature. Some of his essays on Shakespeare were published as a pamphlet (321).

Foote remained as editor of *The Freethinker* and as president of the National Secular Society (a job he inherited after Bradlaugh's death), until his own health began to fail in 1915. His post as NSS president was taken by Chapman Cohen, who had been Foote's assistant for many years.

There is no published biography of G. W. Foote. An attempt at a "literary biography" of Foote was made in the mid-1950s by Cutner, but the manuscript was never published. Any attempt at a biography of the man himself would now be difficult because his papers seem to have disappeared. Some were undoubtedly lost during the Second World War, when the offices of *The Freethinker* were gutted by fire. Strangely enough, there also seem to be no pamphlets about Foote's life. There have been a small number of articles written about him, such as the one by Robertson (388).

William Stewart Ross (1844–1906), who used the pen name "Saladin," was born in Kirkbean, Scotland. He attended school in Scotland and amazed everyone with his excellent memory and prodigious reading habits. In 1861, he left school to become a schoolmaster in Dunscore. He then attended the University of Glasgow. Ross had originally intended to become a clergyman, but his studies soon made him a doubter. While still in college, he managed to sell some of his writings (fiction and poetry) to publishers. His work came to the notice of an Edinburgh textbook publisher, who hired Ross to produce textbooks. After doing this for several years, he decided to establish his own publishing company.

Ross went to London in 1872 and started his company. At the same time, he began contributing articles to *The National Reformer* (207). When the Knowlton trial of 1877 began, Ross took the position that the freethought movement should have nothing to do with the distribution of birth control information or literature, which he considered obscene. This opposition to Bradlaugh's Malthusianism made him into an enemy of Bradlaugh's. Although Bradlaugh did not feel strongly about Ross at first, Ross began to actively oppose and taunt Bradlaugh whenever the opportunity arose.

Ross' support of Charles Watts in the Knowlton case made them friends. Watts severed his relationship with Bradlaugh and Besant and with *The National Reformer* over the Knowlton birth control issue. Watts and Holyoake started *the Secular Review* (414) in 1876. Watts soon became the sole editor. In 1880, Ross became associated with Watts as coeditor. Ross had founded his own freethought magazine, *The Agnostic Journal* (265) in 1884. In 1889, Ross merged the two magazines into *The Agnostic Journal & The Secular Review (265)*.

When the *Life of Charles Bradlaugh, M. P.* (367) was published in 1888, purporting to be by Charles R. Mackay, Bradlaugh sued for libel and launched an investigation to determine who was behind the publication. After a complex series of events, it was determined that W. H. Johnson and Ross had been largely responsible for the publication (and authorship) of the book. Ross was assessed a large fine, which was given by Bradlaugh to charity. The book was ordered destroyed. A small number, however, have escaped destruction. The role of Ross in the production of the libelous biography of Bradlaugh is covered in a pamphlet called *Balak Secundus* (366), purportedly by Charles R. Mackay, but actually George Griffith-Jones ("Lara"). The same author's *Monkanna Unveiled* (335) also discusses Ross' role.

Ross was the author of many books. Almost all of those concerning freethought were published by his own company, W. Stewart & Co. Among the more important of Ross' books (many of which first appeared as a series of articles in one of his freethought magazines) were *God and His Book* (406), *Woman: Her Glory, Her Shame and Her God* (410), *Roses and Rue* (407), *Why I Am An Agnostic* (409), and *The Book of "At Random"* (405). There is little doubt that "Saladin" (as he called himself in almost of his freethought writings) had developed one of the best prose styles of any of the freethought writers. He was a master at the use of sarcasm and irony, and also wrote fairly good poetry. However, Ross was at the center of a divisive struggle which nearly succeeded in splitting the freethought movement at the very time when it was at the numerical peak of its strength.

There has never been a full-length biography of Ross, although there have been a number of biographical pamphlets. Among these are *Sketch of the Life and Character of Saladin (W. Stewart Ross)*

(307) by Flaws, *Sketch of the Life of Saladin (W. Stewart Ross)* by Hithersay and Ernest (339), *Saladin the Little* (352) by Jacob, and *In Memoriam Saladin* (385), edited by Radde.

Joseph Mazzini Wheeler (1850–98) was one of the very few people who could truly be called a scholar of freethought. Although he is now forgotten, his work shows the great erudition and careful research which are the hallmarks of Wheeler's efforts. It can be confidently said that at the time of his death, Wheeler knew more about the bibliography of freethought than any man who ever lived.

Wheeler was born in London, and spent his early working years at Edinburgh, where he was a lithographer. G. W. Foote made his acquaintance when Foote first came to London in 1868. While Wheeler was in Edinburgh, he wrote occasional articles for the freethought press. Foote soon invited him to come to London to be his associate in his freethought publishing ventures. Wheeler became the subeditor of *The Freethinker* (325) when it began publishing in 1881.

Wheeler has been described as weak in body and highly nervous in temperament, but a devoted and profound scholar. He spent much of his free time in the reading room of the British Museum. His specialties can be said to be oriental religions, anthropology, and the history and bibliography of freethought. When Foote was sentenced to prison for blasphemy in 1883, Wheeler became responsible for the day-to-day operations of Foote's business. The strain of overwork, and worry about Foote, became too much for Wheeler's nervous temperament, and his mental health broke down. He recovered after a convalescence of several months.

Wheeler remained closely associated with Foote in all his future publications and activities for freethought. The high point in Wheeler's freethought scholarship can be seen in his *Biographical Dictionary of Freethinkers* (48), containing information about the identity of authors that is not found elsewhere. It is too bad that Wheeler's projected *History of Freethought in England* was never completed, and only a few parts were published as articles in *The Freethinker.*

Among Wheeler's other publications were *Bible Studies* (439), and *Footsteps of the Past* (442), both of which consist of revised articles which had been published in *The Freethinker.* Wheeler was the coauthor with Foote of *Crimes of Christianity* (314) and coeditor with Foote of the English translation of the *Sepher Toldoth Jeschu,* also known as *The Jewish Life of Christ* (319). Wheeler also wrote several pamphlets, including *The Christian Doctrine of Hell* (440), *Satan, Witchcraft and the Bible* (444), and an anthology (still useful) called *Freethought Readings and Secular Songs* (443).

Very little has been written about Wheeler, although he deserves more attention than he has received. There are a few articles which give the details of his life, but there are no books or pamphlets. Among the articles are those by Moss (372) and others.

The early part of the career of George Jacob Holyoake (1817–1906) has been covered in the previous chapter. The period after 1860 will be dealt with here. When Charles Bradlaugh started *The National Reformer* (207) in 1860, he had Joseph Barker as his coeditor. When Barker left the magazine after some disagreements in 1862, Holyoake agreed to become coeditor with Bradlaugh. He lasted only three months, again due to a disagreement.

Holyoake's *The Reasoner* (234) was issued only intermittently after 1864. It appeared in this way until 1872, often with different subtitles (e.g., *The Counsellor, The Secular World, The English Leader*). Holyoake briefly joined with Foote in the production of a periodical called *The Secularist* (416) in 1876. The partnership lasted only three months, after which Foote continued the magazine alone. Holyoake started *The Secular Review* (414), which lasted a year and a half. Another periodical of his, *The Present Day* (382), was more successful, lasting three years.

In 1851, George Jacob Holyoake coined the word "secularism," believing it had much less negative connotation than "atheism." Eventually, he saw that the two terms were no longer synonomous. Holyoake and Bradlaugh even had a public debate (350), later published, over the distinction between the two terms. Holyoake also debated with the Rev. Brewin Grant twice (345) and (346), but his lack of debating skill prompted Holyoake to avoid most challenges.

In the 1860s, Holyoake began his lengthy involvement with the Co-operative Movement. He was one of the central figures in the organization of that group, often working behind the scenes. Holyoake also acted as the historian of Co-operation, writing *Self-Help by the People: History of Co-operation in Rochdale* (348 and 189) and *The History of Co-operation* (347).

In the latter part of his life, Holyoake withdrew from active involvement in the secular movement. He felt that the atheistic and the non-atheistic branches of secularism were irreconcilable. Holyoake considered himself of the nonatheistic school, although it was primarily for reasons that arose out of his feeling that attacks upon Christianity were unproductive, rather than that he had become a theist.

Holyoake died at the age of eighty-eight. He had survived, despite his often precarious health, while all the others who had been his contemporaries in the freethought movement had long since died.

George Jacob Holyoake was buried alongside his brother Austin in Highgate Cemetery, London. A large monument, topped with a bust of Holyoake, marks his grave.

There have been a number of works about Holyoake. A thorough bibliography, *A Descriptive Bibliography of George Jacob Holyoake, With a Brief Sketch of His Life* (13) was compiled by Goss. Holyoake told a partial autobiography in a series of reminiscences (not organized well enough to call a real autobiography), published as *Sixty Years of an Agitator's Life* (351) and as *Bygones Worth Remembering* (344). McCabe wrote the "authorized" biography of Holyoake as *The Life and Letters of George Jacob Holyoake* (19). He also wrote a condensed version of this work as *George Jacob Holyoake* (361). Grugel has written a condensation of his dissertation as *George Jacob Holyoake: A Study in the Evolution of a Victorian Radical* (15). There is also a great deal about Holyoake in Royle's *Victorian Infidels* (35). The papers of George Jacob Holyoake are now at the Cooperative Union in Manchester, England, with a few additional items at the Bishopsgate Institute of London. The papers are available as a commercial microfilm.

Joseph McCabe (1867–1955) was one of the most prolific authors who ever lived. He wrote over 200 books or translations, plus over 200 "Little Blue Books" and a like number of "Big Blue Books" for E. Haldeman-Julius. Not all of these were on freethought topics, but McCabe must still be rated as the most prolific author in the freethought movement.

Joseph McCabe was born in the north of England at Macclesfield. The town was an industrial one, and his family was large and poor. Joseph was a good pupil, and was therefore destined for the clergy. He went through the traditional Catholic training for the priesthood, taking his vows with the Franciscans. His new name was Father Antony. McCabe's jobs as a priest included teaching what passed for philosophy and Latin. Doubts about the validity of Catholic teachings soon surfaced, and, at the age of twenty-seven, McCabe left the church.

Positions for priests who left the church were extremely hard to find in those days. The first employment McCabe obtained as a new rationalist was as secretary to the newly-formed Leicester Secular Society. He held this position for about a year. At about this time, McCabe's first two books appeared. They were *Modern Rationalism* (362) and *Twelve Years in a Monastery* (364). His first fame came when his translation of Ernest Haeckel's *The Riddle of the Universe* (336) became a best seller in 1901. Although the work sold 250,000 copies, McCabe earned $100 for his work. When the Rationalist Press Association was formed in 1898–1899, Joseph McCabe was elected one of the directors. He produced the first book issued by the RPA, namely *The Religion of the Twentieth Century* (363). When the first chairman of the RPA, George Jacob Holyoake, died in 1906, Joseph McCabe was commissioned to write his biography. The result was *The Life and Letters of George Jacob Holyoake* (19), published as two volumes in 1908. Parts of this biography reawakened the dispute between the daughters of Bradlaugh and Holyoake over the motivation for some of their fathers' actions.

McCabe continued to make his living by writing and lecturing. He went on a speaking tour of Australia in 1910, 1913, and 1923, and of the United States in 1914, 1916, and 1925. On his last trip to the United States, McCabe went to Girard, Kansas to meet with Emanuel Haldeman-Julius, at the latter's invitation. From this meeting came a collaboration lasting nearly thirty years that involved McCabe writing an unending series of Little Blue Books and Big Blue Books for E. Haldeman-Julius's publishing company. Several million of McCabe's publications for Haldeman-Julius sold over the years, but this takes us into the next chapter's time period, where we will take up McCabe's subsequent career again.

John Mackinnon Robertson (1856–1933) was another very prolific author. His volume of books sets no records (there were about 125 of them), but the breadth and the depth of his scholarship certainly does. He has been referred to as having had the most encyclopedic knowledge of any author since the French encyclopedist Pierre Bayle, who died in 1706.

Robertson was born at Brodick, on the Isle of Arran in Scotland. He attended school until the age of thirteen, after which he had to help support his family. His early jobs included telegraph clerk, insurance clerk, and finally, newspaperman. At the age of twenty, he obtained a position on the *Edinburgh Evening News*, eventually becoming headline writer and then assistant editor.

Robertson's first contact with organized freethought occurred in 1878, when he heard a lecture by Charles Bradlaugh. By the early 1880s, he had become an active member of the Edinburgh Secular Society. In 1884, Annie Besant was sent by Charles Bradlaugh to try to find an able person who could relieve him of some of his editorial duties on *The National Reformer* (207). The object was to allow Bradlaugh to attend to the many other things he was called upon to do. Mrs. Besant found Robertson in Edinburgh, and invited him to London. He soon became assistant editor of *The National Reformer*.

Robertson's writings were often begun as a series of magazine articles. These were then collected as a book. Among the books which were begun this way were *Christ and Krishna* (390), which was later expanded into *Christianity and Mythology* (391), *Pioneer Humanists* (399), and *Explorations* (392), as well as others. Some of Robertson's books were also originally delivered as speeches, such as *Modern Humanists* (397) and *Spoken Essays* (402).

John M. Robertson was the foremost exponent in the twentieth century (at least so far) of what is called the "myth theory" of Jesus. He held that not only was Jesus not the Messiah, but that the historical character Jesus, as described in the New Testament, never existed. Robertson wrote five books on this subject. They were *Christianity and Mythology* (391), *Pagan Christs* (398), *The Historical Jesus* (393), *The Jesus Problem* (395), and *Jesus and Judas* (394). Robertson also had some notable written battles with clergymen (and others) about his mythological views of Jesus.

Robertson is perhaps best known for his histories of freethought. These have been mentioned in the introduction, and have been discussed at length in the bibliography of the introduction. The masterpieces of Robertson's histories of freethought were the last editions of these works, which ran to four volumes. They are *History of Freethought, Ancient and Modern, To the Period of the French Revolution* (32) and *History of Freethought in the Nineteenth Century* (33). The first of these was posthumously published from Robertson's nearly completed manuscript. The immense reading and knowledge that Robertson displays is immediately obvious to anyone who has opened these histories. Despite some weaknesses and limitations, it is doubtful if the thoroughness of either of these two works will ever be surpassed. His *Courses of Study* (30) are also masterpieces.

Robertson wrote several other books on freethought topics. Among them are *Thomas Paine: An Investigation* (404), *The Dynamics of Religion* (31), *Studies in Religious Fallacy* (403), *A Short History of Christianity* (401), *Rationalism* (400), and *Charles Bradlaugh* (389).

John M. Robertson was elected M. P. for Tyneside in 1906. He served in Parliament for twelve years, becoming a member of the Board of Trade and of the Privy Council. His expertise on free trade (and the number of books he wrote on the subject) were important, but outside the scope of this book. The same could be said about his numerous books of Shakespearean criticism.

Robertson was the assistant editor of *The National Reformer* for a number of years. When Bradlaugh died in 1891, Robertson became the editor. He continued the publication until 1893. At this time it ceased, and Robertson, along with Bradlaugh's daughter Hypatia, published *The Reformer* (387). It ran for several years. Later in his career, Robertson was also the editor of a number of political and economic journals.

There has never been a published biography of Robertson, although one has been in progress for quite some time (see appendix). There is a bibliography of his works (not complete) in the back of volume 2 of *History of Freethought, Ancient and Modern, to the Period of the French Revolution* (32). The front part of volume one of this set also contains "Appreciations" and a sort of biographical sketch. There are also a number of short biographical articles, by Page (381) and others, which have appeared in freethought publications.

John William Gott (1866–1922) was born in Birmingham, England. He passed an uneventful childhood and youth, eventually becoming a dry goods merchant in Bradford. In 1894, he and John Grange (who was editor) began the publication of a freethought magazine called *The Truthseeker* (431). This is *not* the same as *The Truth Seeker* of New York. Gott organized the North of England Secular Federation in 1896, as well as the British Secular League. During this period he maintained his dry goods business and heavily advertised it in his publications. In 1903, Gott was charged with blasphemy for the publication of a cartoon in *The Truthseeker* of October 1903. The charges were later mysteriously dropped.

In 1911, Gott was again charged with blasphemy for a pamphlet called *Rib Ticklers, Or Questions for Parsons* (327). This time Gott was found guilty and sentenced to four months in jail. Towards the end of his term, his wife died. After his release, he resumed both his dry goods business and his freethought activities. In 1917, Gott was again prosecuted for blasphemy for the same *Rib Ticklers* pamphlet. This time Gott was found guilty and sentenced to three months on the blasphemy charge, and an additional three months on an associated obscenity charge.

Gott's last trial for blasphemy occurred in 1921. Again, the pamphlet *Rib Ticklers* was involved. The sentence for Gott this time was nine months at hard labor, even though his health was poor. An appeal did no good. Gott spent most of his time in the prison hospital, too ill to do any hard labor. He died shortly after his prison release.

There has never been a biography of Gott, and the few articles about him deal almost exclusively with his various trials. The most useful single source about Gott is Pack's *The Trial and Imprisonment of J. W. Gott for Blasphemy* (380). There are also a number of articles about the trials, including several in law journals (357). Gott wrote virtually nothing except a few articles in his own magazine. The few pamphlets that his Truthseeker Company published were mostly by others. Gott was known for his magazine and for having gotten into trouble with the law on a charge of blasphemy more times than anyone else, with his right to publish his freethought views being the issue each time.

Arthur B. Moss (1855–1937) was born in London and was a

witness to, and participant in, a very long period of freethought history. He was not a prolific writer, although he did write articles and pamphlets. He also lectured upon occasion, but he was not a leader of the free-thought movement in the usual sense in any of these areas. Rather, he was a loyal worker who often wrote about the people he had known or the events he had witnessed in the freethought movement.

Moss' writings include *The Bible and Evolution* (369), *Christianity and Evolution* (370), a volume of collected pamphlets called *Lectures and Essays* (373), as well as a published discussion with Agnes Rollo Wilke entitled *Was Jesus an Impostor?* (374). He also wrote a series of articles called *Famous Freethinkers I Have Known* (371).

There are two published pamphlet biographies of Moss. One is by Standring (421) and is included in the Moss volume *Lectures and Essays*. The other is by Heaford (338) and was published separately.

Joseph Symes (1841–1906) was a freethought leader on two continents. He was born in Portland, England and began his training to be a Wesleyan minister, after a Methodist upbringing. In 1872, just at the time he was to be ordained as a minister, he refused to go through with the ceremony and resigned. A number of social and political factors had caused Symes to doubt the truth of his denomina-tion. A brief period as a labor organizer, lecturer, and newspaperman followed. He also taught elocution until he became a full fledged free-thought lecturer by 1876.

In May of 1876, Symes began to contribute to Bradlaugh's *The National Reformer* (207). In 1877, Symes found himself squarely behind Bradlaugh in the latter's position in the Knowlton *The Fruits of Philosophy* (354), prosecution. Symes supported the idea of birth control, as did Bradlaugh. His support of Bradlaugh helped Symes become elected a vice-president of the National Secular Society, while Bradlaugh was president. Symes continued as a lecturer for free-thought, as well as a contributor to most of the freethought publications, including *The Freethinker* (325). When Foote was imprisoned for blasphemy in 1883, Symes expected to be named interim editor. He was outflanked, however, by the devious Edward Aveling, who obtained the editorship for himself.

A series of meetings had been held in Melbourne, Australia in late 1882 by a group of freethinkers who were starting to organize. In May 1883, a letter was sent by this group to Charles Bradlaugh, asking him to send someone to Australia to serve as the leader of the new Australian freethought group. Bradlaugh selected Joseph Symes, who accepted the position. Symes left for Australia in December 1883. From February 1884 until June 1906, Symes struggled to build a viable freethought organization in Australia and in New Zealand.

He founded a magazine called *The Liberator* (359). Symes' career in Australia is discussed in the appendix on freethought in Australia.

In 1906, Joseph Symes returned to England for a visit. There he became ill and died. His family returned to Australia, although Symes was cremated in England. There are no full-length biographies of Symes, although he wrote a partial autobiography when he was in Australia, called *From the Wesleyan Pulpit to the Secularist Platform* (425). The most thorough coverage of Symes' interesting life is to be found in a series of pamphlets by Sinnott, the first and most important of which is called *Joseph Symes, the "Flower of Atheism"* (418). Symes was the author of a number of pamphlets, and his debate with the Rev. Brewin Grant (424) was published. Symes' British pamphlets included *Universal Despair* (428), *Hospitals & Dispensaries Not of Christian Origin* (426) and *Philosophical Atheism* (427).

Harriet Frost Law (1831–1897) was born in Essex. She was a strict Baptist until her twenties, when she came in contact with open air freethought lecturers in London. She attempted to answer the freethinkers (who included such leaders as Holyoake, Southwell, and Bradlaugh), but found herself unable to do so effectively. At one of the secular halls Harriet Frost met her future husband, Edward Law. Both Laws soon became secularists.

In 1859, Harriet Law began her career as a freethought lecturer. She was soon acclaimed as one of the best female lecturers who ever spoke for freethought. Although she was not extremely well read, she had a deep knowledge of the Bible and was fearless on the platform. Harriet Law refused to join the National Secular Society or to follow Charles Bradlaugh. Rather, she preferred to remain an independent, with leftish political leanings. Her independence caused her to purchase *The Secular Chronicle* (413) from the estate of the late George Reddalls, its first editor. She was the editor and publisher of that magazine from 1876–1878. During that three year period, she lost £1000 on its publication costs. An editorial association took over publication from her, but was unable to keep it going for very long.

Harriet Law retired from active freethought lecturing in 1878. Ill health had caused her retirement, but she lived quietly in Wallworth and Peckham until she died.

Mrs. Law wrote virtually nothing besides articles in *The Secular Chronicle*. There has been an extraordinarily small amount of material published about her. Moss (371) wrote an article about her in 1915, and there were several obituary notices in the freethought press upon her death, including ones by Foote (315) and Wheeler (441).

Edward Bibbins Aveling (1849–1898) was, by many accounts, one of the worst scoundrels ever to be a leader of the freethought movement. By other accounts, he was not nearly that bad. He was born, the son of a Congregationalist minister, at Stoke Newington, England. He attended University College, London as a medical student, but switched to the science facility. Aveling earned his B.Sc. with honors in zoology, taught science in schools and colleges, and then received his D.Sc. from University College in 1876. He had married in 1872.

Aveling became a secularist (he said) in 1877, but he did not make this fact public until 1879, when he wrote openly for *The National Reformer* (207). In 1883, when Foote was serving his prison term for blasphemy, Aveling was made acting editor of both *Progress* (383) and *The Freethinker* (325). He had been elected a vice-president of the National Secular Society in 1881, largely on the basis of his willingness to teach many of the courses (especially in science) that the NSS offered its members. Aveling has been described as very conscientious about his views about secularism (and later about socialism), but absolutely without conscience when it came to money or women.

In 1883, Aveling started a relationship with Eleanor Marx, the daughter of Karl Marx. Aveling had separated from his wife by this time. He lived openly with Eleanor Marx from 1884 until 1898. In 1897, he secretly married a much younger woman while still living with Eleanor Marx. Aveling used a false name to do this. She committed suicide in 1898, with the suspicion lingering among the public that Aveling had had something to do with her death (although this was never proved). He died four months after Marx did, of kidney disease. Aveling went through huge sums of borrowed money, which he rarely repaid. Exactly what he spent his money on is not clear.

There were many books which bear Aveling's name on the title page. Many were works about socialism which he coauthored or translated with Eleanor Marx. We will concern ourselves only with his freethought works here. One of his most popular books was *The Student's Darwin* (272). He was also the author of a series of pamphlets, some of which were entitled *The Creed of an Atheist* (270), *A Godless Life the Happiest and Most Useful* (271), and *Why I Dare Not Be a Christian* (273).

There are no biographies of Aveling, but there is a wealth of information about him in Kapp's large biography of *Eleanor Marx* (353). The freethought movement seems to have had a very low opinion of Aveling, and has written virtually nothing about him after his early years with Bradlaugh and Foote.

John Watts (1834–1866) was the brother of Charles Watts. Although not nearly as well known as Charles, John Watts made a significant contribution to freethought during his short lifetime. John Watts was born at Bristol, England and his father was a part-time Methodist preacher. Watts was apprenticed to a printer, and learned that trade. Charles Watts visited London and became acquainted with Charles Southwell, who converted him to freethought. John and Charles argued about religious matters for some time after that, with John taking the Christian role. The situation was resolved when John Watts went to London himself to see Southwell. John became a freethinker and was soon the subeditor of Holyoake's *The Reasoner* (234). He then became coeditor with Charles Bradlaugh of *The National Reformer* (207). For some time, Watts was the sole editor and proprietor of that magazine, when Bradlaugh withdrew to attend to other business.

John Watts suffered from "consumption" (tuberculosis) and died at the early age of thirty-two. Watts wrote many articles for *The National Reformer* and *The Reasoner*. He also wrote a number of pamphlets, including *The Christian Doctrine of Man's Depravity Refuted* (436) and *Metaphysical Parallels* (437).

There are no biographies of John Watts. There is an article about him by Law (356), and obituary notices in *The National Reformer*.

William James Ramsey (1844–1916) was born in London. He joined the freethought movement where his abilities as a business manager soon brought him into a role in this capacity within the movement. He was the publisher of *The Freethinker* (325) after the end of 1881 (before that Bradlaugh and Besant were the publishers). When a prosecution for blasphemy was initiated against *The Freethinker* in 1882, Foote, Ramsey, and the printer, H. A. Kemp, were all indicted. Ramsey was also the manager of the Freethought Publishing Company for Bradlaugh and Besant.

Ramsey was tried and convicted of blasphemy, and received a sentence of nine months in jail. He served his time, then was released to resume his former position as business manager. Ramsey wrote about his experiences in jail in a pamphlet called *In Prison For Blasphemy* (386), which is virtually his only publication. There are no biographies or articles about Ramsey, although he continued to serve the freethought movement (being affiliated with G. W. Foote after Bradlaugh's death), and often lectured until his death.

Austin Holyoake (1827–1874) was a younger brother of George Jacob Holyoake. He was brought up in the large and poor Holyoake household at Birmingham and trained as a printer. His skepticism led him to write articles for *The National Reformer* (207), and to become printer of the magazine in London. Prior to that he had been an assistant to James Watson in the printing of *The Reasoner* (234), edited by his brother George Jacob. In 1851, the two Holyoake brothers formed a partnership as printers (and later publishers) under the name "Holyoake & Co." In 1853, a sum of money enabled the brothers to purchase James Watson's printing press and type from his widow. Later, the company was called Fleet Street House, and incorporated publishing activities as well as others. When the Fleet Street House premises were sold, Austin Holyoake opened his own printing and publishing business under the name Austin & Co. in 1862. Upon Austin's death, this company became Charles Watts', and eventually did the printing and publishing for the Rationalist Press Association as Watts & Company.

Austin Holyoake did some lecturing and writing, but he was primarily a printer and publisher. His own writings include a few pamphlets such as *Ludicrous Aspects of Christianity* (342) and *Daniel the Dreamer* (340). He also edited *Facetiae for Freethinkers* (341) and, with Charles Watts, *The Secularist's Manual of Songs and Ceremonies* (343). There is no biography of Austin Holyoake, although Holyoake did issue a memorial pamphlet, called *In Memoriam. Austin Holyoake* (349).

Charles C. Cattell (1830–1910) was one of the founders of the secular movement in Birmingham. He was the person largely responsible for the Birmingham Eclectic Institute, founded in 1852. This Institute was the precursor of the later Birmingham secular groups that occupied Baskerville Hall for a time which included the 1891 period.

Cattell wrote a number of pamphlets both under his own name and that of "Christopher Charles." The pseudonym was used mostly for periodical articles. Among Cattell's publications were *Is Darwinism Atheistic?* (301), *The Dark Side of Christianity* (300), and *Secularism: What It Is* (302). There are no biographies of Cattell, and virtually nothing about him was published in the form of articles either.

Edward Truelove (1809–1899) was one of the most important freethought booksellers and publishers of the nineteenth century. As a young man he came under the influence of Robert Owen. In 1844, Truelove lived at Harmony Hall in Hampshire, one of Owen's utopian communities. After the town was discontinued, Truelove became the secretary of the John Street Institution, where he met George Jacob Holyoake, James Watson, and Henry Hetherington. These men were all members of the freethought movement, as well as publishers, and he was influenced to set up a business in 1852 as a freethought bookseller. In 1858, Truelove was arrested for publishing a pamphlet about tyrannicide. The prosecution was withdrawn six months later (before the trial) as a result of strong public opposition. In 1877,

Edward Truelove was arrested, tried and convicted for selling two pamphlets, one of which was Robert Dale Owen's *Moral Physiology* (379). After conviction in the second trial, Truelove was sentenced to four months' imprisonment and a fine of £50.

He was responsible for introducing Annie Besant to Charles Bradlaugh, after she had come into his bookshop. Truelove made Mrs. Besant go to hear Bradlaugh speak, and a partnership was born. Truelove maintained his bookshop until 1893, when he finally retired. The publishing business of Truelove is discussed in more detail in the section on publishers.

Truelove appears not to have written anything himself, although a report of his trial was published (430). There is also very little which has been written about him. Perhaps the best article about Truelove is "Edward Truelove: Bookseller and Publisher (377) by Neuburg. There was also a catalog of Truelove's own library and bookstock (46), published by his executors after his death, when the library was auctioned.

Robert Forder (1844–1901) was born in Yarmouth, England. He went to work at a young age and was entirely self-educated. At sixteen, Forder went to London. In the suburbs he attended freethought discussions, often arguing the Christian position. He was gradually converted to the freethought position.

In 1877, Forder was appointed National Secular Society secretary by Charles Bradlaugh. He took charge of the publishing business of *The Freethinker* while Foote, Ramsey, and Kemp were in jail for blasphemy in 1883. Forder's job as NSS secretary involved organizing local chapters, speaking at numerous meetings, and handling the correspondence. He also became a publisher in his own right in the 1890s, issuing books with the imprint "R. Forder." There is a further discussion of his role as a publisher in the section on publishers. Forder wrote several pamphlets, among them *There Was a War in Heaven* (323). There are no published biographies other than an anonymous article (267) and an obituary (268) in *The Freethinker*.

George Standring (1855–1924) became associated with the freethought movement after attending Christian Evidence Society lectures which caused him to doubt the truth of Christianity. Attendance at Bradlaugh's lectures in the Hall of Science in 1873 confirmed him as a freethinker. Standring met Foote in 1874, and was soon writing for *The National Reformer* (207). In 1875, he became the Corresponding Secretary of the National Secular Society.

Standring was a popular outdoor speaker for the NSS for many years. He became a founder and secretary of the London Secular

Federation. Standring was also involved in the Malthusian League and in its birth control propaganda. He was the printer and publisher of its journal as well.

Standring also had a brother, Sam, who was active in the free-thought movement, but who died at a relatively early age. George Standring was the author of a number of pamphlets, perhaps the best known of which is *An Atheist at Church* (420). He also wrote a short *Biographical Sketch of Arthur B. Moss* (421), a *Life of Charles Bradlaugh, M.P.* (422), and a life of *Richard Carlile* (423). There are no biographies of George Standring, other than an article by Moss (371) and an obituary by Vance (432).

There are a few freethought books which were important during this period (mostly because of the widespread reaction they produced), but that have not yet been mentioned. These books are in a somewhat unique group because their authors were either not active in the organized freethought movement, or because the books were the only freethought works these authors produced (or both). Blatchford's *God and My Neighbor* (284) is an example of such a book. It had a very wide sale upon its publication in 1903, and for many years afterwards. Many editions were published, and it caused a large controversy when first released. Blatchford was better known as a socialist than as a freethinker.

Another book in this class was Cassels' *Supernatural Religion* (299). The book was published anonymously, and its real author remained unknown from the date of initial publication in 1875 until after the turn of the century, despite much speculation as to his identity. Cassels' book was a learned, detailed, and devastating attack upon the authority of the Bible. He went through a minute analysis, showing why that book was historically and logically inconsistent. A number of responses to *Supernatural Religion* were also published.

A third book that produced somewhat of a stir when it was first published in 1876 was Amberley's *An Analysis of Religious Belief* (266). The author was the father of Bertrand Russell and died soon after the book was written and before the second volume was published.

The periodicals of the freethought movement during the Bradlaugh/Besant/Foote era were quite numerous. Many of these have already been discussed, and so will only be briefly mentioned again here. The others will be added at this point.

The National Reformer (207) and *The Freethinker* (325) were the two most important freethought magazines during this period. *The National Reformer* was founded by Charles Bradlaugh and Joseph Barker in 1860. Bradlaugh took it over in 1866, after John and Charles Watts and Holyoake had been involved for a time. Besant became coeditor with Bradlaugh in 1877. Bradlaugh alone ran it after early 1890. In 1891, upon Bradlaugh's death, Robertson edited the magazine until its suspension in 1893.

The Freethinker was founded in 1881 by Foote. Wheeler was subeditor for many years. When Foote died in 1915, Cohen (and later others) became editor, but this will be discussed in the next chapter. Foote also produced the magazine *Progress* (383) in the 1880s. It was his attempt at a quality magazine. Besant had a similar magazine in her *Our Corner* (378). Robertson's attempt at a quality freethought magazine was his *Reformer* (387).

The Rationalist Press Association produced an annual magazine called *The R. P. A. Annual* (384) from 1908 onwards. It replaced Charles Watts' *Agnostic Annual* (264), which was published from 1884 through 1907. *The R. P. A. Annual* changed its name to *The Rationalist Annual* with the issue of 1927. Watts & Company also published *The Literary Guide* (360) from 1885 onwards. It began as an advertising listing of Watts & Company's new publications, but by 1896 had expanded into book reviews and other literary articles. It became a weekly during the twentieth century.

Law published *The Secular Chronicle* (413), taking over from its founder, Reddalls. It lasted from 1872 until 1879. Gott published *The Truthseeker* (431) irregularly from Bradford from 1894 until 1905. Charles A. Watts was the editor of a short-lived magazine called *The Agnostic* (263), that lasted only a part of 1885.

Among the other briefly-published periodicals of this era were *The Secularist* (416), published by Foote and Holyoake, then by Foote alone. *The Secular Review* (414) of Holyoake, Watts and "Saladin," eventually came under the control of Ross ("Saladin") alone in 1884. He renamed it *The Agnostic Journal* (265), with the subtitle "*& Secular Review*" in 1889. It ceased publishing upon Saladin's death in 1906.

The British Secular Almanac (297) and *The National Secular Society Almanac* (375) have been mentioned in connection with their respective editors, Charles Watts and Bradlaugh/Besant/Foote.

The most important freethought publishing company of this period was Bradlaugh's Freethought Publishing Company. It was formed in 1877 as a partnership between Bradlaugh and Annie Besant. It lasted until 1890, at which time Besant left the freethought movement. Foote had published books and pamphlets as The Progressive Publishing Company from 1881, when *The Freethinker* was first published, until 1899, when he formed The Freethought Publishing Company, Ltd. This was an entirely different company from Bradlaugh and Besant's company of nearly identical name. Foote's new company lasted until 1908. The Pioneer Press was formed in 1908, and took over from The Freethought Publishing Company, Ltd. Robert Forder published freethought books and pamphlets under the imprint "R. Forder" from 1890 until 1899. Among his few book publications was Bradlaugh's *Labour and Law* (292).

Watts & Company started as "C. Watts" in about 1875. After Charles Watts and Charles Bradlaugh split up in 1877, Watts published as "Watts & Co." This company lasted until the 1960s, with the descendants of Charles Watts running the company. The Rationalist Press Association was formed in 1899, and published its first book in 1900. After this time, Watts & Company acted as the actual printer for RPA publications, which sometimes bore a dual imprint.

The imprint "Charles Bradlaugh and Annie Besant" appears on their publications from about 1875 until 1877, when the Freethought Publishing Company was formed. After Charles Bradlaugh's death, his daughter, Hypatia Bradlaugh Bonner, and her husband, Arthur Bonner, published (and often republished Freethought Publishing Company titles) as "A. & H. B. Bonner." This lasted until about 1903. The National Secular Society published a few items under its own imprint. "Austin and Company" (1860–1874) and its predecessor, Holyoake & Company, (1851–1860) were publishers in the early part of this era.

There were several other publishers that also existed during this period. Almost all of Ross's ("Saladin") publications were issued by his own company, called "W. Stewart & Co." This existed from the early 1880s until 1906. Truelove published a number of books as "E. Truelove" or as "The Reformer's Library" from the 1870s until 1899. Abel Heywood was a publisher in Manchester, starting about 1832. The company continued to exist as "Abel Heywood and Son," or the related "J. Heywood" until the mid-1880s. Thomas Scott published about 150 different pamphlets privately from about 1870–1879. He also published at least one book, Scott's *The English Life of Jesus* (412). Farrah sold many freethought books of other publishers, and also published a few under his own imprint.

The Rationalist Press Association had its origins in the Rationalist Press Committee that was formed in 1893. Prior to that, there was a Propaganda Press Fund established by Watts & Company through the medium of its (*Watts'*) *The Literary Guide* (360), founded in 1885. The purpose of the Rationalist Press Committee was " . . . to assist in the production and circulation of Rationalist publications." This committee published a few books during this period.

In 1899, the Rationalist Press Association was organized by Charles A. Watts (son of Charles Watts) and several others. It was incorporated as an organization in which members subscribed a sum in advance and received a certain value of books in return, with the value of the books in proportion to the amount of money subscribed. It was something like an American book club, except that the fees for the year were paid in advance, and the money received was used to finance the publication of the books themselves.

The first chairman of the RPA was Holyoake. Edward Clodd, a banker, was elected chairman of the RPA in 1906, upon Holyoake's death. He served until 1913. The first book published by the RPA was McCabe's *The Religion of the Twentieth Century* (363), published in 1900. In fact, McCabe's book was the only one published during the RPA's first year of existence. In the second year, two books by Robertson, *Christianity and Mythology* (391) and *Studies in Religious Fallacy* (403), and McCabe's translation of Haeckel's *The Riddle of the Universe* (336) were the publications. Fortunately for the survival of the RPA, *The Riddle of the Universe* became a best seller.

In 1902, the RPA Cheap Reprints were launched. These were freethought or science classics printed as double-column paperback books for six pence each (about twelve cents then). Among the earliest authors reprinted as Cheap Reprints were Thomas Huxley, Matthew Arnold, Ernest Renan, Herbert Spencer, and Ernest Haeckel. In 1902 alone, over 150,000 copies of the Cheap Reprints were sold.

The Rationalist Press Association also sponsored a series of speakers, as well as social activities for members. The first lecturers were Charles Watts, McCabe, Hypatia Bradlaugh Bonner, and Robertson. An annual dinner was begun in 1903. The RPA also published, starting in 1908, an annual volume called *The R.P.A. Annual* (384) and later *The Rationalist Annual*. It continued to appear every year until 1967, as will be mentioned in the next chapter. The many other activities of the RPA that occurred after 1915 will also be covered in the next chapter. At the end of 1915, the RPA had about 2,600 paying members. The history of the RPA is told in two different volumes. They are Whyte's *The Story of the R.P.A., 1899–1949* (49), and Gould's *The Pioneers of Johnson's Court* (14).

The National Secular Society was founded by Charles Bradlaugh (with help from Charles Watts), in 1866. It started in London, but soon tried to organize chapters in the major cities and regions of the United Kingdom. It was a slow process to organize such chapters, but eventually there were over 140 chapters formed. One of the major ways in which Bradlaugh organized chapters was simply by going on a speaking tour of the area he wished to organize. Along with Bradlaugh went such erstwhile NSS secretaries as Robert Forder and George Standring to follow-up Bradlaugh's drawing power as a speaker with plans for organizing a chapter. Besant was also a great speaker and organizer from about 1875 to 1890. After Bradlaugh's death, Foote became president of the NSS. Foote was also a powerful lecturer, who was only too glad to carry the NSS message to the "provinces."

In the area of London, the Hall of Science (City Road) was bought from the Owenites in 1843. From that date onwards, it was used by the freethinkers. In the 1850s, the London Secular Society occupied it. In 1865–1866, a fund drive was held to build a new hall. The fund drive was unsuccessful. In 1868, a lease for a building at 142 Old Street was obtained. Improvements were made, including an addition to the building in 1870. This expanded the seating capacity to 1,200. Charles Bradlaugh lectured in this hall regularly. Upon Bradlaugh's death, the lease fell into dispute. There was an attempt to secure or build a new hall to be named after Bradlaugh, but the plan failed, and the ability of the freethinkers to use their old hall was also lost.

In the Provinces of England, there were fairly strong local NSS branches in West Ham, North London, and Edmonton. After the NSS declined in the mid-1880s, Foote organized the London Secular Federation in 1888. It was not successful. There was little activity in South London, the Eastern Counties, or Wales. In the East Midlands, there were successful societies in Leicester and Nottingham.

The Leicester Secular Society was among the most successful anywhere. Its history has been told in a small book entitled *The History of the Leicester Secular Society* (332) by Gould. After a small beginning, a Secular Hall Company was launched to raise money for a hall in 1872. In 1881, the new hall at Humberstone Gate was opened. It is one of the largest freethought buildings ever built in England, and among the few that are still being used for freethought purposes. In 1898, a full-time secretary was appointed. This position was filled by a former priest, who had just left the church. His name was Joseph McCabe, and he would later become an important freethought author and lecturer. After McCabe, Gould took over as secretary, holding the post for the next ten years.

The Birmingham secularists were led for many years by Charles C. Cattell. In 1877, the Birmingham Secular Society opened Baskerville Hall as its own meeting place. This hall was briefly used by Charles Watts upon his return from Canada in 1891, but soon after this it passed out of the secularist's hands.

In 1901, Percy Ward brought together a North of England Secular Federation, which soon became The British Secular League. Its aim was to spread secularism into areas in which the National Secular Society currently did not have chapters. In the 1890s, J. W. Gott and John Grange organized a Bradford freethought group that was also socialist.

There were only a few strong societies in Scotland, namely at Edinburgh, Perth, Dundee, Paisley and Glasgow. The Glasgow society dated back to the "Zetetic Societies" that had existed in the 1820s. It was known as the Glasgow Eclectic Institution. In 1867, at Charles Watts' suggestion, a branch of the NSS was started in Glasgow. The members of the Eclectic Institution feuded with the NSS members in the early 1870s. In 1877, a branch of The British Secular Union was formed in Glasgow. In the 1880s, the NSS branch and the Eclectic Institution seem to have been reunited.

The Edinburgh Secular Society existed during the period, as did the Scottish Secular Union, founded in 1870. This Union was not affiliated with the NSS, although it did maintain cordial relations with it.

J. P. Gilmour of Glasgow was a leading figure in Scottish free-thought from 1879 until his death in 1930. John M. Robertson was born and raised in Scotland, although his connection with freethought was not firm until he came to London. Charles Watts and Annie Besant (as well as Bradlaugh and Foote) often lectured in Scotland.

Ireland was not hospitable to any form of freethought until late in the nineteenth century. There was a small freethought society organized in Boyne in 1875–1876. There was also an NSS branch in Cork in 1883, and there were short-lived societies in Dublin and Belfast in 1875. In 1888, *The National Reformer* (207) admitted that there was no organized freethought group in Ireland at that time. An NSS branch was finally organized in Belfast from late in 1886 to the mid-1890s.

The Ethical Culture movement was founded in New York by Felix Adler (a former rabbi) in 1876. In the United States, several branch groups had been set up by 1880, including one in Chicago, led by William S. Salter. In 1885, an American sociologist distributed some of Salter's writings among some young British philosophers. Stanton Coit, an associate of Felix Adler in America, happened to be in London at about this time. He met with the men whose interest had been aroused, and urged the formation of a London group. In 1886, the first formal attempts at organization of such a society appear to have taken place. A series of lectures was announced as being given in Toynbee Hall, London, beginning November 21, 1886, and under the general title "Morality and Modern Life." Officers for a London Chapter of the Ethical Culture Society were also elected at this time. In 1888, the lectures were transferred to Essex Hall.

The South Place Religious Society was a group which had its start in 1795, when it was founded by Universalists as "The Philadelphians." It became, successively, a Unitarian society, Liberal Unitarian, an Ethical Culture Society, and finally a Humanist group. The name of the group after "The Philadelphians" was "The Universalists," "The

Society of Religious Dissenters," "The South Place Unitarian Society," "The South Place Society," "The Free Religious Society," and "The South Place Ethical Society."

Elhanan Winchester, an American Universalist, had come to London and started a Universalist society in 1795. This was "The Philadelphians." Winchester was succeeded by William Vidler in 1799. In 1816, W. J. Fox, a Unitarian, started a society to continue that group, but he moved it to South Place Chapel. Fox abandoned the ministry for politics after he divorced his wife and married a much younger member of his congregation. When Moncure Conway went on a speaking tour of England in 1863, which included several sermons at South Place Chapel, he was asked to stay to be in charge of the congregation.

Moncure Daniel Conway (1832–1907) was born in Stafford, Virginia, but he spent most of his adult life in England. Conway had trained to be a Methodist minister, but decided to switch to a Unitarian seminary after preaching as a Methodist for a short while. He attended Harvard's divinity school, then took a Unitarian pulpit in Washington, D.C. Conway's openly antislavery sentiments soon got him into trouble in Washington. He went to Cincinnati, where he soon became more heretical, remaining "Unitarian" in name only. Moncure Conway left Cincinnati for Boston in 1862, and Boston for the lecture tour to England in 1863.

Conway found England hospitable, so he sent for his wife and children. He became the leader of South Place, where he remained from 1863 until 1884, at which time he took his family to the Continent, and then to New York. Conway remained in New York for the next seven years. Much of this time he was working on his *The Life of Thomas Paine* (157) and his edition of *The Writings of Thomas Paine* (158), which was published after his return to London in 1892. Conway returned because the congregation at South Place had had difficulty finding a permanent replacement for him. They had tried Stanton Coit from 1888 until 1892, but he had not worked out as well. This time Moncure Conway stayed until 1897, when his wife became terminally ill. He took her back to the United States. After her death, he lived in Paris from 1898 until 1900, then alternated between Paris, London, and New York until his death. He spent those last years writing and lecturing.

Moncure Conway wrote many books. Some were what would be called freethought, others were more about ethics or the history of religion. The ones that relate most closely to freethought are *Demonology and Devil Lore* (304), his biography of Thomas Paine (157) and edition of Paine's works (158), and his two autobiographical studies, *My Pilgrimage to the Wise Men of the East* (305) and *Autobiography: Memories and Experiences* (303).

Besides the autobiographies, there are several biographical studies of Moncure Conway. The best is Burtis' *Moncure Conway: 1832–1907* (298). Another full biography is in preparation. Of interest also are Robertson's *The Life Pilgrimage of Moncure Daniel Conway* (396), Walker's *A Sketch and Appreciation of Moncure Daniel Conway* (433), and d'Entremont's pamphlet *Moncure Conway, 1832–1907* (306).

In the early twentieth century, many other people lectured at the South Place Ethical Society (as it was known after 1888). Stanton Coit, Joseph McCabe, and F. J. Gould were included.

It is hard to know where to best place Frederick James Gould (1855–1938). He was a school teacher who devoted much of his life to the teaching of ethics and morals to children. He served a period of time as secretary of the Leicester Secular Society, was a leader of the Leicester Positivist Society, a founder of the Rationalist Press Association, was associated with the South Place Ethical Society for many years, and wrote a large number of books and pamphlets. A number of his other books have already been mentioned. There was *The Pioneers of Johnson's Court* (14) that told the story of the RPA. There also was *The History of the Leicester Secular Society* (332). Gould also wrote *The Building of the Bible* (329), *The New Testament* (334), a biography of Thomas Paine (168), *A Concise History of Religion* (331), a biography of *Auguste Comte* (328) and the useful set of biographical sketches called *Chats With Pioneers of Modern Thought* (330). Gould wrote his autobiography as *The Life-Story of a Humanist* (333). There is also a biographical study of his last years by Hayward and White, called *The Last Years of a Great Educationist* (337).

The history of the Ethical Culture movement in England has been covered in two books. One is Spiller's *The Ethical Movement in Great Britain* (37), and the other is Ratcliffe's *The Story of South Place* (26).

Although Positivism was not exactly freethought, and although the Positivists themselves often had rather unfriendly relations with the other freethought groups, it is thought advisable to briefly mention a few things about Positivism. Many of the same people (e.g., Gould) moved from Positivism to more traditional freethought. Both groups were opposed to traditional religion.

Positivism was the brainchild of August Comte. It was introduced into England (from France) by the combined efforts of John Stewart Mill and G. H. Lewes. Mill had read Comte in the original French around 1840. Lewes and his friend and later wife, George Eliot, influenced John Morley to open up the columns of his magazine (*The Fortnightly Review*) to Positivist views around 1866. Lewes had evidently been influenced originally by Mill. A group of people later broke away from the South Place Ethical Society and formed The Ethical Church,

Bayswater along Positivist lines. For a short time, there was a fairly strong Positivist movement in England, but it rather quickly lost strength. The English Positivist leaders included F. J. Gould, Richard Congreve, Frederic Harrison, and John Henry Bridges.

The two books which best cover Positivism in England are John Edwin McGee's *A Crusade for Humanity* (365) and Walter M. Simon's *European Positivism in the Nineteenth Century* (417).

The period from 1860 to 1915 saw the peak of the organized freethought movement in the United Kingdom. There were more active members in organized freethought groups, more actual groups themselves, and a greater visibility in both the media and in the awareness of the public than there has been before, or since. Much of the credit for the establishment of this "Golden Age" of freethought belongs with the "temper" of the Victorian Age. In both Britain and the United States (see *Freethought in the United States* [140]), the times were right for the flowering of freethought, and important leaders arose to take command. Leaders such as George Jacob Holyoake, Charles Bradlaugh, Charles Watts, Annie Besant, and G. W. Foote had scarcely been seen before, and would hardly be seen again in the next sixty-five years.

The twentieth century (after 1915, when Foote died) was marked by a great falling away from organized religion by the people of the United Kingdom, and, at the same time, a gradual weakening of the strength of the organized freethought movement. The possible relationship between these two events will be explored in the next chapter.

BIBLIOGRAPHY

263. *Agnostic, The*. A freethought magazine published in London by Charles A. Watts, while Charles Watts was in Canada. It lasted only a part of the year 1885.

264. *Agnostic Annual, The*. A yearly publication, with Charles A. Watts, and W. Stewart & Company as the editor and the publisher, respectively. It was issued from the 1884 volume through the volume for 1907, after which it became *The R.P.A. Annual* (384). The volumes for 1884 and 1885 were published by H. Cattell & Company.

265. *Agnostic Journal & The Secular Review, The*. A freethought magazine published in London by W. Stewart Ross. This double title was given to the publication by Ross in 1889. It continued under this title until 1906, at which time it stopped publishing. Prior to 1889, the names had been *The Secular Review* (414), and *The Agnostic Journal*.

266. Amberley, Viscount [John Russell]. *An Analysis of Religious Belief*. 2 vols. London: Trübner & Co., 1876.

267. Anonymous. "Robert Forder." *The Freethinker* 24 September 1893.

268. Anonymous. "Robert Forder." *The Freethinker* 25 August 1901.

269. Arnstein, Walter. *The Bradlaugh Case*. London: Oxford University Press, 1965. About Bradlaugh's fight to take his seat in the House of Commons.

270. Aveling, Edward B. *The Creed of an Atheist*. London: Freethought Publishing Co., [1881].

271. Aveling, Edward B. *A Godless Life the Happiest and Most Useful*. [London: A. Besant & C. Bradlaugh, 1882].

272. Aveling, Edward B. *The Student's Darwin*. Freethought Publishing Co., 1881.

273. Aveling, Edward B. *Why I Dare Not Be a Christian*. London: Freethought Publishing Co., [1881].

274. Besant, Annie. *Annie Besant: An Autobiography*. London: T. Fisher Unwin, 1893. There were a number of later editions.

275. Besant, Annie (and others). *The Atheistic Platform*. London: Freethought Publishing Co., 1884–1888. A collection of pamphlets, reprinted later in a uniform format, and with continuous pagination, but often with the original dates of publication still on the title page. The following pamphlets by Annie Besant were included in *The Atheistic Platform: The Myth of the Resurrection, The Story of the Soudan, What Is the Use of Prayer?, Why I Am a Socialist*, and *Why Should Atheists Be Persecuted?* Also included were pamphlets by Charles Bradlaugh, Edward Aveling, and Arthur B. Moss.

276. Besant, Annie. *Autobiographical Sketches*. London: Freethought Publishing Co., 1885.

277. Besant, Annie. *The Freethinker's Text-Book, Part II: Christianity: Its Evidences, Its Origin, Its Morality, Its History*. London: Freethought Publishing Co., 1877. Part I was by Charles Bradlaugh (#288), and was published in 1876. Part III was by Charles Watts (#47).

278. Besant, Annie. *The History of the Great French Revolution*. London: Freethought Publishing Co., 1883. This volume was made from the second edition of the first series of these lectures, (which were originally published by C. Watts in London in 1876), plus the second edition of the second series of lectures (originally published in 1879 by the Freethought Publishing Co.).

279. Besant, Annie. *The Law of Population: Its Consequences, and Its Bearing Upon Human Conduct and Morals*. London: Freethought Publishing Co., 1877. Mrs. Besant's plea for birth control.

280. Besant, Annie. *My Path to Atheism*. London: Freethought Publishing Co., 1877. A reprint of all of the anonymous pamphlets

written by Besant, which were originally published by Thomas Scott.

281. Besant, Annie. *A Selection of the Social and Political Pamphlets of Annie Besant*. New York: Augustus M. Kelley, 1970.

282. Besant, Annie. *Theological Essays and Debates*. London: Freethought Publishing Co., [c. 1885]. A collection of previously-published pieces.

283. Besterman, Theodore. *Mrs. Annie Besant: A Modern Prophet*. London, Kegan Paul, Trench Trübner & Co., 1934.

284. Blatchford, Robert. *God and My Neighbor*. London: The Clarion Press, 1903. There were many subsequent British and American editions.

285. Blavatsky, Helena. *The Secret Doctrine: The Synthesis of Science, Religion and Philosophy*. 2 vols. London: The Theosophical Publishing Co., 1888.

286. Bradlaugh, Charles. *Debates in Theology*. London: A & H. Bradlaugh Bonner, 1892. A reissue (and in some cases a reprinting) of a number of earlier debates between Bradlaugh and assorted clergymen. There are five debates: Bradlaugh with Rev. Baylee, Thomas Cooper, Rev. A. J. Harrison, Rev. R. A. Armstrong, and a written debate with the Bishop of Peterborough (W. C. Magee).

288. Bradlaugh, Charles. *The Freethinker's Text-Book. Part I: Man: Whence and How? Religion: What and Why?* London: Freethought Publishing Co., 1876. Part II was by Annie Besant (#277) and Part III was by Charles Watts (#47).

289. Bradlaugh, Charles. *Genesis: Its Authorship and Authenticity*. London: Austin & Co., 1861. An enlarged edition was issued by the Freethought Publishing Co. (London) in 1882. The book was originally a section of Bradlaugh's *The Bible: What It Is*, which was expanded into the first part of a projected series of books on the Bible. The other parts were never expanded past the pamphlet stage.

290. Bradlaugh, Charles. *Humanity's Gain From Unbelief*. London: Freethought Publishing Co., 1889. Originally published as a magazine article (*North American Review*, [1889], pp. 294–306), it was published along with a number of additional essays as *Humanity's Gain from Unbelief and Other Selections From the Works of Charles Bradlaugh* in the Thinker's Library edition (Watts & Co., London, 1929). This is probably the most widely read Bradlaugh selection, because of its inclusion in the Thinker's Library.

291. Bradlaugh, Charles. *The Impeachment of the House of Brunswick*. London: Austin & Co., 1872. Revised editions were published in 1873 and 1888. An attack on the Monarchy.

292. Bradlaugh, Charles. *Labour and Law* London: R. Forder, 1891. Includes "Memoir" by J. M. Robertson.

293. Bradlaugh, Charles. *A Plea for Atheism*. London: Austin & Co., 1864. Reissued in 1865, and in revised and enlarged editions in 1877, 1880, and 1883 (Freethought Publishing Co.). It was also published in an American edition by Asa K. Butts of New York.

294. Bradlaugh, Charles. *A Selection of the Political Pamphlets of Charles Bradlaugh*. New York: Augustus M. Kelley, 1970. A reprint of twenty-seven of Bradlaugh's individual pamphlets, including those which were originally issued as a collected edition called *Political Essays* 2 vols. London: Freethought Publishing Co., 1888–1889.

295. Bradlaugh, Charles. *Speeches By Charles Bradlaugh*. London: Freethought Publishing Co., 1890. A later edition was annotated by J. M. Robertson.

296. Bradlaugh, Charles. *Theological Essays*. London: A & H. Bradlaugh Bonner, 1895. A reissue (and in some cases a reprinting) of a number of Bradlaugh's earlier pamphlets about theological subjects.

297. *British Secular Almanac, The*. Edited by Charles Watts and W. S. Ross ("Saladin"), it was published in London by Watts & Co. from 1878 through 1883 as an annual. It was published for The British Secular Union.

298. Burtis, Mary Elizabeth. *Moncure Conway: 1832–1907*. New Brunswick, N.J.: Rutgers University Press, 1952.

299. [Cassels, Walter Richard]. *Supernatural Religion: An Inquiry Into the Reality of Divine Revelation*. 2 vols. London: Longmans, Green & Co., 1874. Issued anonymously, the authorship of Cassels was not revealed until after 1902.

300. Cattell, Charles C. *The Dark Side of Christianity, Showing It Unreasonable and Impracticable*. London: C. Watts, [1875?].

301. [Cattell, Charles C.]. *Is Darwinism Atheistic*? London: Freethought Publishing Co., 1884. A part of *The Atheistic Platform* series of pamphlets (#275).

302. [Cattell, Charles C.]. as "Christopher Charles." *Secularism: What It Is*. London: Austin & Co., [1870?].

303. Conway, Moncure D. *Autobiography: Memories and Experiences*. 2 vols. Boston: Houghton, Mifflin & Co., 1904.

304. Conway, Moncure D. *Demonology and Devil Lore*. 2 vols. New York: Henry Holt & Co., 1879.

305. Conway, Moncure D. *My Pilgrimage to the Wise Men of the East*. Boston: Houghton, Mifflin & Co., 1906.

306. d'Entremont, John. *Moncure Conway 1832–1907*. London: South Place Ethical Society, 1977.

307. Flaws, Gordon G. *Sketch of the Life and Character of Saladin (W. Stewart Ross)*. London: Watts & Co., n.d. [c. 1882].

308. Foote, G. W. *Arrows of Freethought*. London: H. A. Kemp,

n.d. [c. 1882]. A collection of some of Foote's best short pieces from *The Freethinker* (#325).

309. Foote, G. W. and Ball, William Platt. *The Bible Handbook for Freethinkers and Inquiring Christians*. London: Progressive Publishing Co., 1888. Many subsequent editions, most of them published by Pioneer Press, London. One of the most often reprinted of freethought books, it is easily Foote's most popular book.

310. Foote, G. W. *Bible Heroes*. London: Progressive Publishing Co., 1887. These satires originally appeared as a series of articles in *The Freethinker* (#325). They were then published as a series of separate pamphlets. Finally, the entire series was issued as a single volume.

311. Foote, G. W. *Bible Romances*. London: Progressive Publishing Co., 1888. A series of articles from *The Freethinker* (#325), then a series of pamphlets, and finally, a single volume. It went through many editions.

312. Foote, G. W. and McCann, James. *Christianity and Secularism: Which Is True*? London: Progressive Publishing Co., 1886. The verbatim report of a debate which occurred at the Hall of Science in London on April 8, 15, and 29, and May 6, 1886.

313. Foote, G. W. and Woffendale, Z. B. *Christianity V. Secularism*. London: A. Woffendale, n.d. [c. 1879]. Issued by Woffendale without Foote's review or approval. Its contents were repudiated by Foote as an inaccurate report of the debate held at the South Place Chapel on the 6th and 7th of February, 1879.

314. Foote, George William and Wheeler, J. M. *Crimes of Christianity*. Vol. 1. London: Progressive Publishing Co., 1886. Vol. 2 was published in 1886, but two weeks later the entire stock was destroyed in a fire. It was not republished, and there may be no extant copies.

315. Foote, G. W. "Death of Harriet Law." *The Freethinker*, August 8, 1897.

316. Foote, G. W. *Flowers of Freethought*. London: R. Forder, 1893 (First Series), and 1894 (Second Series). Two volumes of Foote's best articles from *The Freethinker* (#325).

317. Foote, G. W. *The Grand Old Book: A Reply to the Right Hon. W. E. Gladstone's "The Impregnable Rock of Holy Scripture."* London: Progressive Publishing Co., 1891.

318. Foote, G. W. *Infidel Death Beds*. London: Progressive Publishing Co., 1886. Later editions (London: Pioneer Press, 1933 and onward) were revised and enlarged by A. D. McLaren. True accounts of the last moments of well-known freethinkers, written to refute the Christian tale that they all recanted at death.

319. Foote, G. W. and Wheeler, J. M. eds. *The Jewish Life of Christ, Being the Sepher Toldoth Jeshu or Book of the Generation of Jesus*. London: Progressive Publishing Co., 1885.

320. Foote, G. W. *Letters to the Clergy*. London: Progressive Publishing Co., 1890. A series of articles in *The Freethinker* (#325) originally.

321. Foote, G. W. *Shakespeare and Other Literary Essays*. London: Pioneer Press, 1929. A posthumous publication of a number of Foote's literary articles from *The Freethinker* and *The English Review*.

322. Foote, G. W. and Lee, W. T. *Theism or Atheism: Which Is the More Reasonable?* London: R. Forder, 1896. A report of a debate held in the Temperance Hall, Derby, May 15 and 16, 1896.

323. Forder, Robert. *There Was a War in Heaven. An Infidel Sermon*. London: R. Forder, 1886.

324. *Free Review, The*. A magazine published in London by J. M. Robertson, from 1893 to 1897. In March 1897, it changed its name to *University Magazine & Free Review*. This was published until September 1900.

325. *Freethinker, The*. A freethought magazine founded in London in 1881 by G. W. Foote. Foote was editor from its founding until 1915. From 1882 until the 1960s, it was a weekly. The editors after Foote were Chapman Cohen (1915–1951), F. A. Ridley (1951–1954), a Committee (1954–59), Colin McCall (1959–65), David Tribe (1966), Kit Mouat (1966–1967), David Collis (1967), Karl Hyde (1967–1968), David Reynolds (1968–1970), William McIlroy (1970–1971, 1975–1976), Nigel Sinnott (1972–1973), Chris Morey (1973–1974), Jim Herrick (1977–).

326. Gilmour, J. P. "Charles Watts (1836–1906), A Reminiscence and an Appreciation." *The Literary Guide*, August 1935: 147–148.

327. Gott, J. W., ed. *Rib Ticklers, Or Questions for Parsons*. Bradford, England: Truthseeker Co., [1903]. The subject of several blasphemy prosecutions.

328. Gould, F. J. *Auguste Comte*. London: Watts & Co., 1920.

329. Gould, F. J. *The Building of the Bible*. London: Watts & Co., 1907.

330. Gould, F. J. *Chats With Pioneers of Modern Thought*. London: Watts & Co., 1898.

331. Gould, F. J. *A Concise History of Religion*. 3 vols. London: Watts & Co., 1897.

332. Gould, F. J. *The History of the Leicester Secular Society*. Leicester: The Leicester Secular Society, 1900.

333. Gould, F. J. *The Life-Story of a Humanist*. London: Watts & Co., 1923.

334. Gould, F. J. *The New Testament*. London: Watts & Co., 1914.

335. Griffith-Jones, George C. *Monkanna Unveiled. An Essay on Charles R. Mackay's "Life of Charles Bradlaugh, M. P." With an Addendum on Secularism and Politics*. London: "D. J. Gunn & Co.," [1888]. Fictitious imprint. In this and the Mackay pamphlet *Balak Secundus* (#366), "Lara" explains much of the background of the libelous life of Bradlaugh.

336. Haeckel, Ernest. *The Riddle of the Universe at the Close of the Nineteenth Century*. London: Watts & Co., 1901. Translated from the original German by Joseph McCabe.

337. Hayward, F. H. and White, E. M. *The Last Years of a Great Educationist. A Record of the Work and Thought of F. J. Gould From 1923 to 1938*. Bungay, England: Printed by Richard Clay & Co., [1942]. Privately published?

338. Heaford, William. *Biographical Sketch: Arthur B. Moss*. Bradford [England]: Truth Seeker Co., n.d. [c. 1900].

339. Hithersay, Richard B. and Ernest, George. [Pseudonym of George Giffith-Jones ("Lara")]. *Sketch of the Life of Saladin (W. Stewart Ross)*. London: W. Stewart & Co., n.d. [c. 1887].

340. Holyoake, Austin. *Daniel the Dreamer*. London: Austin & Co., n.d. [1873].

341. Holyoake, Austin. *Facetiae for Freethinkers*. London: Austin & Co., n.d. [1873].

342. Holyoake, Austin. *Ludicrous Aspects of Christianity*. London: Austin & Co., n.d. [c. 1873].

343. Holyoake, Austin and Watts, Charles. eds. *The Secularist's Manual of Songs and Ceremonies*. London: Austin & Co., n.d. [c. 1873].

344. Holyoake, George J. *Bygones Worth Remembering*. 2 vols. London: T. Fisher Unwin, 1905. A partial autobiography, consisting of unconnected recollections.

345. Holyoake, G. J. and Grant, Rev. Brewin. *Christianity and Secularism: Report of a Public Discussion Between Rev. Brewin Grant, B. A., and George Jacob Holyoake, Esq., Held in the Royal British Institution, Cowper Street, London, on Six Successive Thursday Evenings, Commencing January 20 and Ending February 24, 1863 on the Question "What Advantages (to) . . . Mankind by the Removal of Christianity and the Substitution of Secularism . . . ?"* London: Ward & Co., 1853.

346. Holyoake, G. J. and Grant, Rev. Brewin. *Discussion on Secularism: Report of a Public Discussion Between Rev. Brewin Grant, B. A. and George Jacob Holyoake, Esq., Held in the City Hall*

Glasgow, on Monday and Thursday Evenings, Commencing October 2, and Ending October 19, 1854, on the Question "Is Secularism Inconsistent With Reason & the Moral Sense, and Condemned by Experience?" Glasgow: Robert Stark, n.d. [c. 1854].

347. Holyoake, G. J. *The History of Co-operation in England: Its Literature and Its Advocates.* London: Trübner & Co., 1875 (vol. 1) and 1879 (vol. 2). The first volume covers the pioneer period, from 1812 to 1844. The second volume covers the period from 1845 to 1878.

348. Holyoake, G. J. *The History of the Rochdale Pioneers.* London: Swan Sonnenschein & Co., 1893. This book was known, in earlier editions, as *Self-Help By the People: History of Co-operation in Rochdale* (#189), and was originally published by Holyoake & Co. (London) in 1858.

349. Holyoake, G. J. *In Memoriam. Austin Holyoake. Died April the 10th, 1874.* London: no publisher, [1874].

350. Holyoake, G. J. and Bradlaugh, Charles. *Secularism, Skepticism and Atheism.* London: Austin & Co., 1870. A debate.

351. Holyoake, G. J. *Sixty Years of an Agitator's Life.* 2 vols. London: T. Fisher Unwin, 1892. A partial autobiography, consisting of unconnected remembrances.

352. Jacob, T. Evan. *Saladin the Little: An Exposure.* London: Robert Forder, 1887. A criticism of Ross' criticisms of the Malthusian stand of the National Secular Society.

353. Kapp, Yvonne. *Eleanor Marx.* London: Lawrence and Wishart, 1972 (vol. 1) and 1976 (vol. 2). There was also an American edition, which came out later. Contains much on Edward B. Aveling.

354. Knowlton, Charles. *The Fruits of Philosophy.* London: Free-thought Publishing Co., 1877. The prosecuted edition (with the subtitle *"An Essay on the Population Question"*). The original edition was published in New York in 1832. There were also a number of earlier British editions.

355. Law, Harriet. "Charles Watts." *The Secular Chronicle* 9 (1878): 181–83 (21 April 1878).

356. Law, Harriet. "John Watts." *The Secular Chronicle* 9 December 1877.

357. *Law Times, The.* (London) "Occasional Notes." 11 Feb 1922, pp. 105–06. Also *Justice of the Peace.* "John William Gott." 25 April 1908, pp. 188–89. An obituary of Gott appears in *The Freethinker* of 12 Nov 1922, p. 730, and 19 Nov. 1922, p. 750.

358. *Liberal, The.* A mostly political magazine, published in London by G. W. Foote, from January 1879 to December 1879.

359. *Liberator, The.* A freethought magazine, published weekly in Melbourne, Australia by Joseph Symes from June 1, 1884 until February 6, 1904. Two final issues were published on March 5, and March 12, 1904.

360. *Literary Guide, The.* A freethought magazine published by Watts & Co. in London from 1885 until September 1956. At that time, its title was changed to *The Humanist* (#488). It began as a small announcement of new Watts & Co. publications, but by 1896 it had become a book review and literary journal. From 1894 until 1954, it carried the subtitle *"and Rationalist Review."* In its first few years, it was called *"Watts' Literary Guide."* The editors of *The Literary Guide* were Charles A. Watts (1885–1930), Frederick C. C. Watts (1930–1953) and Hector Hawton (1953–1956).

361. McCabe, Joseph. *George Jacob Holyoake.* London: Watts & Co., 1922. A condensation of McCabe's two-volume biography, *Life and Letters of George Jacob Holyoake* (#19).

362. McCabe, Joseph. *Modern Rationalism.* London: Watts & Co., 1909.

363. McCabe, Joseph. *The Religion of the Twentieth Century.* London: Watts & Co., 1900. The first publication of the RPA.

364. McCabe, Joseph. *Twelve Years in a Monastery.* London: Smith, Elder & Co., 1897.

365. McGee, John Edwin. *A Crusade for Humanity. The History of Organized Positivism in England.* London: Watts & Co., 1931.

366. "Mackay, Charles R." [really by George Griffith-Jones]. *Balak Secundus. Being a Preliminary Exposure of William Stewart Ross, Trading as W. Stewart & Co. . .* London: "D.J. Gunn & Co.," [1888]. Fictitious imprint. About the libelous biography of Bradlaugh (#367).

367. Mackay, Charles R. *Life of Charles Bradlaugh, M.P.* London: "D.J. Gunn & Co.," 1888. This book was really by William Harral Johnson and a small part was added by William Stewart Ross. It was printed in Edinburgh, with the "D.J. Gunn & Co." imprint being fictitious. Mackay really existed, but he was paid to allow his name to be put as author. The book was found libelous (as well it should have been), and Ross was ordered to pay a large fine to Bradlaugh (who gave it to charity). Copies were ordered destroyed.

368. Micklewright, F. H. A. "The Humanism of Bradlaugh." *Humanist* (London) September 1958, pp. 16–18. There is also Marshall Gauvin's "Charles Bradlaugh: Giant of Freethought" in *The Truth Seeker* (New York) September 1960, pp. 133–35. Also, Hypatia Bradlaugh Bonner's "Letters from W. E. Gladstone to Charles Bradlaugh" in *The Literary Guide*, May 1933, pp. 83–84 and F. J.

Gould's "Charles Bradlaugh (1833–1891) Breaker and Builder," *The Literary Guide* October 1933, pp. 179–81.

369. Moss, Arthur B. *The Bible and Evolution*. London: Watts & Co., n.d. [c. 1890].

370. Moss, Arthur B. *Christianity and Evolution*. London: Watts & Co., [1900].

371. Moss, Arthur B. "Famous Freethinkers I have Known." A series of twelve articles in *The Freethinker* of 11 April, 18 April, 2 May, 23 May, 6 June, 4 July, 1 August, 5 September, 3 October, 24 October, 14 November, and 12 December 1915. The titles of the articles vary somewhat.

372. Moss, Arthur B. "Famous Freethinkers I have Known'— X. Joseph Mazzini Wheeler." *The Freethinker* 24 October 1915, pp. 676–77. There are also articles about Wheeler in *The Freethinker* May 1956, p. 157 and in *The Reformer* 15 May 1898. *The Freethinker* 15 May 1898 reports Wheeler's death and has obituaries.

373. Moss, Arthur B. *Lectures and Essays*. London: Watts & Co. *and* Freethought Publishing Co. [dual imprint], n.d. [c. 1889]. Collected pamphlets which were published separately before.

374. Moss, Arthur B. and Wilke, Agnes, Rollo. *Was Jesus an Impostor?* London: Watts & Co., n.d. [c. 1890]. A discussion.

375. *National Secular Society Almanac, The*. An annual volume, published in London from 1870 until 1904. From 1870 to 1874, the editors were Charles Bradlaugh and Austin Holyoake. From 1875 until 1878, they were Charles Bradlaugh and Charles Watts. From 1879 until 1890, the editors were Charles Bradlaugh and Annie Besant. From 1891 until 1898, it was edited by G. W. Foote and J. M. Wheeler. After 1898 (through 1904), Foote and Chapman Cohen edited it. The Freethought Publishing Company was the publisher from 1877 until 1890, with the National Secular Society as publisher after that.

376. Nethercot, Arthur H. *The Last Four Lives of Annie Besant*. Chicago: The University of Chicago Press, 1962.

377. Neuburg, Victor E. "Edward Truelove: Bookseller and Publisher." *The Truth Seeker* (New York) February 1953 p. 30.

378. *Our Corner*. A magazine published in London from 1883 until 1888 by Annie Besant. It was a weekly. The magazine was largely literary, although there was much freethought material as well. Among the contributors were Charles Bradlaugh, J. M. Robertson and George Bernard Shaw.

379. Owen, Robert Dale. *Moral Physiology, Or a Brief Treatise on the Population Question*. New York: Wright & Owen, 1831. There were many editions.

380. Pack, Ernest. *The Trial and Imprisonment of J. W. Gott for Blasphemy*. Bradford, England: The Freethought Socialist League, [1912].

381. Page, Martin. "The Paradoxical 'Genius' of J. M. Robertson," *The Ethical Record* (London), September 1970, pp. 5–10. There was also a series of short articles on J. M. Robertson by Herbert Cutner, as follows: *The Freethinker* 9 November 1956, pp. 362–63 and 16 November 1956, pp. 370–71.; *The Literary Guide*, March 1955, pp. 36–37. John Hastings also had an article on Robertson in *The Freethinker*, 12 October 1956, p. 330. Obituary articles on J. M. Robertson appeared in *The Literary Guide*, February 1933, pp. 35–39 and in March 1933, pp. 53–54. *The Literary Guide* for April 1933 carries a report about the Robertson Memorial Meeting held at Conway Hall (p. 74).

382. *Present Day, The*. A magazine published in London by George Jacob Holyoake, from 1883 until 1886. It was devoted to secularism, but not to religious criticism.

383. *Progress*. A freethought and literary magazine, published in London by G. W. Foote from 1883 until 1887.

384. *R.P.A. Annual, The*. A yearly volume published by the Rationalist Press Association from 1908 until 1926. It then changed its name to *The Rationalist Annual* in 1927, and was published under this title through the issue of 1967. In 1968, it was replaced with *Question* (#517).

385. Radde, Carl Otto, ed. *In Memoriam Saladin (William Stewart Ross)*. Hamburg, Germany: Artushof, Carl Otto Radde, [1906].

386. Ramsey, W. J. *In Prison for Blasphemy*. London: R. Forder, n.d. [c. 1883].

387. *Reformer, The*. A magazine (mostly freethought) published in London by Hypatia Bradlaugh Bonner. John M. Robertson was the editor. It was published from 1898 until 1904.

388. Robertson, Archibald. "Foote of 'The Freethinker.'" *The Literary Guide*, September 1950, pp. 183–84. There are also articles about Foote in *The Secular Chronicle* of 17 March 1878 (by Harriet Law); in *The Spur*, February 1916 pp. 73–75 ("Richard and the Georges" by Guy Aldred); in *Progressive World*, September 1958 pp. 9–16 (by Peter Charlton); and in *The Freethinker* 31 October 1915 ("G. W. Foote Memorial Number").

389. Robertson, John M. *Charles Bradlaugh*. London: Watts & Co., 1920. A revised version of the section on Bradlaugh's political career which Robertson contributed to the biography of Hypatia Bradlaugh Bonner (#4).

390. Robertson, John M. *Christ and Krishna*. London: Freethought Publishing Co., 1889. Not actually published until 1890. This originally was a series of articles in *The National Reformer* (#207). It was later incorporated in a slightly modified form into *Christianity and Mythology* (#391).

391. Robertson, John M. *Christianity and Mythology*. London: Watts & Co., 1900. Second edition published in 1910.

392. Robertson, John M. *Explorations*. London: Watts & Co., [1923]. A collection of seven previously published essays.

393. Robertson, John M. *The Historical Jesus: A Survey of Positions*. London: Watts & Co., 1916.

394. Robertson, John M. *Jesus and Judas: A Textual and Historical Investigation*. London: Watts & Co., 1927. The final of five volumes of Robertson's investigation of the historicity problem.

395. Robertson, John M. *The Jesus Problem: A Restatement of the Myth Theory*. London: Watts & Co., 1917.

396. Robertson, John M. *The Life Pilgrimage of Moncure Daniel Conway*. London: Watts & Co., 1914.

397. Robertson, John M. *Modern Humanists*. London: Swan Sonnenschein & Co., 1891. Contains essays on Carlyle, Mill, Emerson, Arnold, Spencer, and Ruskin.

398. Robertson, John M. *Pagan Christs: Studies in Comparative Hierology*. London: Watts & Co., 1903. Second edition, 1911.

399. Robertson, John M. *Pioneer Humanists*. London: Watts & Co., 1907. Contains essays on Machiavelli, Bacon, Hobbes, Spinoza, Shaftesbury, Mandeville, Gibbon, and Mary Wollstonecraft.

400. Robertson, John M. *Rationalism*. London: Constable & Co., 1912.

401. Robertson, John M. *A Short History of Christianity*. London: Watts & Co., 1902. An abridged edition was published in The Thinker's Library.

402. Robertson, John M. *Spoken Essays*. London: Watts & Co., 1925. Contains eight essays, which had originally been speeches.

403. Robertson, John M. *Studies in Religious Fallacy*. London: Watts & Co., 1900.

404. Robertson, John M. *Thomas Paine: An Investigation*. London: Freethought Publishing Co., 1888. Written in refutation of Leslie Stephen's section on Thomas Paine in his *History of English Thought in the Eighteenth Century* (#39). Stephen later admitted his errors and changed the section.

405. Ross, W. Stewart. *The Book of "At Random."* London: W. Stewart & Co., [1905]. A collection of Ross' "At Random" columns from *The Agnostic Journal* (#265).

406. [Ross, W. S.] "Saladin." *God and His Book*. London: W. Stewart & Co. [1887].

407. Ross, W. Stewart. *Roses and Rue: Being Random Notes and Sketches*. London: W. Stewart & Co., [1894].

408. [Ross, W. Stewart] "Saladin." *Sketch of the Life and Character of C. Watts*. London: W. Stewart & Co., [1897].

409. [Ross, W. Stewart] "Saladin" and Taylor, Joseph. *Why I am an Agnostic*. London: W. Stewart & Co., [1889].

410. [Ross, W. Stewart] "Saladin." *Woman: Her Glory, Her Shame and Her God*. 2 vols. London: W. Stewart & Co., [1894].

411. Royle, Edward, ed. *The Papers of Charles Bradlaugh (Index)*. Microfilm edition of the Papers, held in the library of the National Secular Society (London). The microfilm and *Index* were published by EP Microforms, Wakefield, England, 1975. The *Index*, compiled by Royle, contains an abstract of each item in the collection, along with a short biography of Bradlaugh.

412. Scott, Thomas. *The English Life of Jesus*. Ramsgate, England: Thomas Scott, 1869. Probably written largely by G. W. Cox.

413. *Secular Chronicle, The*. A freethought magazine, published at Birmingham, England by George H. Reddalls in 1872. When he died in 1875, Harriet Law took over the magazine, and ran it for three years. A committee tried to run it after that, but was unsuccessful. It closed in 1879.

414. *Secular Review, The*. A freethought magazine published at London from 1876 until 1889. It was started by George Jacob Holyoake, and edited by Charles Watts from February 1877. G. W. Foote was coeditor from June 1877 until February 1878. Watts was joined by W. S. Ross as coeditor in 1882. In August 1884, Ross became the sole owner. It was renamed *The Agnostic Journal* (#265) in 1889, and continued with the subtitle "*& Secular Review*" until his death in 1906.

415. *Secular Thought*. A magazine founded in Toronto, Canada in 1885 by Charles Watts, who edited it from 1885 until 1891. After Watts returned to England, it was edited by J. Spencer Ellis, from 1891 until it closed in 1911. It was largely a weekly.

416. *Secularist, The*. A weekly freethought periodical, published in London from January 1876 until June 1877 by George Jacob Holyoake and G. W. Foote. Holyoake's involvement ceased in March 1876.

417. Simon, Walter M. *European Positivism in the Nineteenth Century: An Essay in Intellectual History*. Ithaca, N.Y.: Cornell University Press, 1963. Reprinted by Kennikat Press.

418. Sinnott, Nigel. *Joseph Symes, The "Flower of Atheism."* Lidcome North, NSW, Australia: Atheist Society of Australia, 1977. This pamphlet contains the best biography of Symes to date. Additional information on Symes and his family is contained in two additional pamphlets by Sinnott: *Matilda, Agnes and Stella Symes* (same publisher, 1978) and *Joseph Skurrie's Freethought Reminiscences* (same publisher, 1977).

419. [Smith], Adolph Headingley. *The Biography of Charles Bradlaugh*. London: Remington & Co., 1880. The first attempt at a book-length biography of Bradlaugh.

420. Standring, George. *An Atheist at Church*. London: R. Forder, 1894.

421. Standring, George. *Biographical Sketch of Arthur B. Moss*. London: G. Standring, [1889]. Included as a preface to Moss's *Lectures and Essays* (#373).

422. Standring, George. *Life of Charles Bradlaugh, M.P.* London: Freethought Publishing Co., n.d. [1889].

423. Standring, George. *Richard Carlile: A Brief Sketch of His Public Life*. London: E. Truelove, n.d. [c. 1885?].

424. Symes, Joseph and Rev. Brewin Grant. *Christianity V. Secularism. The Authorized Verbatim Report of the Debate Between The Rev. Brewin Grant, B.A. and Joseph Symes, Esq., Held at the Hartlepools, on February 24, 1980 and Three Following Nights*. London: J. Britnell, [1880].

425. Symes, Joseph. *From the Wesleyan Pulpit to the Secularist Platform: Or, the Life and Death of My Religion*. Melbourne: The "Liberator" Printing & Publishing Co., 1884. An autobiography.

426. Symes, Joseph. *Hospitals & Dispensaries Not of Christian Origin*. London: Freethought Publishing Co., n.d. [c. 1879?].

427. Symes, Joseph. *Philosophical Atheism: A Bundle of Fragments*. London: Freethought Publishing Co., [1879].

428. Symes, Joseph. *Universal Despair; Or, Who Will Be Damned If Christianity Be True*? London: Charles Bradlaugh & Annie Besant, 1883.

429. Thomson, James. *The City of Dreadful Night*. This long poem first appeared serially in *The National Reformer*, in the issues of March 22, April 12 and 26, and May 17, 1874. It was first published in book form in 1880 (London: Reeves and Turner).

430. Truelove, Edward. *The Queen Vs. Edward Truelove*. London: E. Truelove, 1878. A report of his obscenity trial.

431. *Truthseeker, The*. A freethought magazine, published at Bradford, England by J. W. Gott, and edited by John Grange at first,

and then by Gott. It was started in 1894. A. B. Wakefield was also involved in the publishing at the beginning. Gott became editor in 1900. The paper was entirely cartoons by 1905, and folded shortly thereafter. The cartoons were from *The Truth Seeker* (New York).

432. Vance, Edith M. "Obituary" [George Standring]. *The Freethinker*, March 16, 1924.

433. Walker, Edwin C. *A Sketch and Appreciation of Moncure Daniel Conway, Freethinker and Humanitarian*. New York: Edwin C. Walker, 1908.

434. Watts, Charles and Sexton, George. *Debate on Christianity. Christianity & Secularism: Which is the Better Suited to Meet the Wants of Mankind?* London: Smart & Allen, [1881]. A written debate, reprinted from *The Secular Review*.

435. Watts, Charles. *The Meaning of Rationalism and Other Essays*. London: Watts & Co., 1905. Collected essays.

436. Watts, John. *The Christian Doctrine of Man's Depravity Refuted*. London: Austin & Co., 1865.

437. Watts, John. *Metaphysical Parallels; Or, Arguments in Juxta-Position, for and Against the Existence of God; the Immateriality and Immortality of the Soul, &c*. London: J. Watson, n.d. [c. 1855].

438. "West, Geoffrey" [G. Welles]. *Mrs. Annie Besant*. London: Gerald Howe, 1927.

439. Wheeler, J. M. *Bible Studies. Essays on Phallic Worship and Other Curious Rites and Customs*. London: Progressive Publishing Co., 1892.

440. Wheeler, J. M. *The Christian Doctrine of Hell*. London: R. Forder, 1890.

441. Wheeler, J. M. "Death of Harriet Law." *The Freethinker* 1 August 1897.

442. Wheeler, J. M. *Footsteps of the Past: Essays on Human Evolution*. London: Progressive Publishing Co., 1895. Partial reprint issued by Pioneer Press (London) in 1931, with the same title. The remainder of the original book was republished by Pioneer Press in 1932, under the title *Paganism in Christian Festivals*.

443. Wheeler, J. M., ed. *Freethought Readings and Secular Songs*. London: R. Forder, 1892.

444. Wheeler, J. M. *Satan, Witchcraft and the Bible*. London: R. Forder, n.d. [c. 1890].

445. Williams, Gertrude. *The Passionate Pilgrim: A Life of Annie Besant*. New York: Coward-McCann, 1931.

4
Freethought After Foote
━━━━━━ (1915-present) ━━━━━━

With the death of G. W. Foote in October 1915, the leadership of the British freethought movement passed to Chapman Cohen. It was an excellent choice, as Cohen was an experienced platform speaker, a lucid writer, and a hard worker. Cohen also lived to a ripe old age (eighty-six), thereby remaining in charge of the National Secular Society (and its publication, *The Freethinker* [325]) for a very long time. Cohen's longevity, (plus his native talents, of course) makes him the single most influential individual active in British freethought after Foote.

There were a few other "old timers" who remained active. Most important among them were Joseph McCabe, John M. Robertson, Adam Gowans Whyte, Charles A. Watts, Hypatia Bradlaugh Bonner, Arthur B. Moss, and F. J. Gould. By the late 1930s, all of these (except Cohen and McCabe) were dead. McCabe had, by then, drifted away from the RPA, the NSS and organized freethought in general. A new group of people (except for Chapman Cohen) moved into leadership roles at this time. In the early 1950s, after Cohen's death, the new faces were in charge. They included such people as F. A. Ridley, F. J. Corina, Fred Watts, Charles Bradlaugh Bonner, Herbert Cutner, Nigel Sinnott, David Collis, David Tribe, Hector Hawton, H. J. Blackham, Kit Mouat, William McIlroy, Len Ebury, Chris Macy, Nicolas Walter, Barbara Smoker, and Jim Herrick.

The RPA was to grow steadily, reach its peak, and then decline. A similar situation was to occur with the NSS. Yet, both groups would be operating in an increasingly secular British society; one that was to become filled with empty churches. Rationalist publications sold in the millions; perhaps they were partly responsible. There were a number of new freethought magazines, and an increasing respectability to membership in a freethought organization. Perhaps these also had an effect. It is certainly hard to measure these influences, and to separate them from the other secularizing influences present at the same time.

Let's begin with the death of Foote in 1915, and trace the recent history of freethought in the United Kingdom from that point.

Foote's death was proceeded by a fairly lengthy illness. During that time, Chapman Cohen, who had been in the freethought movement for about twenty years, took over Foote's editorial and speaking duties. When Foote died, it was logical that Cohen should continue what he was already doing.

Chapman Cohen (1868–1954) probably spent more time in a leadership capacity in the freethought movement than any other man. He was active in freethought for over sixty years, with thirty-four of those years being spent as president of the National Secular Society. He was also editor of *The Freethinker* (325) for thirty-five years.

Chapman Cohen was born in the British midlands region, into a family which had no longer any religion. Thus, as he often remarked, he had no religion to unlearn or reject in order to accept freethought. He was an omnivorous reader, with philosophy being one of his favorite subjects. The philosopher who seems to have influenced him most was George Berkeley.

It is exceedingly difficult to give the facts of Cohen's early life, even though he wrote a book-length autobiography, called *Almost an Autobiography* (457). This is true because Cohen seems to have little reportable life outside of his reading, writing, thinking, and lecturing for freethought. He did marry and have two children, but his autobiography gives almost nothing in the way of facts about his private life. It is really a sort of "justification" for having indulged himself by doing exactly what he wanted to do (reading, writing, thinking, and talking about philosophical topics), and nothing more. His life was a total commitment to the freethought cause.

Nevertheless, we do know a few things about Cohen's life. He was almost entirely self-educated. He started out in the freethought cause in about 1890, when he first appeared at open-air meetings at which freethinkers spoke. Cohen was soon asked to speak for the freethought cause. In about 1895, Cohen became assistant editor of J. W. Gott's *The Truthseeker* (431). He soon disagreed with Gott, however, over Gott's policy of taking large sections of his publications to advertise the clothing and other items which he sold in his dry goods business. Cohen then became largely a platform orator and lecturer. The one publication of his, from this period, which can be mentioned is a debate with the Rev. W. Hetherington, called *Christianity V. Secularism* (459), dating from about 1892. Cohen also published a few pamphlets, the earliest of which seems to be *The Decay of Belief* (460), which was published in about 1895. His first publication for the London freethought press was *An Outline of Evolutionary Ethics* (466) in 1896.

Chapman Cohen was a regular contributor to Foote's *The Free-thinker* (325). His early contributions for publication (until about 1910) were signed "C. Cohen." The Bowman Case, responsible for finally deciding that bequests left for the propagation of freethought were legal, and a major victory for freethought, was argued all the way up to the House of Lords. The battle was largely fought by Cohen in its last stages, since Foote was too ill to take a very active role in the fight. When it was finally settled by the House of Lords in 1916, Foote had just died. The full story of this important case is told in *A Fight For Right* (463), with an introduction by Cohen, published in 1917.

Cohen's tenure as editor of *The Freethinker* (from 1915 until 1951) was marked by an enormous productivity. G. H. Taylor, in his *A Chronology of British Secularism* (41), has calculated that during this period Cohen contributed 2,696 articles to *The Freethinker*. Cohen resigned as president of the National Secular Society in 1949, a position he had held since 1915. R. H. Rosetti was made acting president.

Chapman Cohen often reprinted his articles in *The Freethinker* as pamphlets, or cumulated them as books. Some of his best contributions to *The Freethinker* over the years were issued as a series of five volumes called *Essays In Freethinking* (462). Another series of pamphlets was bound together and issued as *Pamphlets for the People* (467). A totally original volume (i.e., not previously published in magazines) was *Religion and Sex* (468). Chapman Cohen's articles commemorating the centenary of the birth of Bradlaugh and Ingersoll (1933) were published as *Bradlaugh and Ingersoll* (458). His *A Grammar of Freethought* (464) remains a useful introduction to the philosophical basis of nontheism. Cohen's *Theism Or Atheism* (469) exemplifies his clear writing style, especially when applied to philosophically difficult problems. There were also two written debates published. One was *Materialism: Has It Been Exploded?* (465), with C.E.M. Joad. The other was *Does Man Survive Death?* (461), with Horace Leaf. Chapman Cohen was also a prolific pamphleteer. A few of his approximately forty pamphlets have already been mentioned. There is a series of articles about Cohen by Cutner (472).

The earlier career of Joseph McCabe (1867–1955) has already been traced in the previous chapter. It was mentioned that on one of his lecturing trips to the United States, McCabe met with Emanuel Haldeman-Julius, and agreed to write a large number of Little and Big Blue Books for him, with the subjects of the booklets being almost at the discretion of Haldeman-Julius.

During the same trip to the United States (in 1925) in which the arrangements with Haldeman-Julius were drawn, McCabe had delivered some lectures in Chicago, under the auspices of Percy

Ward. Ward had ordered several hundred dollar's worth of books from the Rationalist Press Association for sale during McCabe's lectures. When McCabe returned to England, he was told that Ward had defaulted on payment for the books, and that McCabe was therefore responsible. The entire matter is far too complex to explain here, but McCabe felt it was an excuse to expel him from the RPA. He had made a number of powerful enemies there, partly because of his defense of Holyoake against Bradlaugh. The result was that McCabe's books were no longer published by Watts & Co. for the RPA after McCabe's expulsion from that group. This strengthened the agreement between Haldeman-Julius and McCabe, and explains why Haldeman-Julius virtually became McCabe's exclusive publisher from 1926 through 1951.

Among the publications which Joseph McCabe wrote for Haldeman-Julius were the fifty Little Blue Books that were later published in collected form as *The Story of Religious Controversy* (503), *The Key to Culture* (500), *The True Story of the Roman Catholic Church* (505), *The Freethinker's Library* (496), and number of periodical publications, including *The Joseph McCabe Magazine* (499) and *The Militant Atheist* (501).

In the late 1940s, McCabe was reconciled with the RPA, mostly because he had outlived his former enemies. The one notable book that came out of this reconciliation was *A Rationalist Encyclopedia* (20), although Watts and Co., as McCabe's publisher again, also issued *A History of the Popes* (497) and *The Testament of Christian Civilization* (504).

Among the more important freethought books which McCabe had written before his break with the RPA were the following: *The Sources of the Morality of the Gospels* (502), *A Biographical Dictionary of Modern Rationalists* (17), *The Bankruptcy of Religion* (489), and *Is Spiritualism Based on Fraud?* (498). Joseph McCabe also had a number of his books about religion published by traditional publishers. These books include *A Candid History of the Jesuits* (491), *The Decay of the Church of Rome* (494), *Church Discipline* (492), and *Crises in the History of the Papacy* (493). McCabe also translated about forty works from German, French, Italian or Latin. The most famous of these translations was Haeckel's *The Riddle of the Universe* (336).

Some of the work that Joseph McCabe did for E. Haldeman-Julius has been briefly mentioned. Besides pamphlets in series, McCabe did scores of individual Little and Big Blue Books for Haldeman-Julius. They ranged in subject matter from history, freethought, literature, and sexology to science and encyclopedias. Perhaps the most important, from the point of view of freethought history and bibliography, were his *Biographical Dictionary of Ancient, Medieval and Modern Freethinkers* (490), which is not the same as his earlier biographical dictionary (20), and his partial autobiography, *Eighty Years a Rebel* (18). This is virtually the only work telling the facts of McCabe's life. There also have been no bibliographies detailing McCabe's huge written output.

Almost nothing *about* McCabe has ever been written. An exception is Goldberg's pamphlet, *Joseph McCabe: Fighter for Freethought* (478), published by Haldeman-Julius. There were also a few articles in the freethought periodicals published when McCabe died in 1955. A long-projected biography of McCabe by Michael Lloyd-Jones (see appendix) has not yet appeared.

Hypatia Bradlaugh Bonner (1858–1935) was the younger daughter of Charles Bradlaugh. Her elder sister, Alice, died of typhoid fever in 1888. She served as her father's secretary during some of his busiest years, towards the end of his life and also taught a number of classes in the Halls of Science. Her own higher education was obtained at the City of London College, where briefly, she was a student until a public outcry was made against having the daughter of a public atheist in attendance. As a result, all women were refused admission for a few years. Both Hypatia Bradlaugh and Annie Besant had to leave the school.

Hypatia Bradlaugh made her first public speech during the time when Charles Bradlaugh was being prosecuted for having published *The Fruits of Philosophy* (354). That was in 1877. Miss Bradlaugh studied science with Edward Aveling, and then taught this subject herself at the Hall of Science schools. She also lectured regularly, usually about nonfreethought subjects. Hypatia Bradlaugh also wrote regularly for *The National Reformer* (207) and other freethought magazines. She married Arthur Bonner, a printer and former mathematics student of hers, in 1885.

Hypatia Bradlaugh spent much of her life honoring her father. She and J. M. Robertson wrote the first full-length biography of him, *Charles Bradlaugh: A Record of His Life and Work* (4). She was always ready to publicly refute the persistent deathbed repentance stories told about her father, and she constantly fought against the lies told about him in the libelous *Life of Charles Bradlaugh, M.P.* (367). She also edited a freethought periodical, called *The Reformer* (387), for several years.

In addition to the biography of her father, Hypatia Bradlaugh Bonner wrote several other books. Among them were *The Christian Hell* (449), *Christianizing the Heathen* (450), and *Penalties Upon Opinion* (452), a study of blasphemy prosecutions. She lived long enough to take an active role in the celebration of the centenary of Bradlaugh's birth in 1933. A biography, entitled *Hypatia Bradlaugh Bonner* (447), was written by Arthur Bonner and Charles Bradlaugh Bonner (her son). There were also obituary notices by Gilmour and others (476).

Edward Clodd (1840–1930) was a banker who wrote for the freethought cause. Clodd also gave financial advice and contributions. His banking career eventually led to his becoming Secretary of the London Joint Stock Bank.

Clodd was born in Margate, the child of a long line of seafaring men. He was largely self-educated, with a special interest in anthropology and folklore that led to several books written in that field. His activities for freethought included being one of the founders of the Rationalist Press Association, and its Chairman after George Jacob Holyoake died in 1906. Clodd served as Chairman from 1906 until 1913. He tells of his career (briefly) and of his acquaintences, both in and out of freethought, in his autobiography, *Memories* (455), published in 1916.

Edward Clodd was also the author of a rationalistic biography of Jesus, called *Jesus of Nazareth* (454). He also wrote a work about spiritualism, entitled *The Question: If a Man Die, Shall He Live Again?* (456). Clodd died in 1930. There is a biography of him by McCabe, which is called *Edward Clodd: A Memoir* (495). There were also obituary notices in the freethought press, including a tribute by Robertson (521).

Adam Gowans Whyte (1875–1950) was born in Glasgow, Scotland. He came to London in 1898, where he met Charles A. Watts. This friendship led to Whyte becoming one of the founders of the Rationalist Press Association the next year. He had studied geology in college, then became a newspaperman before he came to London. In London, Whyte became well known as a scientific journalist. He wrote for the freethought press as well. Whyte contributed a column, called "The Open Window," to almost every issue of *The Literary Guide* (360) for nearly fifty years. He was the last survivor of the original Board of Directors of the Rationalist Press Association.

Whyte often wrote his articles in the freethought press under the name "Protonius." His autobiography, *Personal Pie* (537), was also written under that pseudonym. Whyte used his own name on his numerous other books. These included *The Religion of the Open Mind* (538), *The Natural History of Evil* (536), and his history of the Rationalist Press Association, *The Story of the R.P.A.* (49). There are no other biographical works about Whyte, although there were a number of obituary tributes published in *The Literary Guide* of September 1950, including one by Pike (510).

Charles A. Watts (1858–1946) was the son of Charles Watts. He began work as a printer's apprentice before he was twelve years old. At age thirteen, Watts went to work as a printer for Austin Holyoake. When Holyoake died in 1876, Charles Watts (the father) took over the business, and the younger Watts worked for him. In 1885, he published the short-lived magazine *The Agnostic* (263). In that same year, he started *The Literary Guide* (360), which was initially known as *Watts' Literary Guide*. He remained as the editor of *The Literary Guide* from 1885 until 1930. C. A. Watts was also the editor of *The Agnostic Annual* (264), that eventually became known as *The R.P.A. Annual* (384) and then as *The Rationalist Annual*.

In 1890, C. A. Watts founded the Rationalist Press Committee, becoming the Rationalist Press Association in 1899. He was Vice-Chairman of the RPA for many years. The Cheap Reprints series of the RPA was his idea. He guided the publishing fortunes of Watts & Company (later called C. A. Watts and Company) through the difficult years from its formation until 1930. C. A. Watts did not write any books or pamphlets of his own. Much of his biography is covered in F. J. Gould's *The Pioneers of Johnson's Court* (14) and A. G. Whyte's *The Story of the R.P.A.* (49). He did write two articles on his career (535).

Frederick Charles Chater Watts (1896–1953) was the son of Charles A. Watts. He joined his father in the publishing business of Watts & Company, along with the publishing activities of the Rationalist Press Association. The idea of the Thinker's Library series of small hardbound cheap books was F. C. C. Watts' idea in 1929. When C. A. Watts retired in 1930, his son took over the editorship of *The Literary Guide* (360). He remained the editor until his death. Upon his death, he had made provisions that the Watts family holdings in C. A. Watts and Company were to be transferred to the RPA. Fred Watts never wrote any books or pamphlets himself, but he carried on the Watts tradition of freethought publishing. There is an obituary article about him by Bonner (448).

Hector Hawton (1901–1975) was born in Plymouth, England. He became a professional journalist, moving to London when he was twenty. He worked as a reporter on Fleet Street for ten years, then moved to the countryside to write fiction. Hawton produced at least a book a year (sometimes as many as five a year) for over thirty years. Many of these were produced under pseudonyms (one of which was "Virginia Curzon"). In his thirties, Hawton became a freethinker (he had previously been a Calvinist and a Catholic). He first started to work and write for the Rationalist Press Association in 1940. He continued to act as ghostwriter as well. In 1948 he became secretary of the South Place Ethical Society. Hawton played a role in the formation of the International Humanist and Ethical Union in 1952.

Hector Hawton became general editor of the RPA in 1952, and a director of the organization in 1953. He became editor of *The Literary Guide* (360) in June 1953, and managing editor of the RPA later that year. In 1956, he became the RPA's managing director. In 1956, he changed the name of *The Literary Guide* to *The Humanist* (488). In 1960, the "Watts & Co." imprint was sold to the Pitman Publishing Group. Finally, the Pemberton imprint was started in 1962, all under his leadership.

Hawton wrote several books for freethought as well. These included *The Thinker's Handbook* (486), *Men Without Gods* (485), and *The Humanist Revolution* (484). *The Thinker's Handbook* was revised twenty years after its original publication and reissued as *Controversy* (483).

Hawton retired in 1971 as editor of *The Humanist* and as managing director of the RPA. He continued to edit *Question* (517), the new name and format given to *The Rationalist Annual* (384) in 1968. There are no biographies of Hector Hawton, but there is a detailed obituary of him that appeared in *The New Humanist* in 1976 (446).

Bertrand Arthur William Russell (1872–1970) was involved in so many causes, wrote prolifically on so many subjects, and led such a long and busy life, that it is difficult to know exactly where to place him. Part of his efforts were definitely given over to the support of the freethought movement, so he belongs in this history. Only his involvement with freethought will be discussed here, however. The other aspects of his life and work can be examined elsewhere.

Russell's parents were the Amberleys. His father was John Russell, Viscount Amberley, a freethinker and the author of *An Analysis of Religious Belief* (266). Both of his parents died when he was a small child, and he was raised by his paternal grandmother. Bertrand's father had appointed two freethinkers as his guardians, but the court set aside that portion of his father's will. Bertrand Russell was given a Christian upbringing, but lost his belief in God as a result of reading John Stuart Mill's autobiography. He became interested in mathematics and philosophy, attending Cambridge to study these subjects. His subsequent career as a philosopher of mathematics and activist need not be of concern here. He was associated with the Rationalist Press Association for many years, becoming one of its Honorary Associates.

Russell's own writings run to many volumes. They deal with mathematics, philosophy, social reform, sociology and many other topics. The ones that relate to freethought and religion are his *A Free Man's Worship* (523), *Sceptical Essays* (529), *Freethought and*

Official Propaganda (524), *Has Religion Made Useful Contributions to Civilization?* (525), *Mysticism and Logic* (527), *Why I am Not a Christian* (530), *Religion and Science* (528), and several pamphlets done for E. Haldeman-Julius (526).

Bertrand Russell wrote an *Autobiography* (522) of sorts, but it is mostly a collection of letters to and from him. The first volume deals the most with his ideas about religion. The best source for information on Russell's life is Clark's *The Life of Bertrand Russell* (453). Also helpful are Wood's *Bertrand Russell the Passionate Sceptic* (539), Crawshay-Williams' *Russell Remembered* (470), and Gottschalk's *Bertrand Russell: A Life* (482).

Charles Turner Gorham (1856–1933) was an educator and author who served the Rationalist Press Association as secretary for many years. He was the author of several popular freethought books, among which were *A Plain Man's Plea for Rationalism* (481), *The First Easter Dawn* (480), and *Christianity and Civilization* (479). There are no published biographies of Gorham.

Arthur Bonner (1861–1939) was the husband of Hypatia Bradlaugh Bonner. He married her in 1885. Bonner had joined the National Secular Society in 1881, and was a printer of many of the freethought books published by the Freethought Publishing Company in the 1880s. After Bradlaugh's death, Hypatia and Arthur Bonner published a number of freethought books under their imprint of "A. & H. Bradlaugh Bonner." Arthur Bonner was also the author of a biography of his wife (447), which was completed by his son.

Charles Bradlaugh Bonner (1890–1966) was the son of Hypatia Bradlaugh Bonner. He was a teacher, and served as the president of the World Union of Freethinkers for many years. He translated a number of the WUF proceedings into English from French for the British freethought press. Many of these translations were published in *The Freethinker* (325) and *The Literary Guide* (360).

The Welsh poet Llewelyn Powys (1884–1933) was a freethinker. He was not an active participant in organized freethought, although he did express his atheism in several of his works published by the freethought press. The most open expression of his freethought views is found in his books *Glory of Life* (513), *Damnable Opinions* (512), *Now that the Gods are Dead* (515), *The Pathetic Fallacy* (516), and *An Hour on Christianity* (514). There is a good biography of the Powys brothers by Kenneth Hopkins (487).

Henry Stephens Salt (1852–1939) was known more for whom he knew than for what he did or wrote for freethought. He seems to have had a wide spectrum of friends, many of them famous people. Salt wrote about some of them (including some freethinkers) in his autobiographical *Company I Have Kept* (531). He also wrote a biography of James Thomson (532).

Sydney Ansell Gimson (1860–1938) was the son of Josiah Gimson. Both were engineers, and together they built and sustained the Leicester Secular Society for fifty years. The father was one who planned the building of the Society's Secular Hall, which opened in 1881. The son was a financial contributor, officer, and host for visiting speakers at the Society for many years.

James Pinkerton Gilmour (1860–1941) was born in Glasgow. He was probably the leading organizer of freethought in Scotland during the period from 1880 to 1930. He was secretary of the Glasgow Secular Society, and lectured at the other Scottish societies. Gilmour also wrote a number of articles for the freethought press. In 1925, he was elected to the board of directors of the Rationalist Press Association, eventually becoming chairman. There is no biography of Gilmour, but there is an article about him by Bonner (451) in *The Literary Guide*.

David Tribe (1931–) was born in Australia. He came to England in 1955 to write and teach about vocational education. Tribe moved to London in 1959, where he was soon speaking for the freethought cause in Hyde Park. He became increasingly involved with freethought, becoming chairman of the Humanist Group Action in 1961. In 1963, Tribe was nominated for the job of president of the National Secular Society, and won. He also acted as the movement's official historian and biographer while in office (1963–1971). Tribe wrote *100 Years of Freethought* (43) and rediscovered the existence of the Bradlaugh Papers, using them to write his *President Charles Bradlaugh, M.P.* (44). The papers of Bradlaugh were subsequently microfilmed and are commercially available. David Tribe was also the editor of *The Freethinker* (325) in 1966. He retired from the freethought movement in 1971, returning afterwards to Australia. Tribe's office in British freethought was marked by a movement towards social activism.

Francis Joseph Corina (1904–1976) was a leader of the freethought movement in Bradford. He published a freethought magazine called *Freethought News* (475) for several years. Corina had a number of disagreements with Chapman Cohen during the early 1950s, some of which caused a split in the National Secular Society for a while. Other than in his own magazine, Corina does not seem to have written anything of a freethought nature.

Len Ebury (1897–1977) was one of the most popular outdoor freethought lecturers of the twentieth century. He originally came to London from Yorkshire in 1912. He became a member of the National Secular Society in 1926, and was soon speaking for them at open-air meetings. He delivered over 1000 formal lectures (and many more informal ones) during his speaking career of over fifty years. The most popular spots at which he lectured were Hyde Park, Hamstead, and Tower Hill, all in London. In 1941, he was prosecuted and fined for blasphemy. He did not write anything of note, but there is a published interview with him, which was conducted by Taylor (533).

Robert Henry Rosetti (1880–1951) gave his first freethought lecture in 1908. He eventually became president of the West Ham branch of the National Secular Society, and then general secretary of the NSS when Chapman Cohen resigned that post in 1949. He served in the office until his death.

Francis Ambrose Ridley (1897–) was born in North Wales. He was originally trained to be a clergyman. After his seminary days, he decided that he did not believe in Christianity. Ridley came to London and was soon lecturing in Hyde Park on socialism and freethought topics. He wrote many articles for socialist publications and contributed articles to *The Freethinker* (325) for many years. Ridley became the editor of *The Freethinker* upon Chapman Cohen's retirement in 1951. He remained as editor until 1954. Ridley became president of the National Secular Society in 1951 and remained as president until 1963. He is the author of *Julian the Apostate* (520), *Evolution of the Papacy* (518) and *The Jesuits* (519) among other books.

Vivian Phelips (1860–1939) lost his belief in Christianity while working in India. After retiring from a career with the Indian Public Works Department, he began devoting his full efforts to writing for freethought. Of his freethought writings, *The Churches and Modern Thought* (509) enjoyed the largest circulation.

Herbert Cutner (1881–1969) was a freethought book collector and professional artist. He was the author of many articles in *The Freethinker* (325), especially ones concerning freethought, history, and biography as well as the historicity of Jesus. Cutner was a proponent of the myth theory of Jesus. He wrote a book on the subject, called *Jesus: Man, God or Myth?* (471), as well as a biography of Taylor (161) and an unpublished biography of Foote.

John S. L. Gilmour (1906–) is a botanist who has made a special interest of the bibliography of freethought. He has written a number of journal articles about freethought bibliography and book collecting (477), and at one time had one of the largest collections of freethought books and materials in England. The collection was auctioned off or sold in 1974.

Robert W. Morell (1938–) is an authority on Thomas Paine. He is the secretary of the Thomas Paine Society and has collected and displayed many Paine items at different exhibits. He also sold freethought books at one time.

Kit Mouat (1920–) is the pen name of a former professional dancer, who has written a number of books for the freethought movement. Among her books are *What Humanism is About* (507) and *An Introduction to Secular Humanism* (506). She was also the editor of *The Freethinker* (325) from 1966 to 1967. She has run an out-of-print freethought book service and the Humanist Letter Network, a sort of pen pal service for Humanists.

Nicolas Walter (1934–) is a journalist and editor who was chief subeditor of the *Times Literary Supplement* for a number of years before becoming Managing Director of the Rationalist Press Association and editor of its magazine, *The New Humanist* (508) in 1975. He continues to hold both of those positions at the present time.

Jim Herrick (1944–) has a background in theater. He attended Cambridge, then began writing film and theater reviews for *The Freethinker* (325). Herrick then became assistant editor of *The Freethinker*, and then editor of that magazine in 1977. He also became the General Secretary of the National Secular Society at that time, a position he relinquished late in 1979.

Barbara Smoker (1923–) had a traditional Catholic education. Her doubts about her religion grew, especially after she heard some of the outdoor speakers from the National Secular Society. She was soon a familiar speaker at those meetings herself. Smoker was elected president of the National Secular Society in 1972, a position which she continues to hold at the present time.

The two major freethought organizations in the United Kingdom in the period after 1915 were the Rationalist Press Association and the National Secular Society. The origin of both of these organizations has been discussed in the previous chapter. Their growth and activities after 1915 will be of concern here.

The Rationalist Press Association reached its peak membership of 5,000 in 1947. Up until that time, it showed a slow but gradual growth. From 1947 until 1956, it experienced a steep decline in both membership and profits. By 1956, membership was down to less than 3,000. The RPA moved to new premises in Drury Lane, selling the old buildings in Johnson's Court. The staff was cut at the same time from thirty-two to eight. The unprofitable C. A. Watts and Company was sold to the Pitman Publishing Group. In 1962, the Pemberton Publishing Company was set up as the RPA's new publishing division. The RPA's Memorandum of Association was revised so that it could be recognized as an educational charity.

By 1963, the RPA had recovered much of its membership and financial stability. In 1967, the RPA gave up its lease on the Drury Lane property and bought a building on Islington High Street. The building was remodeled and continues to house the RPA at the present time.

The publishing activities of the Rationalist Press Association during this period will be discussed under the publishers section. The major contribution that the RPA made to freethought publishing during this time was the publication of the Thinker's Library series. This began in 1929, as an idea of Fred Watts. He continued to expand the series of small, cheap hardbound books until 1951, when publication ceased. By that time, about 150 titles had been published, and the sales of the series numbered in the millions of volumes.

The RPA issued an annual report in which it detailed its activities for the year, financial condition, and officers. Many people held office in the organization. It is sufficient here to merely give the names of the managing directors and the chairmen/presidents. The managing directors of the RPA were C. A. Watts (1899–1930), F. C. C. Watts (1930–1953), Hector Hawton (1953–1971), Christopher Macy (1971–1974) and Nicolas Walter (1975–present).

The title of RPA "chairman" was not used after 1952. Prior to that time, the chairmen were George Jacob Holyoake (1899–1906), Edward Clodd (1906–1913), Herbert S. Leon (1913–1922), George Whale (1922–1925), J. P. Gilmour (1925–1941), Ernest Thurtle (1941), and F. C. C. Watts (1942–1952). The presidents were Graham Wallas (1926–1929), Harold J. Laski (1930–1933), Lord Snell of Plumstead (1933–1940), C. M. Beadnell (1940–1947), C. D. Darlington (1948), A. E. Heath (1949–1954), The Earl Russell (1955–1968), Baroness Barbara Wootton (1968–1971), and Lord Ritchie-Calder (1971–present).

The National Secular Society started the period after Foote's death with a victory. The Bowman case decision of the House of Lords that legacies could legally be left to freethought organizations provided a significant amount of financial support over the years. Chapman Cohen's term as president of the NSS was marked by a number of small advances. The right to sell literature of a freethought type in the London parks was obtained, Humanist/rationalist programs were allowed on the BBC, the Pioneer Press (publishing company for the NSS) issued a large volume of books and pamphlets, with financial condition remaining sound.

Every year, the NSS held an annual conference in some part of England. For example, the 1949 conference was in Nottingham, the 1953 conference in Leicester, and the 1956 conference in Liverpool. The National Secular Society celebrated its 100th anniversary in 1966. The presidents of the NSS since its founding have been Charles Bradlaugh (1866–1890), G. W. Foote (1890–1915), Chapman Cohen (1915–1949), R. H. Rosetti (1949–1951), F. A. Ridley (1951–

1963), David Tribe (1963–1971), and Barbara Smoker (1972–present).

The magazine *The Freethinker* (325) continues to be the official publication of the NSS. The book and pamphlet publications of the National Secular Society are discussed under the publishing section of this chapter.

In 1938, an International Congress of the World Union of Free-thinkers was held in London. Conway Hall, the home of the South Place Ethical Society, was the site of this world meeting. Among the British freethinkers who addressed the meeting were Joseph McCabe, J. P. Gilmour, J. B. S. Haldane, H. J. Bridges, and G. D. H. Cole.

The period from 1915 until the present time (1980) has seen a rather large drop in the number of freethought periodicals published in the United Kingdom. *The Freethinker* (325) and *The Literary Guide* (360) have survived until the present, with *The Literary Guide* becoming known as *The Humanist* (488) in 1956, and as *The New Humanist* (508) in 1976. *The RPA Annual* (384) became known as *The Rationalist Annual* in 1927, and changed its name and format to become *Question* (517) in 1968. *Free Mind* (474) was published briefly by Watts and Company from 1947 to 1948. F. J. Corina published *Freethought News* (475) from Bradford from 1947 to 1952. The South Place Ethical Society published *The Ethical Record* (473) and the Ethical Union published *The Plain View* (511). The Thomas Paine Society publishes its *Thomas Paine Society Bulletin* (534).

There were several publishers who specialized in freethought books during this period. The biggest of these was Watts and Company, and its affiliated membership organization, the Rationalist Press Association. Watts and Company published most of the works of McCabe (until his break with them in 1928), Robertson, Gorham, and Gould. In its Thinker's Library series, which sold over 3 million copies during the 1929 to 1951 period in which they were published in 150 titles, most of the famous freethinker's works were republished. Included were Bradlaugh, Ingersoll, Paine, Robertson, McCabe, Gorham, Hawton, Whyte, Hypatia Bonner, and Clifford. After the Watts imprint was sold to Pitman in 1960, the Pemberton Publishing Company was formed to publish RPA books. For a time, Pemberton was affiliated with the the Elek Publishing Company, which issued both of David Tribe's books, *100 Years of Freethought* (43) and *President Charles Bradlaugh, M.P.* (44). Barrie and Rockcliff was also affiliated with Pemberton for a period of time.

The National Secular Society had as its publishing company in the twentieth century The Pioneer Press. The company was officially a part of G. W. Foote & Company, that, in turn, was the official company which owned *The Freethinker* (325). Among the authors whose works were published by The Pioneer Press, can be mentioned Chapman Cohen, reprints of G. W. Foote's works, Walter Mann, George Whitehead, Herbert Cutner and F. A. Ridley. The South Place Ethical Society also published a number of pamphlets during this period.

The South Place Ethical Society built Conway Hall as its meeting place, and moved into it in 1929. They still occupy the building, and it is often the site for meetings of other freethought groups as well. The Society did not have a single leader for many years after Moncure Conway left for the second time. Rather, it had a series of lecturers who alternated on weekends. Among the men who acted as lecturers were Joseph McCabe, J. M. Robertson, Herbert Burrows, Cecil Delisle Burns and J. A. Hobson. A later group of such lecturers included S. K. Ratcliffe, Archibald Robertson and W. E. Swinton. The present leader of the South Place Ethical Society is Peter Cadogan, who succeeded H. J. Blackham.

After Stanton Coit left the South Place Ethical Society (where he had replaced Moncure Conway, when Conway left for New York), he formed the West London Ethical Society. In 1896, that group joined with three others to form the Union of Ethical Societies. This was incorporated as the Ethical Union in 1928. In 1963, the Rationalist Press Association and the Ethical Union jointly formed the British Humanist Association. All of these organizations were recognized as charities at the time. In 1965, the Ethical Union was removed by the Government from the list of charities. That was soon followed by the removal of the British Humanist Association from the charities list. That meant that the RPA could no longer support the BHA without endangering its own charitable status. As a result, the RPA severed its connection with the BHA, except for the fact that members of the BHA receive a subscription to *The New Humanist* (508) along with their membership in the BHA. The Ethical Union published the magazine *The Plain View* (511), with H. J. Blackham as the editor, for many years. The South Place Ethical Society publishes *The Ethical Record* (473).

In early 1980, there were Humanist groups in the following areas of the United Kingdom: Belfast, Berkshire, Brighton & Hove, Harrow, Havering, Lewisham, London, Merseyside, Muswell Hill, Nottingham, Warwickshire, West Glamorgan, Worthing, Sutton, and Tyneside. There were also inactive or semi-active groups in Ealing, Leeds, and Portsmouth. All of these groups were affiliated with the National Secular Society.

At the present time, freethought in the United Kingdom is in a relatively weak condition. Membership in the RPA and the NSS are far below their highest levels. The British Humanist Association is having financial difficulties, and the South Place Ethical Society is threatened with the possible loss of Conway Hall. It is not the brightest picture possible, but there are other factors to consider. The secularization of British society is at an all time high. True, there are still goals which have not been met: there is still an official established religion in the United Kindgom; that established religion is still shown a great deal of favoritism; the airwaves are still not really open to the presentation of freethought views; there is still Church of England religious instruction in the schools; the blasphemy laws are still enforceable and convictions can still occur; finally, there is still a reservoir of distrust and suspicion at the idea of accepting freethought, rationalism, and Humanism as legitimate ways of life or outlooks on the world.

BIBLIOGRAPHY

446. Anonymous. "Obituary: Hector Hawton." *The New Humanist*, February 1976, pp. 259–260. This article is followed by "Remembering Hector Hawton" by H. J. Blackham, which is also of interest.

447. Bonner, Arthur and Bonner, Charles Bradlaugh. *Hypatia Bradlaugh Bonner: The Story of Her Life*. London: Watts & Co., 1942.

448. Bonner, C. Bradlaugh. "Frederick Charles Chater Watts." *The Literary Guide*, December 1953, pp. 210–11.

449. Bonner, Hypatia Bradlaugh. *The Christian Hell*. London: Watts & Company, 1913.

450. Bonner, Hypatia Bradlaugh. *Christianizing the Heathen*. London: Watts & Company, 1922.

451. Bonner, Hypatia Bradlaugh. "J. P. Gilmour." *The Literary Guide*, January 1930, pp. 17–18.

452. Bonner, Hypatia Bradlaugh. *Penalties Upon Opinion*. London: Watts & Company, 1912. About blasphemy prosecutions.

453. Clark, Ronald W. *The Life of Bertrand Russell*. New York: Alfred A. Knopf, 1976.

454. Clodd, Edward. *Jesus of Nazareth*. London: C. Kegan Paul, 1880.

455. Clodd, Edward. *Memories*. London: Chapman & Hall, 1916. American edition published by G. P. Putnam's Sons (New York, 1916).

456. Clodd, Edward. *The Question: If a Man Die, Will He Live Again?* London: Grant Richards, 1917.

457. Cohen, Chapman. *Almost an Autobiography*. London: The Pioneer Press, 1940.

458. Cohen, Chapman. *Bradlaugh and Ingersoll: A Centenary Appreciation of Two Great Reformers*. London: The Pioneer Press, 1933.

459. Cohen, Chapman and Hetherington, Rev. W. *Christianity V. Secularism: Which Has Benefitted the World Most? A Full Report of the Remarkable Debate. . . . at the Workman's Hall, Walthamstow.* London: W. B. Whittingham & Co., n.d. [c. 1892].

460. Cohen, Chapman. *The Decay of Belief*. Bradford [England]: Truthseeker Company, n.d. [c. 1896].

461. Cohen, Chapman and Leaf, Horace. *Does Man Survive Death?* London: The Pioneer Press, n.d. [c. 1920]. A debate.

462. Cohen, Chapman. *Essays in Freethinking*. London: The Pioneer Press, 1923 (Series 1), 1927 (Series 2), 1928 (Series 3), 1938 (Series 4) and 1939 (Series 5). Reprints of some of Cohen's best contributions to *The Freethinker*.

463. Cohen, Chapman, ed. *A Fight for Right. The Decision of the House of Lords in re Bowman and Others Vs. the Secular Society, Ltd.* London: The Pioneer Press, n.d. [1917].

464. Cohen, Chapman. *A Grammar of Freethought*. London: The Pioneer Press, 1921.

465. Cohen, Chapman and Joad, C. E. M. *Materialism: Has It Been Exploded?* London: Watts and Company, 1928. A written debate.

466. Cohen, Chapman. *An Outline of Evolutionary Ethics*. London: R. Forder, 1896.

467. Cohen, Chapman. *Pamphlets for the People*. London: The Pioneer Press, n.d. [c. 1938]. Contains eighteen pamphlets bound into one volume. None are dated.

468. Cohen, Chapman. *Religion and Sex*. London: T. N. Foulis, 1919.

469. Cohen, Chapman. *Theism or Atheism: The Great Alternative*. London: The Pioneer Press, 1921.

470. Crawshay-Williams, Rupert. *Russell Remembered*. London: Oxford University Press, 1970.

471. Cutner, Herbert. *Jesus: Man, God or Myth?* New York: Truth Seeker Company, 1950.

472. Cutner, Herbert. "The Two Contemporaries." *The Freethinker* 15, 22, 29 March, 5 and 12 April, 1957. A series of articles comparing Joseph McCabe and Chapman Cohen.

473. *Ethical Record, The*. A monthly magazine, published by the South Place Ethical Society in London, from 1895 until the present.

474. *Free Mind*. A freethought periodical published by Watts and Company, London, from 1947 until 1948.

475. *Freethought News*. A monthly freethought magazine, pub-

lished at Bradford, England from 1947 until 1952, and edited by F. J. Corina.

476. Gilmour, J. P. "Hypatia Bradlaugh Bonner (1858-1935)." *The Literary Guide*, October 1935, pp. 179–82. There was an additional obituary tribute by Chapman Cohen in the November 1935 issue of *The Literary Guide* (p. 202). Another article about her, while still alive, appears in *The Literary Guide* of August 1927, pp. 133–34. It is also by J. P. Gilmour.

477. Gilmour, John S. L. "A Freethought Collection and Its Predecessors." *The Book Collector* (London) 11 (1962): 184–96. Gilmour has also published bibliographies of Charles Blount (see #85), Julian Hibbert (see #167), and William Winwood Reade [*The Book Collector* 6 (1957): 62–66].

478. Goldberg, Isaac. *Joseph McCabe: Fighter for Freethought.* Girard, Kansas; Haldeman-Julius Publications, 1936.

479. Gorham, C. T. *Christianity and Civilization.* London: Watts and Company, 1914.

480. Gorham, C. T. *The First Easter Dawn: An Inquiry Into the Evidence for the Resurrection of Jesus.* London: Watts and Company, 1908.

481. Gorham, C. T. *A Plain Man's Plea for Rationalism.* London: Watts and Company, 1919. This was later rewritten and published as *The Gospel of Rationalism* (London: Watts and Company, 1949).

482. Gottschalk, Herbert. *Bertrand Russell: A Life.* London: John Baker, 1965. A translation from the German edition of 1962.

483. Hawton, Hector. *Controversy.* London: Pemberton Books, 1971. A revision and reissue of *The Thinkers Handbook* (see #486).

484. Hawton, Hector. *The Humanist Revolution.* London: Barrie and Rockcliff, 1963.

485. Hawton, Hector. *Men Without Gods.* London: Watts and Company, 1948. Thinker's Library #126.

486. Hawton, Hector. *The Thinker's Handbook.* London: Watts and Company, 1951. Later republished in a revised form as *Controversy* (see #483).

487. Hopkins, Kenneth. *The Powys Brothers: A Biographical Appreciation.* Madison, N. J.: Fairleigh Dickinson Unviersity Press, 1967.

488. *Humanist, The.* A freethought periodical, published monthly in London by the Rationalist Press Association from 1956 until 1972. It had formerly been called *The Literary Guide* (see #360), but completely changed its format with the new title. The editor for most of its lifetime was Hector Hawton.

489. McCabe, Joseph. *The Bankruptcy of Religion.* London: Watts and Company, 1917.

490. McCabe, Joseph. *Biographical Dictionary of Ancient, Medieval and Modern Freethinkers*. Girard, Kansas: Haldeman-Julius Publications, 1945.

491. McCabe, Joseph. *A Candid History of the Jesuits*. New York: G. P. Putnam's Sons, 1913.

492. McCabe, Joseph. *Church Discipline: An Ethical Study of the Church of Rome*. London: Duckworth & Company, 1903.

493. McCabe. Joseph. *Crises in the History of the Papacy*. New York: G. P. Putnam's Sons, 1916.

494. McCabe, Joseph. *The Decay of the Church of Rome*. London: Methuen & Company, 1909.

495. McCabe, Joseph. *Edward Clodd: A Memoir*. London: John Lane at the Bodley Head, 1932.

496. McCabe, Joseph. *The Freethinker's Library*. Girard, Kansas: Haldeman-Julius Publications, 1936. A series of ten different pamphlets, with different titles.

497. McCabe, Joseph. *A History of the Popes*. London: Watts and Company, 1939.

498. McCabe, Joseph. *Is Spiritualism Based Upon Fraud?* London: Watts and Company, [1920].

499. McCabe, Joseph. *The Joseph McCabe Magazine* (Girard, Kansas). Edited and largely written by McCabe. It was published as a monthly from 1930-1931.

500. McCabe, Joseph. *The Key to Culture*. Girard, Kansas: Haldeman-Julius Publications, 1927-1928. A series of thirty-eight separate pamphlets.

501. McCabe, Joseph, ed. *The Militant Atheist*. (Girard, Kansas). A newspaper-format monthly, which ran for only nine issues in 1933.

502. McCabe, Joseph. *The Sources of the Morality of the Gospels*. London: Watts and Company, 1914.

503. McCabe, Joseph. *The Story of Religious Controversy*. Boston: Stratford Company, 1929. This book was the result of compiling the texts of the first fifty Little Blue Books on religion which Joseph McCabe wrote for E. Haldeman-Julius.

504. McCabe, Joseph. *The Testament of Christian Civilization*. London: Watts and Company, 1946.

505. McCabe, Joseph. *The True Story of the Roman Catholic Church*. Girard, Kansas: Haldeman-Julius Publications, 1930, twelve vols. in six. Parts of this first appeared as entire issues of *The Haldeman-Julius Monthly* in 1930.

506. Mouat, Kit. *An Introduction to Secular Humanism*. Haywards Heath [England]: Charles Clarke, n.d. [c. 1973].

507. Mouat, Kit. *What Humanism Is About*. London: Barrie and Rockliff, 1963.

508. *New Humanist, The*. A freethought periodical, which was formed in 1972 by a change in the name and the format of *The Humanist* (see # 488). It continues to be published by the Rationalist Press Association of London. Nicolas Walter is the present editor. It was originally a monthly, then became a bimonthly, then a quarterly, then a bimonthly again.

509. Phelips, Vivian. *The Churches and Modern Thought*. London: Watts and Company, 1906.

510. Pike, Royston. "Adam Gowans Whyte: In Tribute." *The Literary Guide*, September 1950, pp. 192-93.

511. *Plain View, The*. A monthly magazine published by the Ethical Union, London, from 1944 until 1965. H. J. Blackham was the editor for much of this time.

512. Powys, Llewelyn. *Damnable Opinions*. London: Watts and Company, 1935.

513. Powys, Llewelyn. *Glory of Life*. London: Golden Cockerel Press, [1934].

514. Powys, Llewelyn. *An Hour on Christianity*. Philadelphia: J. B. Lippincott, 1930.

515. Powys, Llewelyn. *Now that the Gods are Dead*. New York: Equinox, 1932.

516. Powys, Llewelyn. *The Pathetic Fallacy: A Study of Christianity*. London: Longmans Green and Company, 1930.

517. *Question*. An annual volume, published by the Rationalist Press Association. It began in 1968 and replaced *The Rationalist Annual* (see # 384).

518. Ridley, F. A. *Evolution of the Papacy*. London: The Pioneer Press, [1949].

519. Ridley, F. A. *The Jesuits: A Study in Counter-Revolution*. London: Secker and Warburg, [1938].

520. Ridley, F. A. *Julian the Apostate and the Rise of Christianity*. London: Watts and Company, 1937.

521. Robertson, J. M. "In Memoriam: Edward Clodd (1840-1930)." *The Literary Guide*, May 1930, pp. 81-82.

522. Russell, Bertrand. *The Autobiography of Bertrand Russell. Volume 1: 1872-1914*. London: Allen and Unwin, 1967. American edition published by Little, Brown & Company (Boston, 1967). There are two additional volumes (same publisher), but they contain little concerning Russell's religious views.

523. Russell, Bertrand. *A Free Man's Worship*. Portland, Maine: T. B. Mosher, 1923.

524. Russell, Bertrand. *Free Thought and Official Propaganda*. London: Watts and Company, 1922. Conway Memorial Lecture.

525. Russell, Bertrand. *Has Religion Made Useful Contributions to Civilization?* London: Watts and Company, [1930].

526. Russell, Bertrand. *Is Materialism Bankrupt?: Mind and Matter in Modern Science.* Girard, Kansas: Haldeman-Julius Publications, [1946]. Also published by Haldeman-Julius were Russell's *An Outline of Intellectual Rubbish* [1943], *Am I an Atheist or an Agnostic?* [1947], *The Faith of a Rationalist* [1947], *On the Value of Scepticism* [1947], and *The Value of Free Thought* [1944].

527. Russell, Bertrand. *Mysticism and Logic and Other Essays.* London: Longmans, Green and Company, 1918.

528. Russell, Bertrand. *Religion and Science.* London: Thornton Butterworth, [1935].

529. Russell, Bertrand. *Sceptical Essays.* London: Allen and Unwin, 1928. American edition published by W. W. Norton (New York, 1928).

530. Russell, Bertrand. *Why I am Not a Christian and Other Essays.* London: G. Allen, [1957]. American edition published by Simon and Shuster (New York, 1957). The title essay was originally published by Watts and Company in 1927.

531. Salt, Henry Stephens. *Company I Have Kept.* London: George Allen and Unwin, 1930.

532. Salt, Henry Stephens. *The Life of James Thomson ("B.V.")* London: A. & H. B. Bonner, 1903.

533. Taylor, G. H. "Len Ebury." *The Freethinker,* 7 May 1954, p. 147.

534. *Thomas Paine Society Bulletin, The.* A quarterly (though, in fact, irregularly issued) magazine relating to Paine, especially in his work for freethought. Edited by Robert W. Morrell, and published since 1967.

535. Watts, Charles A. "Some Reminiscences of No. 17 Johnson's Court." *The Literary Guide,* January 1924, pp. 19-20. The article was continued as "Twilight Thoughts" in *The Literary Guide* of April 1924, pp. 69-70.

536. Whyte, Adam Gowans. *The Natural History of Evil.* London: Watts and Company, 1920.

537. Whyte, Adam Gowans (as "Protonius"). *Personal Pie.* London: Watts and Company, 1938. An autobiography.

538. Whyte, Adam Gowans. *The Religion of the Open Mind.* London: Watts and Company, 1915.

539. Wood, Alan. *Bertrand Russell the Passionate Sceptic.* London: George Allen and Unwin, 1957.

APPENDICES

Appendices I through V give a very brief and encapsulated introduction to the history of freethought in various Commonwealth countries. These introductions are intended to merely sketch the high points of freethought history in these countries. Those interested in freethought in New Zealand, Australia, Canada, and India will find that the appendices on those areas will help them get started in the right direction.

In the case of Appendix V, "Freethought in Other Commonwealth Countries," there may well have been other Commonwealth countries in which some manifestation of freethought occurred that are not included. It was impossible to investigate the history of every country that has ever been in the Commonwealth. There are a few such countries in which there may well have been a freethought movement, but in which no traces of such a movement have been found in investigations conducted (unfortunately) entirely from the United States and the United Kingdom. These countries include Zimbabwe-Rhodesia, Kenya, Ghana, Hong Kong, Jamaica, Bermuda, Malta, Cyprus, and Barbados.

APPENDIX
I

Freethought in
New Zealand

The history of freethought in New Zealand is long and honorable. The full history has never been told in a single place, although there are a number of articles in freethought journals which cover segments of that history.

The first publication which could be called freethought in New Zealand (although not antireligious *per se*) was Charles Southwell's *Auckland Examiner* [129], which Southwell published during the last four years of his life in Auckland. It was unrelated to any organized group, and was virtually a one-man operation. It ceased publication shortly before Southwell died in 1860, having started in 1857.

There does not seem to have been an organized freethought movement in New Zealand until after it became a crown colony, and until after the Maori Wars were over. The first trace of organization seems to have been in 1855, when an Auckland Secular Society was founded by Archibald Campbell. It was dormant by 1859. In 1870, the Dunedin Mutual Improvement Association used its auspices to have an independent "committee of gentlemen" sponsor a number of speeches by "liberal theological lecturers." They also had freethought spiritualist speakers. The organization was definitely heterodox, if not strictly a freethought group. There was at this time a freethought magazine, *The Echo* [540], started and edited by Robert Stout, later to be Prime Minister and Chief Justice of New Zealand.

The Mutual Improvement Association was replaced by the Spiritual Investigation Society, that, in turn, became the Eclectic Society in 1876. This last society became popular, and lasted for a number of years. In 1878 a new group, called the Freethought Association, replaced the Eclectic Society, but the exact date and circumstances of this change are not clear. The presence of Charles Bright (1832-1903) as one of the early lecturers for the Eclectic Society (his first lectures for the Society were given in 1876), helped make the meetings popular. Bright was heavily involved in the early history of the free-thought movement in both New Zealand and Australia.

By 1881, the Dunedin Freethought Association had grown so much that they were thinking of building their own hall. A committee was set up to raise funds, and in April of 1882 the Lyceum Hall was officially opened. In addition to lectures, the Lyceum later also conducted a Freethought Sunday School, and published a textbook called *The Lyceum Guide* (545). There was a similar book called *The Australasian Secular Association Lyceum Tutor* (545), by Bernard O'Dowd, issued from Melbourne.

By June of 1881, there were small freethought groups in Auckland, Wellington and Nelson. In the latter part of 1881, the first freethought group in Christchurch was formed. This group was known as the Canterbury Freethought Association. On the 10th, 11th, and 12th of March 1884, a meeting of all the freethought societies then active in New Zealand (i.e., Dunedin, Auckland, Wellington, Wanganui, Nelson, Picton, and Woodville), with the exception of Christchurch, which did not send delegates, was held in Dunedin. At this meeting, a New Zealand Freethought Federal Union was formed. Robert Stout was elected president, and John Ballance vice-president of the Union. Both men would be future Prime Ministers of New Zealand.

The Dunedin Freethought Association finally collapsed in 1890 as a result of the friction occurring between the always incompatible combination of freethinkers and spiritualists that had formed the original alliance. In February 1889, the title to the Lyceum Hall, built by the freethinkers, passed into the hands of nonfreethought groups. It was used for lectures for many years, and was still standing in Dunedin at last report.

The Auckland Rationalistic Association was formed in January 1884. In June 1885, a weekly magazine, *The Rationalist* (546), edited by "Ivo" (Joseph Evison) was started. The magazine lasted only about one year.

In 1890, William Whitehouse Collins (1853-1923), another figure important in the early freethought history of both Australia and New Zealand, arrived in New Zealand from Australia. He had originally come from England, where he had been associated with Charles Bradlaugh and the National Secular Society. Collins settled in Christchurch, where he became the editor of an iconoclastic magazine called *The Tribune* (547) in 1894-1895. He also edited another magazine, *The Examiner* (541) from Christchurch from 1907 until 1917. Collins returned to Australia in 1917.

The Wellington freethought group began in 1881, when an organization called the Freethinkers of Wellington met. In July of 1883, the Wellington Freethought Association was formed. The name was changed later in the year to the Wellington Secular Society. This group lasted until the 1890s, when the general economic depression seems to have finished it off.

In Wanganui, a freethought magazine, *The Freethought Review* (542), was published, starting in 1883. It was founded by A. D. Willis, but John Ballance later became the editor. It lasted until 1885.

From the mid-1890s until 1913, New Zealand freethought was in a period of virtually total inactivity. The only notable exception was W. W. Collins, with his magazines and the organization at Christchurch. The lecturing tour of Joseph McCabe to New Zealand (and Australia) in 1913 seems to have revived some freethought activities and organizations there.

In 1923, McCabe made another visit to New Zealand and Australia. An announcement of his visit in the Auckland newspapers stirred the formation of a Rationalist Association there. The Association prospered while McCabe was there, but it went into dormancy about a year later. In 1927, the Auckland Rationalist Association was revived. It published a journal, *The Truthseeker* (549). This time the Rationalist Association was successful, and it endured. In 1939, it changed the title of its journal to *The New Zealand Rationalist* (544). In 1964, *The New Zealand Rationalist* incorporated the recently formed *The New Zealand Humanist* (543) to become *The New Zealand Rationalist & Humanist*. It is still being published.

The Wellington branch of the N.Z. Rationalist Association was formed in 1938. In October 1939, the society's name was changed to the Wellington Rationalist Association. The New Zealand Rationalist Association has its headquarters in its own building on Symonds Street in Auckland. In 1968, a Humanist Society of New Zealand was organized in Christchurch.

There are a number of articles in the New Zealand freethought magazines that tell bits and pieces of the history of freethought in New Zealand. The story of the Dunedin Freethought Association is told by J. Trower (548) and by Harry Pearce (as "Profanum Vulgus"). There are also articles by A. E. Carrington and James O. Hanlon, all listed under the Trower entry. There seems to have never been a book (or even a pamphlet) written about the history of freethought in New Zealand, although the lives of some of the people involved in the movement there (e.g., Charles Southwell) have been covered in their other contexts.

BIBLIOGRAPHY

540. *Echo, The.* A freethought weekly newspaper (daily at first), edited by Robert Stout, and published in Dunedin from November 27, 1869 until March 8, 1873, and then again (as a monthly, from March 1880 until November 1883.

541. *Examiner, The.* A monthly (later bimonthly) freethought magazine, published at Christchurch and edited by W. W. Collins, from April 1907 until May/June 1917.

542. *Freethought Review, The.* A monthly freethought magazine, published at Wanganui by A. D. Willis, and edited by John Ballance. It was published from October 1, 1883 until September 1885.

543. *New Zealand Humanist, The.* A monthly freethought magazine, published until 1964, at which time it was incorporated into *The New Zealand Rationalist* (see # 544) to form *The New Zealand Rationalist & Humanist.* There is a separate bimonthly newletter-style magazine, also called *The New Zealand Humanist,* which is still produced at Christchurch by the Humanist Society of New Zealand.

544. *New Zealand Rationalist, The.* A monthly freethought magazine (recently issued only semi-annually), which was formed as a results of a change of name by *The Truthseeker* (see #548) in September 1939. It was published at Auckland from then until November 1964, at which time it incorporated *The New Zealand Humanist* (see #543), and became known as *The New Zealand Rationalist & Humanist.* It is still being published.

545. O'Dowd, Bernard. *The Australian Secular Association Lyceum Tutor.* Melbourne: Australasian Secular Association, 1888. A textbook for the children in the Secular Sunday Schools. In N.Z. the textbook was called *The Lyceum Guide.* Dunedin: Freethought Assn., 1881.

546. *Rationalist, The.* A weekly freethought magazine, published at Auckland by Joseph Evison ("Ivo") from June 21, 1885 until August 8, 1886.

547. *Tribune, The.* An iconoclastic magazine, published in 1894-1895 by W. W. Collins at Christchurch.

548. Trower, J. "The Beginning & End of the 'Dunedin Freethought Association.'" *New Zealand Rationalist & Humanist,* November 1977, pp. 8-9. See also the series of articles by "Profanum Vulgus" (Harry Pearce) in the *New Zealand Rationalist* (Vol. 9 # 21 [Dec 1938] through Oct 1941) "Early Dunedin Freethought." There is also an article by Charles Alldritt (as "C.A."), entitled "Early Rationalist Journals," in the *N.Z. Rationalist & Humanist* of May 1977 (pp. 4 and 13), "Recollections of a Rationalist" by James O. Hanlon (*N.Z.*

Rationalist & Humanist, May 1977, pp. 1-2), and A. E. Carrington's "Rationalism in Auckland—Struggles and Achievements" (*N.Z. Rationalist & Humanist*, August 1977, pp. 1-2, 4) and P. Campbell's "Early New Zealand Freethought" (New Zealand Rationalist & Humanist, January/February 1963, pp. 7-8, 14.)

549. *Truthseeker, The.* A monthly freethought magazine, published at Auckland from July 3, 1927 until August 1939, when it changed its name to *The New Zealand Rationalist* (see # 544). The first editor was A. E. Carrington.

APPENDIX
II

Freethought in
Australia

There has been a considerable amount of freethought activity in Australia. Rapid colonization began in the mid-1830s. In the 1850s, there was a gold rush which caused another large influx of settlers. The separate states comprising Australia did not confederate into a single government until 1901. As a result of this pioneer-like situation, the early antireligious activity in Australia was largely characterized by anticlericalism, especially towards the Catholic clergy. Anticlericalism was not an organized movement, of course. Settlement had begun after deism had disappeared, so there was no deistic period in Australia.

Freethought did not exist as an organized movement in Australia until 1865. Prior to that, there were a few isolated freethought activities. For example, in 1859 a small group of freethinkers met in Sydney to celebrate Thomas Paine's birthday. They also held public discussions in the parks there in 1863. In 1861, a freethought society was formed at Newcastle. It had a library, but whether it had any regular activities is unclear. A Newcastle Secular Society was formed in 1865. In 1869, B. S. Naylor started a spiritulist/freethought magazine in Victoria (probably Melbourne). It was called *The Glow-Worm* (563). The paper lasted only five issues, published over six months.

In 1873, John Tyerman (?-1883) began the publication of *The Progressive Spiritualist and Freethought Advocate* (566) in Melbourne. It was a weekly and lasted for twenty-three issues. Tyerman was a former clergyman, who became a spiritualist and theistic freethinker. In 1870, the spiritualists of Melbourne invited him to become their lecturer. He evidently felt that straight spiritualism was too narrow for him, because in 1871 he founded the "Spiritualist and Freethought Propagandist Association." Tyerman was the author of several freethought/spiritualist books and pamphlets. Among them were *Free-*

thought Vindicated (576), a *Hymn Book for the Use of the Spiritualist and Freethought Propagandist Society* (577), and a number of published lectures, including *Is There a Devil?* (578) and *Is There a Hell?* (579).

In December of 1874, Joseph Wing, an important figure in Australian freethought, began the publication of *The Spiritual Inquirer* (574) at Sandhurst (now Bendigo), Victoria. It was a weekly and lasted about a year. The paper was again spiritualist/freethought in nature. Wing then dropped his spiritualist orientation, and became a secularist. He later published *The Reformer* (569), a freethought magazine. Wing was later to become a member of the Executive Council of the Australasian Secular Association.

The Stockwhip (575) was a freethought journal published at Sydney by John E. Kelly. It began in 1875, and appeared in 1876 as *The Stockwhip and Satirist*. This title lasted only two months. In November 1876, the magazine became *The Satirist*. It was to last until 1877. Early in 1876, the "Adelaide Secular and Free Discussion Society" was formed. It published a magazine called *The Adelaide Secular and Free Discussion Society's Review* (550) from 1878 until 1879. It was edited by Henry Oliver.

E. Cyril Haviland published a freethought magazine called *Freethought* (561) in Sydney in 1880. It lasted only about one year. The Australasian Secular Association was formed in Melbourne by Thomas Walker (1858-1932) in 1881. Walker was a freethought leader who wrote *Orthodoxy Unmasked* (581) and several other pamphlets. The Australasian Secular Association had started a campaign to have libraries and museums open on Sunday. In 1883, they asked Charles Bradlaugh, in a letter, to send them a lecturer/leader. Bradlaugh picked Joseph Symes (see below) and he arrived in 1884. In 1882-1883, William Denton had a successful lecturing tour in Australia, causing a great growth in the Association's membership, especially in Sydney. Denton was an American.

The Liberal (565) was a weekly freethought magazine, published by the Liberal Association of New South Wales (Sydney) in 1882. It ran until 1884, and the editors were George Lacy and Charles Bright. Bright has been mentioned as an important early freethought lecturer in New Zealand. *Freedom* (558) was a monthly, published in Brisbane by W. Taylor in 1883. It lasted only a few issues. The short-lived Brisbane Freethought Association seems to have been involved in its publication. E. Skinner also published his *A Secularist's Guide* (572).

The Freethinker and New South Wales Reformer (560) was published at Sydney, starting in 1886. It was edited by William Whitehouse Collins (1853-1923). Collins later went to New Zealand and became an important figure in freethought there. In Australia, Collins, who was an associate of Charles Bradlaugh's in England, became a freethought lecturer with the sponsorship of the Liberal Association of New South Wales. He went to New Zealand on a lecture tour in 1890, and decided to stay. *The Freethinker* (as the magazine was usually called) was merged with *The Liberator* (359) in late 1886. Collins also published another freethought journal in Australia. This was *Freedom* (559), issued from Sydney from February 1889 until February 1890, at which time Collins left for New Zealand. Collins also published several freethought pamphlets in Australia. Included among these were *Can the Design Argument be Vindicated?* (555), *The Church of Rome* (556) and *A Search for a Soul* (557).

The story of Joseph Symes' (1841-1906) trip to Australia from England to become a lecturer and leader of the freethought group in Melbourne has already been told in the chapter which includes Symes in the United Kingdom. Symes arrived in Melbourne in February of 1884. In June of that year he started a magazine called *The Liberator* (359), which was to become the best Australian freethought journal. It was a weekly and survived until 1904.

Joseph Symes was an excellent speaker, who succeeded in drawing large crowds to his freethought lectures. The membership of the Australasian Secular Association (ASA) also increased greatly. Symes was elected president of the Victoria branch of the ASA. He attended the Australasian Freethought Congress held in Sydney in September 1884, and was elected president of that. Symes was so successful in organizing a freethought group in Melbourne that trouble soon began. A freethought hall was built in 1889 upon land whose deed was held by a dissident faction in Symes' group. Eventually, this group was expelled from membership, and they (the anti-Symes group) brought suit to take over the hall built upon their land. They eventually won in court, and Symes was expelled from the hall. After seven years, Symes was able to reacquire the hall, when the anti-Symes group collapsed. They then sold the hall, and a wealthy acquaintance of Symes' was able to buy it for him.

The Liberator (359) continued to be published until March 1904. The fortunes of the freethought movement in Melbourne were steadily declining. After *the Liberator* ceased publication, Symes retired to a farm outside Melbourne. He stayed there for two years. After that, he became restless and decided to return to England for a visit. When he arrived, he was welcomed by G. W. Foote, whom he had last seen when Foote was in prison for blasphemy in 1883. Symes lectured and wrote for the freethought press. In December of 1906, he developed pneumonia while in Newcastle, and died later that month. He was cremated and buried in England, while his family returned to Australia.

There is a partial autobiography of Symes, entitled *From the Wesleyan Pulpit to the Secularist Platform* (425). The best study of Symes' life is a series of pamphlets by Sinnott, especially the one entitled *Joseph Symes: The Flower of Atheism* (418). There is also an article by F. B. Smith about Symes (573) in *Labour History*.

The trips of Joseph McCabe to Australia and New Zealand in 1904, 1910, and 1913 brought about a revival of organized freethought in both of those countries. The Rationalist Association of New South Wales was founded in 1912. Thomas Walker was heavily involved in the formation of the organization. In 1919, the Australian Rationalist Association was formed in Sydney. J. S. Langley was its leader. Rationalist groups were also formed about this time in Queensland (1914), Western Australia, Victoria, and South Australia (1918).

J. S. Langley (1889-1959) was also the editor of the magazine *Freethought* (562), that started in Melbourne in 1939. Langley had a fight with the Rationalist Society of Australia in the late 1930s over the control of the finances of the Society and about their use for Axis powers propaganda. As is usual in struggles of this sort, both parties really lost the fight in the end. Langley finally formed a separate "Freethought Society."

Some of the freethought magazines that were published in Australia in the twentieth century were *Ross' Magazine* (570), a freethought and radical publication of Robert Samuel Ross; *The Rationalist* (567), started in Melbourne in 1924; *The Ingersoll News* (564); *Rationalist News* (568); *The Atheist Journal* (551); *The Australian Rationalist* (554); *The Westralian Secularist* (582); and *The Australian Atheist* (552).

Some attempts at formation and existence (often short-lived) were made by the following groups in the twentieth century: The [Australian] National Secular Society (1966), The Atheist Foundation of [South] Australia (1971), The Atheist Society of Australia (1971), and The Freethinker's Association of New South Wales (1973). The Secular Society of Victoria (briefly called The Victorian Secular Society) existed from 1978 to 1979.

Humanism in Australia began with the formation of the Sydney Humanist Group in 1960. This group later changed its name to the N. S. W. Humanist Society. Soon after this, Humanist groups were formed in Victoria, South Australia, Canberra, Queensland, and Western Australia. In 1965, a Council of Australian Humanist Societies was formed. *The Australian Humanist* (553), a quarterly, was the publication of that group. *The Victoria Humanist* (580) was another major Australian Humanist publication. There are also several newsletter-type publications, including *Viewpoints* (NSW), *The Humanist Post* (South Australia), and *The Queensland Humanist*.

There are almost no books or pamphlets which tell the history of freethought in Australia. J. S. Langley issued a couple of pamphlets detailing his fight with the Rationalist Society of Australia, but these could not very well be called histories of freethought. There have been a few articles in the Australian and New Zealand freethought magazines which touch on aspects of Australian freethought history. Included among these are those by Nigel Sinnott on Joseph Symes (571), David Tribe on freethought in Australasia, and Joseph McCabe on his trip to Australia.

BIBLIOGRAPHY

550. *Adelaide Secular and Free Discussion Society's Review, The.* A freethought monthly magazine published at Adelaide, and edited by Henry Oliver. It was published as a monthly from March 1878 until April 1879.

551. *Atheist Journal, The.* A freethought magazine published by the Atheist Society of Australia at Lidcombe North, N. S. W. It is edited by Alan Rickard and has been published since 1973.

552. *Australian Atheist, The.* A freethought magazine published by the Atheist Foundation of Australia. It was published at Adelaide from about 1971. Last date of issue unknown.

553. *Australian Humanist, The.* A quarterly magazine published at Adelaide from 1966 until late 1975. The editor was Bruce Muirden.

554. *Australian Rationalist, The.* A monthly freethought magazine published at Malvern, Victoria from 1969 until about 1975. The editor was W. Glanville Cook, and it evolved from *The Rationalist* (see #567).

555. Collins, W. W. *Can the Design Argument Be Vindicated? A Reply to the Christian Evidence Society* . . . Sydney: Liberty Publishing Company, n.d. [c. 1888].

556. Collins, W. W. *The Church of Rome, the Enemy of Science, and the Foe of Progress.* Sydney: Sydney Freethought Press, 1890.

557. Collins, W. W. *A Search for a Soul, and What I Found on the Way.* Sydney: "Freedom" Office, n.d. [c. 1889].

558. *Freedom.* A monthly freethought magazine, published at Brisbane by W. Taylor in 1883. It lasted three issues.

559. *Freedom.* A monthly freethought magazine, published at Sydney by W. W. Collins from February 1889 until February 1890.

560. *Freethinker and NSW Reformer, The*. A semi-monthly freethought magazine, published at Sydney by W. W. Collins in 1886. It merged with *The Liberator* (see #359) after publishing for twenty-three issues.

561. *Freethought*. A monthly freethought magazine, published in Sydney by E. Cyril Haviland in 1880. It lasted about one year.

562. *Freethought*. A monthly freethought magazine, published at Melbourne by J. S. Langley, starting in September 1939. It ran intermittently until 1944, with the last few issues mimeographed.

563. *Glow-Worm, The*. A spiritualist/freethought magazine, published in Victoria (Melbourne?) by B. S. Naylor in 1869-1870. It was a monthly, and lasted five issues.

564. *Ingersoll News, The*. A freethought magazine, published in Melbourne from about 1946 until 1948 by H. Scott Bennett.

565. *Liberal, The*. A weekly freethought magazine, published in Sydney from 1882-1884 by George Lacy and Charles Bright.

566. *Progressive Spiritualist and Freethought Advocate, The*. A spiritualist/freethought magazine, published in Melbourne by John Tyerman from 1873 until 1874. It was a weekly, with twenty-three issues being published.

567. *Rationalist, The*. A freethought monthly, published at Melbourne by J. S. Langley and others from 1924 until 1969. It changed its name to *The Australian Rationalist* (see #554) in 1969.

568. *Rationalist News*. A bimonthly freethought magazine, published at Chippendale, N.S.W. by the Rationalist Society of New South Wales, since 1967. Ron Marke is the editor.

569. *Reformer, The*. A freethought magazine, published by Joseph Wing in Melbourne from 1880 until 1883. It was a monthly, then became a biweekly.

570. *Ross' Monthly of Protest, Personality and Progress*. A freethought/radical magazine, published by Robert Samuel Ross in Melbourne, from 1915 until 1923. It later changed the *"Monthly"* in its title to *"Magazine,"* finally becoming part of *The Socialist* magazine.

571. Sinnott, Nigel. "A Tribute to Joseph Symes." *New Zealand Rationalist & Humanist*, August 1977, pp. 14-15, 23. Other articles about freethought in Australia include David Tribe's "Freethought in Australasia" in the *New Humanist*, July/August 1976, pp. 46-50, and Joseph McCabe's "Diary of a Pilgrim" in *The Literary Guide*, 1 September 1910, pp. 131-32, 1 October 1910, pp. 146-48 and 1 November 1910, pp. 162-63.

572. Skinner, E. *A Secularist's Guide: A Book for Young and Old*. Sydney: Sydney Lyceum Committee, n.d. [c. 1886?].

573. Smith, F. Barry. "Joseph Symes and the Australasian Secular Association." *Labour History* (Canberra), November 1963, pp. 26-47.

574. *Spiritual Inquirer, The.* A spiritualist/freethought weekly magazine, edited by Joseph Wing, and published by him from Sandhurst (now Bendigo), Victoria from December 1874 until mid-1875.

575. *Stockwhip, The.* A weekly freethought periodical, published in Sydney by John E. Kelly. It began in February 1875. In October 1876, it became called *The Stockwhip and Satirist.* In November 1876, it became called simply *The Satirist.* It ceased publication in January 1877.

576. Tyerman, John. *Freethought Vindicated.* Melbourne: no publisher, 1880.

577. Tyerman, John. *Hymn Book for the Use of the Spiritualist and Freethought Propagandist Society.* Melbourne: E. Purton & Co., 1874.

578. Tyerman, John. *Is There a Devil? Or, The Scarecrow of Christianity Unmasked.* 2nd ed. Melbourne: W. H. Terry, 1875.

579. Tyerman, John. *Is There a Hell? Or, the Doctrine of Eternal Punishment Examined in the Light of Reason, Justice and Benevolence.* Melbourne: E. Purton & Co., [1873].

580. *Victoria Humanist, The.* A magazine published at East Malvern, Victoria from 1967, and edited by M. Beadnell.

581. Walker, Thomas. *Orthodoxy Unmasked; Or, Clerical Arguments Refuted: An Open Reply and Appendix to the Last Letter of the Rev. J. A. Dowie, Recently Published.* Melbourne: Author, 1882.

582. *Westralian Secularist, The.* A freethought magazine, published at Perth from about 1958 to an unknown date.

APPENDIX
III

Freethought in
Canada

Canadian freethought was not especially noteworthy with regard to the extent of activity which occurred in that country. The activity that did occur can be divided into two distinct sections: freethought in English-speaking Canada, and freethought in French-speaking Canada. The activities, history, and problems of these two groups are quite distinct.

The two centers of English-language freethought in Canada were Toronto and Montreal. The first organized freethought group seems to have been the Toronto Freethought Association, founded in 1873. It remained quite small in membership for many years. In 1875, a freethought magazine called *Both Sides* (593) was briefly published at Alymer, Ontario. In 1877, a magazine called *Freethought Journal* (595) was published in Toronto. In 1881, the Toronto group was reorganized and renamed the Toronto Secular Society. Before it adopted that name, it went through a brief phase when it was called the General Freethought Association and the Toronto Association of Freethinkers. The president at that time was Alfred Piddington.

In 1882, Charles Watts, the British freethought lecturer, spoke in Toronto and impressed the members of the Toronto Secular Society enough that they invited him to become their permanent lecturer. Watts agreed, and brought his family over from England, arriving with them in Toronto in 1884.

With the arrival of Charles Watts, freethought became active and vital. Watts lectured regularly all over Canada and the northern United States. He began publishing his own freethought magazine, called *Secular Thought* (415), in 1885. Watts also published a number of his lectures in pamphlet form. Some of these were reprints of earlier lectures delivered in England.

While Watts was in Canada, he organized a number of annual conventions of secularists and freethinkers of Canada. The first of these was held in 1887, in Toronto. A Canadian Secular Union was formed, with J. A. Risser as secretary and Robert Chamblett Adams (1839-1902) as president. *Secular Thought* was made the official organ of the Canadian Secular Union. The Union was first formed in 1877, then reformed in its functioning form in 1885. The Union held a convention in 1890. An attempt was made to form a Secular Publishing Company in Toronto in 1887, by selling shares, but the effort failed when the Ontario Government refused to charter the company on the grounds that "Christianity is a part of the law of the land." Their thought was that they could give no sanction ". . . to the incorporation of any company known or considered to be in opposition to Christianity." The first Canadian edition of *The Age of Reason* (599) was published in 1887.

When Charles Watts returned to England in 1891, upon the death of Charles Bradlaugh, J. Spencer Ellis carried on the publication of *Secular Thought*, which lasted until 1911.

In Montreal, the Pioneer Freethought Club was formed in 1880. Mr. Boaz was an early president, but the main force behind the Club was Captain Robert Chamblett Adams. The Club lasted until about 1903. Adams wrote several books, all published in the United States. *Good Without God* (583), *Pioneer Pith* (584), and his autobiography, *Travels in Faith from Tradition to Reason* (585) are his principal works. An obituary of Adams appears in *The Truth Seeker* (608).

Alan Pringle published several pamphlets in support of Ingersoll in Canada. *Ingersoll in Canada* (601) and *The Mail's Theology* (602) were his most important works.

There were a number of times in the early 1900s when the Canadian postal authorities prohibited the entry of the American freethought magazine *The Truth Seeker* (608) into Canada. The ban was later lifted in each case. From 1928 until 1933 or so, Marshall Gauvin (1881-1978) held a series of regular lectures in Winnipeg, under the auspices of the Winnipeg Rationalist Society. The Society remained rather weak, however. In Regina, Saskatchewan, there was a small Rationalist Club in 1939, with Dr W. A. Waddell as president. A freethought magazine, *The Rationalist* (605), was published in Vancouver, British Columbia, in 1914.

The Humanist movement in Canada has been a fairly recent phenomenon. The group "Humanists of Canada" has its headquarters in Vancouver, where it publishes its magazine *Humanists in Canada* (597). There was also a quarterly called *The Victorian Humanist* (609).

Freethought in French-speaking Canada took an entirely different course. Quebec was under a very strong Roman Catholic influence, especially in its educational system. For this reason, much of the freethought activity has involved attempts to obtain freedom from the yoke of clericalism and to obtain secular education for the children of non-Catholics or nonbelievers. This phase of freethought activity, occurring almost exclusively in the twentieth century (with regard to secular education), has been called the Mouvement Laïque (or "secularization movement").

During the nineteenth century, freethought activity was confined to the sort of anticlericalism which usually occurs in a heavily Catholic country. The main support for the anticlericalism came from L'Institut Canadien, a group run by a branch of le Parti Rouge, the forerunner of the Parti Libéral. The Parti Rouge was formed in 1837 in a preliminary way. The Institut published a journal called L'Avenir (590), anticlerical and expressing the ideology of the Institut. This journal was published from 1847 to 1857. Shortly after this, the Catholic Church in Quebec put a great deal of pressure on the Government. The Institut published another journal, Le Pays (600), before the Church's pressure on the Government grew sufficient to force the Government to dissolve the Institut. Théophile Hudon's book (596) goes into more detail about the Institut. There are also books by M. Ayearst (591), Susan N. Robertson (606) and Charles Lindsey (598) about L'Institut Canadien and le Parti Rouge. The anticlerical phase of Quebec freethought is discussed in several books as well. J-P Bernard's Le Rouges, Libéralisme, Nationalisme et Anti-Cléricalisme au Milieu du XIXᵉ Siécle (592) and Claude Racine's L'Anti-Cléricalisme dans le Roman Québecois (603) are examples. There are discussions of anticlericalism in modern Quebec in the two articles by Richard Ares (589).

In 1961, there was the birth of le Mouvement Laïque de Langue Française, organized to help secularize the schools in Quebec. A democratic movement called "La Revolution Tranquile" also pressed for secular schools. There have been several books published which detail the fight for secular education in Quebec. Among these are Arthur Buies' Lettres sur le Canada (594), L'École Laique (587), and École Confessionelle et la Dissidence (586), both of which are anonymous. The "problem" of freethought and unbelief from the viewpoint of the Catholic educators of Quebec is discussed in L'Incroyance au Québec (588).

In 1979, the first French Canadian freethought magazine of modern times appeared. It was called La Raison (604), published at Montreal. Attempts have been made recently to form an Association Rationaliste du Québec.

While a few books or pamphlets detailing the early history of freethought in French-speaking Canada have been mentioned, there do not seem to be any books or pamphlets which discuss the overall history of freethought in Canada. There is virtually nothing (not even magazine articles) which covers the history of freethought in English-speaking Canada.

BIBLIOGRAPHY

583. Adams, Robert Chamblett. *Good Without God*. New York: The Peter Eckler Company, 1902.

584. Adams, Robert Chamblett. *Pioneer Pith: The Gist of Lectures on Rationalism*. New York: Truth Seeker Company, 1889.

585. Adams, Robert Chamblett. *Travels in Faith From Tradition to Reason*. New York: G. P. Putnam's Sons, 1884.

586. Anonymous. *École Confessionelle et la Dissidence*. Montreal: La Centrale de l'Enseignement du Québec, [1978].

587. Anonymous. *L'École Laïque*. Montreal: Les Éditions du Jour, 1961.

588. Anonymous: *L'Incroyance au Québec*. Montreal: Les Éditions Fides, 1973. Written from the Catholic point of view.

589. Ares, Richard. "Le Problem de l'Anti-cléricalisme au Canada Français." *Relations* (Montreal) 143 (1952): 282-85. The article is continued as "Anti-Cléricalisme, Cléricalisme, et sense de l'église." In *Relations* 144 (1952): 310-14.

590. *Avenir, L'*. An anticlerical journal, published at Montreal from 1847 until 1857.

591. Ayearst, M. "The Parti Rouge and the Clergy." *Canadian Historical Review* 15 (1934): 390-405.

592. Bernard, Jean-Paul. *Les Rouges, Libéralisme, Nationalisme et Anti-Cléricalisme au Milieu du XIXᵉ Siécle*. Montreal: Presse de L'Universite du Québec, 1971.

593. *Both Sides*. A freethought periodical, published at Alymer, Ontario in 1875. No copies known.

594. Buies, Arthur. *Lettres sur le Canada*. Montreal: Editions L'Etincelle, 1978.

595. *Freethought Journal*. A freethought magazine published at Toronto in 1877. No copies known to exist now.

596. Hudon, Théophile. *L'Institut Canadien de Montréal et l'Affaire Guibord*. Montreal: Beauchemin, 1938.

597. *Humanist in Canada*. A quarterly Humanist periodical, published in Vancouver, British Columbia, from 1967 until the present. Lloyd Brereton was the editor until 1977.

598. Lindsey, Charles. *Rome in Canada: The Ultramontane Struggle for Supremacy Over Civil Authority*. Toronto: Lovel Brothers, 1887.

599. Paine, Thomas. *The Age of Reason*. Toronto: [Office of Secular Thought?], 1887. No copies known.

600. *Pays, Le*. An anticlerical journal, published at Montreal from 1910 until 1921.

601. Pringle, Alan. *Ingersoll in Canada*. Napanee, Ontario: Standard Book and Job Company, 1880.

602. Pringle, Alan. *The Mail's Theology, Being a Reply to the Saturday Sermons of the Toronto Mail, Including a Vindication of Charles Bradlaugh, M. P. Against the Mail's Aspersions*. Napanee, Ontario: Standard Book and Job Company, [c. 1882].

603. Racine, Claude. *L'Anti-Cléricalisme dans le Roman Québecois*. Montreal: Éditions Hurtubise-HMH, 1972.

604. *Raison, La*. A freethought monthly magazine, in French, published from March 1979 until the present at Montreal. The editor is Gabriel Dubuisson.

605. *Rationalist, The*. A freethought magazine, published at Vancouver, B.C., from October 1914. Date of last issue unknown. The editor was E. V. Cook.

606. Robertson, Susan Nancy. *The Institut Canadien: An Essay in Cultural History*. London, Ontario: University of Western Ontario, 1965.

607. *Secular Thought*. A freethought magazine, published at Toronto from 1885 until 1911. It was founded and edited by Charles Watts until early in 1891. After that, J. Spencer Ellis became the editor and publisher. It was a weekly at first, then became a monthly during its last few years.

608. *Truth Seeker, The*. An American Freethought magazine, published weekly from 1873 until 1930, and then monthly after that. It was founded by D. M. Bennett. It moved from New York to San Diego in 1964. An obituary of Robert C. Adams appears in the issue for 23 August 1902, p. 536.

609. *Victorian Humanist, The*. A quarterly Humanist magazine, published from 1964 to 1967 in Victoria, British Columbia.

APPENDIX
IV

Freethought in
India

Freethought tradition in India extends further into the past than any-where else. There is a serious problem when it comes to discussing the earliest forms of materialistic and atheistic thought in India: almost all of the writings of these groups have been destroyed. It is known that the major school of materialistic thought was a philosophical system known as Charvaka (Cārvāka), popular about 600 B.C. The main book or text of Charvakan doctrine was called *Brhaspati Sutra*, and it has not survived. The *Tattvopaplavasimha* (from about 650 A.D.). is considered to be the only authentic Charvakan text to survive. It is by Jayarasi Bhatta.

The ideas of the Charvakan system can be partially reconstructed from the works critical of it which have survived. The major doctrine of Charvaka was called Lokāyata. It holds that only this world exists, and that there is no supernatural or afterlife. Perception is held to be the only source of knowledge. The "soul" has no existence apart from the body. It is really only another name for "intelligence." Nature is indifferent to good and evil, and there are no absolutes, only agreed-upon values. Charvaka did not draw its doctrines from either the *Veda* or the *Upanisads*, as did all the other Indian native religions except Buddhism and Jainism.

There is some problem with terminology that has not yet been mentioned. One name for Charvaka and Lokāyata, used more fre-quently in the past, was Bārhaspatya. This was supposedly derived from the name of the founder of the school, Brhaspati. However, there is some dispute as to whether this name refers to a real or mythical person. One school of thought holds that the real founders of Charvaka were a man named Cārvaka, and another named Ajita Kesakambalin. There is also the term Nastika-mata, which is also used (incorrectly) as a synonym for Charvaka. "Nastika" means "atheist" and the "-mata" makes it into the equivilent of "atheism." The trouble here is that the term Nāstika-mata is just as correctly applied to early Buddhism and early Jainism as well. It is properly a term for any non-theistic system, not just Charvaka.

There have been a number of books and articles about Charvaka and its associated doctrines. The most important include Chatto-padhyaya's *Lokāyata: A Study in Ancient Indian Materialism* (618), Shastri's *A Short History of Indian Materialism, Sensationalism and Hedonism* (657), Mittal's *Materialism in Indian Thought* (639), Tucci's *Linee di una Storia del Materialismo Indiano* (660), Chattopadhyaya's *Indian Atheism: A Marxist Analysis* (617) and Riepe's *The Naturalistic Tradition in Indian Thought* (653). There are also important articles or chapters on ancient Indian materialism by Bhattacharya (615) and Shastri (656). Selections from surviving texts are found in Radhakrish-nan's *Source Book in Indian Philosophy* (647).

In one of the true ironies of history, the rebirth of the freethought movement in India in modern times seems to have been a direct result of the work of Christian missionaries trying to discredit Hindu beliefs in an attempt to convert the Hindus to Christianity. In the first half of the nineteenth century, a missionary effort was made in southern India. The work of the missionaries had the dual result of destroying the Hindu beliefs of many people, leaving them with no religion, while at the same time making them hostile to the new religion of Christianity that was being forced upon them. Some activists imported large amounts of Paine's *The Age of Reason* (216) into India, where it became quite popular. Its contents were used against the missionaries in a direct challenge. Hindu freethought was at first merely anti-Christian, but by the mid-1800s there were programs and organizations.

American freethinkers had an important influence upon the development of freethought in south India. In the 1870s, there was an important contribution made by Moncure Conway, who visited India and compiled a book of ethical scriptures from India, called *The Sacred Anthology* [619], Robert G. Ingersoll (whose works were widely translated and republished in India), D. M. Bennett (who visited India, wrote about it and whose works were also distributed in India), and Henry Steel Olcott (who was a cofounder of Theosophy, lived in Ceylon and India, and was largely responsible for the success of Theosophy as a movement). Olcott represented the rationalistic branch of Theosophy (as opposed to Mrs. Blavatsky's mystical branch). When Olcott went to live in Ceylon from 1880 to 1882, he introduced Western freethought literature (Bennett, Besant, Ingersoll, and Bradlaugh). He also spent much time in India, where he probably did the same thing. The Theosophical Society first set up its Indian headquarters in Bombay, then moved to Madras, where it still has its world headquarters.

In 1875, the Indu Suyagnana Sangam (Hindu Freethought Union) was formed in Madras. It began publishing the first real Indian free-thought magazine, *The Philosophical Inquirer* (646) in 1878. This magazine was a weekly bilingual Tamil-English publication, probably inspired by the British and American freethought weekly magazines of the time. Ingersoll and Bennett were among the American freethinkers frequently featured in its pages. The editor was also the secretary of the Hindu Freethought Union, namely P. Murugesa Mudaliar. The Hindu Freethought Union was affiliated with the National Secular Society. There is an article about the Union by B. Rajannan (649).

The Brahmin caste was the special target of Hindu freethinkers, since they represented the entire repressive social order. The Brahmins were to the Hindu freethinker what the clergy was to the American or British freethinker.

In 1882, the Theosophical Society moved its headquarters from Bombay to Madras, This caused the Madras freethinkers to suspect that Theosophy was Christianity in disguise. The editor of *The Phil-osophical Inquirer* (646) called Olcott an atheist and Theosophy was viewed as an interfering competitor to freethought. However, the editor (Murugesa Mudaliar) changed his mind and joined the Theo-sophical Society, continuing to publish *The Philosophical Inquirer* as a Theosophical/atheist magazine. This was a fatal blow for the Hindu Freethought Union, that had also been headed by Mudaliar. The transition period, during which many freethinkers joined the Theoso-phical society, was marked by much argument over whether a secu-larist could be a Theosophist. In the end, most freethinkers joined the Theosophical Society because they thought it was atheistic. In fact, it was opposed to Christianity, but it was occult/spiritualistic. Olcott did support antimissionary activities. Annie Besant's arrival in Madras to head the Theosophical Society in 1893 did not help the freethought cause either. Even though Mrs. Besant had been a free-thought leader, she soon brought increased support of Hindu orthodoxy into Theosophy. By 1894, Hindu freethought was dead.

After 1900, there was a gradual revival of freethought in India, brought about by the growth of an anti-Bramin feeling, which can be called "Dravidian freethought." In 1925, the Self-Respect Movement (Suyamariadai Iyakkam) was started by Erode V. Ramaswami (1879-1973), usually called "Periyar" or "E.V.R." In 1934, Periyar issued the first of a series of lectures by Robert G. Ingersoll in Tamil. Inger-soll's writings were used extensively by the Self-Respect Movement.

They also held a strongly anti-Brahmin position. Periyar was the editor of several freethought journals, including *Viduthalai* (662), *Pakutharivu* (644) and *Kudi Arasu* (636). By the early 1940s, freethought had become nearly a mass movement, and the Indian constitution, when independence was granted, made India a secular state. The Justice Party, very important in the fight for independence, merged with the Self-Respect Movement, and in 1944 took the name Dravida Kazhagam (Dravidian Federation). By 1949, the Federation was the largest free-thought organization in India.

Periyar was one of the most important leaders of the atheist move-ment in India. It should be understood that in the twentieth century, Indian freethought was heavily intertwined with anticaste, independence, and social reform movements. Periyar was active in all of these causes, and in educational reform as well. Periyar elevated the ancient Tamil classic text, called the *Tirukkural*, to an exalted status among his Tamil-speaking followers. This volume, although ancient, was rather modern in its secularistic, noncaste, and equality of the sexes ap-proach to life. Periyar was the author of a number of books. His col-lected works (650) were issued in three volumes in 1974. There have been a number of pamphlets and articles about Periyar, such as Anaimuthu's *Contribution of Periyar E. V. R. to the Progress of Atheism* (611). Some of the articles about Periyar include those of Dharma-lingam (620), Lavanam, and others listed with the first of these in the bibliography section.

The other major freethought leader in twentieth century India was Gora. Gora was the adopted name of Goparaju Ramachandra Rao (1902-1975). He was born into an orthodox Hindu Brahmin family. He studied botany at college where he lost his religious beliefs. He reacted strongly to the caste system, working constantly for its elimina-tion. He was dismissed from one teaching post because of his atheism. In 1936, Gora began to actively propagate his atheism among the masses. He conducted intercaste and interreligious dinners and events. Intercaste marriages were encouraged, especially when one of the parties was an "untouchable." Gora encouraged the break-down of the prohibitions against Hindus eating beef or Moslems eating pork. He also attacked the very prevalent superstitions, es-pecially fear of ghosts, which permeated Indian society. Gora also held a series of discussions with Gandhi, which were later published as *An Atheist With Gandhi* (623). Gora set up the first Atheist Centre in India, at Patamata, near Vijayawada. It is still functioning. He founded the magazine *The Atheist* (613).

Gora wrote a number of books, including *I Learn* (624), *Positive Atheism* (626), and *We Become Atheists* (627). His native language was Telugu, and there are also a number of books by him published in that language. The earliest was *Nastikatvamu* (625), which is probably the first book about atheism to be written in an Indian language. There is a biography of Gora, called *Sri Gora* (634), written in Telugu. There is also a biography called *Gora—An Atheist* (651), and a number of articles about him in freethought periodicals (661).

In 1930, a group called the Anti-Priestcraft Association was formed in Bombay. In 1931, the group changed its name to the Rationalist Association of India. In October of that year, it launched its magazine *Reason* (652), edited by C. L. D'Avoine, and later by R. D. Karve. The magazine expired in 1942, and the group became inactive. In 1950, the Rationalist Association of India merged with the Indian Rationalist Association. The two people most responsible for the merger with the IRA (formed in 1949) were R. P. Paranjpye and S. Ramanathan. The IRA now publishes a magazine called *Freethought* (621), and issued *The Indian Rationalist* (630). There is an article about the history of the Indian Rationalist Association by Suryanarayana (659).

The Radical Humanist Movement was launched in 1948 by M. N. Roy. It was initially operated through the auspices of the Indian Renaissance Institute. The Institute published the journal *The Radical Humanist* (648), which M. N. Roy edited.

In 1968, A. B. Shah started the Indian Secular Forum, which became the Indian Secular Society later that year, in Bombay. It began publication of its magazine *The Secularist* (655) in 1969. A. B. Shah is the editor of the magazine.

There are a number of other freethought groups in India. One is the Atheist Society of India, located in Visakhapatnam. It tends to have more of a Marxist orientation, and published *The Age of Atheism* (610). The editor and president of the Society is Jayagopal. The Indian Atheist Centre started in 1979. It publishes the magazine *Indian Atheist* (629) and the editor/director is Sanal Edamaruku. It is located in New Delhi. The Indian Humanist Union was established in 1960. It is located in Lucknow. In 1966, it began publishing its journal, *The Humanist Outlook* (628). The founder of the Union was Narsingh Narain, and the editor of *The Humanist Outlook* is Chitra Narain.

There are a number of other magazines that are either still being published in native Indian languages, or that were formerly published. One additional freethought magazine still being published in English which should be mentioned is *The Modern Rationalist* (640), a publication of the Self-Respect Propaganda Institution in Madras, founded originally by Periyar. Non-English freethought journals include *Yuk-*

thivadi (665) in Malayalam, *Charvaka* (616) in Telugu, *Arivu Vazhi* (612) in Tamil, *Nasthika Yugam* (643) in Telugu, *Nasthika Mitra* (642) in Telugu, *Nasthika Margam* (641) in Telugu, *Yukthi Vicharanam* (664) in Malayalam, *Vikasam* (663) in Telugu, *Sinthanayaian* (658) in Malayalam, *Insaan* (633) in Hindi, and *Sangam* (654) in Telugu.

There were at least two notable meetings of a freethought nature held in India. One was the First Convention of Indian Rationalists, held in Madras in 1949. The chairman of the meeting was S. Ramanathan, and the Proceedings were published as a pamphlet (632). The other was the First World Atheist Conference, held at Vijayawada in 1972. The chairman for that meeting was Gora. A Second World Atheist Conference was held in December 1980, also in Vijayawada.

The history of freethought in India has never been told in any sort of an overall fashion. Some books and articles about ancient Indian materialism have already been mentioned. There is virtually nothing in print about the period from 1800 to 1900. An exception is H-J Klimkeit's *Anti-religiöse Bewegungen im modernen Südindien* (635). The unpublished dissertation by Rajannan (see Appendix VIII) is also very useful. In the case of twentieth century freethought history, there are only a few pamphlets and magazine articles. It is possible that something is available in some of the Indian languages, but a partial search of that material has revealed little of value. Lavanam's (638) *Nasthikatvam Adhivruddhi Charita [History and Progress of Atheism]* (638) is of some help, although it is in Telugu. Of some use as well are Bharati's *History and Growth of Rationalist Movement in Tamil Nadu* (614), *The History and Growth of Rationalist Movement* (631), and *Rationalists of Maharashtra* (645), although each of these pamphlet's titles promises more than it delivers.

There are a number of magazine articles on aspects of Indian freethought history. Most of them are not very detailed, however. Several of the better articles have already been mentioned. A few others that can be added are "Pioneers of Freethought in India," a special issue (December 1974) of the magazine *Freethought* (621); Paul Kurtz' "A Passage Through India" (637), which reports on Humanism in India; and the report on "The Indian Rationalist Convention" of 1949 (622) in *The Literary Guide*.

BIBLIOGRAPHY

610. *Age of Atheism, The.* A freethought magazine (monthly) published at Visakhapatnam from 1974 until 1979. Jayagopal was the editor, and the publication was from the Atheist Society of India.

611. Anaimuthu, V. *Contribution of Periyar E. V. R. to the Progress of Atheism*. Tiruchirappalli: Periyar Publications, 1976.

612. *Arivu Vazhi*. A Tamil language freethought magazine, published from 1975 until the present.

613. *Atheist, The*. A monthly freethought magazine, published from Vijayawada from 1969 until the present. The first editor was Gora, then Lavanam became the editor upon Gora's death.

614. Bharati, S. Lakshmirathan. *History and Growth of Rationalist Movement in Tamil Nadu*. Madras: Indian Rationalist Association, 1974.

615. Bhattacharya, Naren. "Philosophic Consequences of Ancient Indian Atheistic Movements" and "Ancient Indian Atheistic Movements." *The Radical Humanist*, 26 (1962): 285-86, 299-300, 311-12, 322, 335, 344, 354, 366, 372, 376, 407, 412, 419-20, 475-76, 484.

616. *Charvaka*. A Telugu freethought magazine, published at Vijayawada from 1976 until 1979. The editor was "T. R."

617. Chattopadhyaya, Debiprasad. *Indian Atheism: A Marxist Analysis*. Calcutta: Manisha Granthalaya, 1969. Most of the Marxism is confined to the last few chapters.

618. Chattopadhyaya, Debiprasad. *Lokāyata: A Study in Ancient Indian Materialism*. New Delhi: People's Publishing House, 1959.

619. Conway, Moncure D. *The Sacred Anthology*. London: Trübner & Company, 1873.

620. Dharmalingam, A. M. "E. V. Ramaswami: A Great Revolutionary." *The Atheist* (Vijayawada), October 1978, pp. 133-35. Other articles about Periyar are Lavanam's "Atheist Leader Periyar E. V. R." in *The Atheist*, March 1980, pp. 24 and 38; P. Ramanathan's "Indian Iconoclast" in *The Humanist* (London) of December 1971, pp. 358-60; Lavanam's "Periyar E. V. Ramaswami: A Saga of Indomitable Courage." in *The Atheist*, October 1979, pp. 160-63; and Lavanam's "Periyar and Gora: Outstanding Atheists of Modern India." in *The Atheist*, November 1979, pp. 177-79, 186-89.

621. *Freethought*. A monthly magazine published at Madras, from 1970 until the present, by the Indian Rationalist Association.

622. Ghosh, S. "The Indian Rationalist Convention." *The Literary Guide*, April 1950, pp. 71-72.

623. Gora. *An Atheist With Gandhi*. Ahmedabad: Navajivan Publishing House, 1951.

624. Gora. *I Learn*. Vijayawada: Atheist Centre, 1976.

625. Gora. *Nastikatvamu* [Atheism]. Mudunuru: Author, 1940. In the Telugu language. Gora's first book.

626. Gora. *Positive Atheism*. Vijayawada: Atheist Centre, 1972.

627. Gora. *We Become Atheists*. Vijayawada: Atheist Centre, 1975.

628. *Humanist Outlook, The*. A magazine (quarterly) published at Lucknow by the Indian Humanist Union from 1966 until the present.

629. *Indian Atheist*. A monthly magazine published at New Delhi from 1979 until the present by Sanal Edamaruku.

630. *Indian Rationalist, The*. A monthly freethought magazine, published by the Indian Rationalist Association at Madras from 1952 until 1965.

631. Indian Rationalist Association. *The History and Growth of Rationalist Movement*. Madras: Indian Rationalist Association, 1974. A mimeographed version of papers presented at the Eighth Convention of Indian Rationalists. It covers rationalism in Kerala, Bombay, Punjab, and Maharashtra.

632. Indian Rationalists. *The First Convention of Indian Rationalists, Rajaji Hall, Madras. Proceedings, 18 December 1949*. [Madras: Indian Rationalist Association, 1950].

633. *Insaan*. A monthly Hindi freethought magazine, published at Vijayawada from 1956 until 1962. The editor was Lavanam.

634. Kafi Viswanatham, V. *Sri Gora*. Eluru: Praja Prchuranalu, 1965. A biography of Gora in Telugu. There is also an anonymous biography of Gora in Hindi, called *Gora Vyakti Vyaktitua* [*Gora: the Man and the Personality*], published at Agra by Sytyagraha Samaj in 1962.

635. Klimkeit, Hans-Joachim. *Anti-Religiöse Bewegungen im modernen Südindien: Eine religionssoziologische untersuchung zur Säkularisierungsfrage*. Bonn: Ludwig Röhrscheid Verlag, 1971.

636. *Kudi Arasu*. A weekly Tamil language freethought magazine, edited by Periyar, and published from 1924 until an unknown date.

637. Kurtz, Paul. "A Passage Through India." *New Humanist* May/June 1976, pp. 6-8. Also published in *The American Humanist* of March/April 1976, pp. 12-14.

638. Lavanam. *Nasthikatvam Adhivruddhi Charita* [*History and Progress of Atheism*]. Vijayawada: Nastika Kendram, 1978. In Telugu.

639. Mittal, Kewal Krishan. *Materialism in Indian Thought*. New Delhi: Munshiram Manoharlal, 1974.

640. *Modern Rationalist, The*. A monthly magazine, published at Madras by the Periyar Self-Respect Propaganda Institution from about 1973 until the present. The editor is K. Eeramani.

641. *Nasthika Margum*. A Telugu language freethought magazine, published at Vijayawada from 1977 until the present by Mythri and Hemalata Lavanam.

642. *Nasthika Mitra*. A quarterly Telugu language magazine, edited by Y. Phanu, and published since 1979 at Vijayawada.

643. *Nasthika Yugam*. A Telugu language freethought magazine, published at Visakhapatnam by Jayagopal from 1972 until 1979.

644. *Pakutharivu*. A Tamil language magazine, published from 1935 until an unknown date by Periyar at Madras.

645. Phatak, N. R., Johsi, T. L. S., and Pradhan, G. P., *Rationalists of Maharashtra*. Calcutta: Renaissance Publishers, 1962. Indian Renaissance Institute Monograph #3. A chapter by each author.

646. *Philosophical Inquirer, The*. A weekly Tamil/English freethought magazine, published at Madras from 1878 until about 1888, and edited by Murugesa Mudaliar. It was the first Indian freethought magazine, although it later became Theosophist/freethought.

647. Radhakrishnan, Sarvepalli and Moore, Charles A. *A Source Book in Indian Philosophy*. Princeton, N.J.: Princeton University Press, 1957.

648. *Radical Humanist, The*. A magazine published at Bombay, then Calcutta, then New Delhi, from 1937 to the present, as a monthly. M. N. Roy was the founder and editor, followed by V. M. Tarkunde at present. It was called *Independent India* from 1937 to 1948.

649. Rajannan, B. "Hindu Freethought Union: Pioneer of South Indian Free Thought." *Freethought* (Madras) November-December 1976, pp. 189-90.

650. Ramaswami, E. V. ("Periyar"), ed. *Thoughts of Periyar EVR*, 3 vols. Tiruchirappalli: Thinker's Forum, 1974. Collected works of Periyar.

651. Rao, G. S. *Gora—An Atheist*. Vijayawada: Atheistic Centre, n.d. [c. 1971].

652. *Reason*. A freethought magazine, published in Bombay from 1931 to 1942 (with a gap in part of 1936) by the Rationalist Association of India and edited by C. L. D'Avoine and then by R. D. Karve.

653. Riepe, Dale M. *The Naturalistic Tradition in Indian Thought*. Seattle: University of Washington Press, 1961.

654. *Sangam*. A Telugu language freethought magazine, published by Gora from 1949 to 1952, and then by Lavanam from 1960 to 1967.

655. *Secularist, The*. A freethought magazine, published from Bombay by A. B. Shah and the Indian Secular Society from 1969 until the present.

656. Shastri, Dakshinaranjan B. "Materialists, Sceptics and Agnostics." *The Cultural Heritage of India*. 3 vols. Calcutta: Ramakrishna Mission Institute of Culture, 1953, 2nd edition. Vol. 3, pp. 168-86.

657. Shastri, Dakshinaranjan B. *A Short History of Indian Materialism, Sensationalism and Hedonism*. Calcutta: Calcutta Book Company, 1930.

658. *Sinthanayaian*. A Tamil language freethought magazine, published by V. Anaimuthu from 1974 until the present.

659. Suryanarayana, A. "Genesis of I.R.A." *Freethought* (Madras) May 1978, pp. 139-40. About the Indian Rationalist Association.

660. Tucci, Giuseppe. *Linee di una Storia del Materialismo Indiano*. 2 vols. Rome: R. A. N. dei Lincei [Academia National dei Lincei], 1924 and 1929.

661. Turner, Jill. "Positive Atheist." *New Humanist*, November 1974, pp. 236-37. Also, see "Gora." by B. Venugopal in *Freethought*, December 1974, pp. 26-28.

662. *Viduthalai*. A Tamil language daily newspaper, published by Periyar from 1931, and still being produced.

663. *Vikasam*. A Telugu language freethought magazine, edited by M. V. Ramamurti and produced at Hydrabad from 1975 to the present.

664. *Yukthi Vicharanam*. A Malayalam language freethought magazine, produced from 1976 to the present.

665. *Yukthivadi*. A Malayalam language freethought magazine, edited by M. C. Joseph from Iranjalakuda, beginning in 1929 and still being published.

APPENDIX
V

Freethought in Other
===== Commonwealth Countries =====

CEYLON/SRI LANKA

Although some of the ancient philosophical traditions of India were shared by Ceylon, the modern period of freethought in Ceylon dates from the early 1950s. At that time, the Ceylon Rationalist Association (later the Sri Lanka Rationalist Association) was formed. It soon became inactive. In 1962, the Association was revived by Abraham T. Kovoor (1898-1978), who became the leading figure in Sri Lankan freethought. Kovoor was born in Kerala, India, and raised a Christian. He studied biology in college, and became a biology teacher. He moved to Ceylon in 1928, becoming a lecturer in botany. Kovoor became convinced of the dangers of religiously-based superstitions, especially in the case of so-called "holy men." He viewed them as confidence men of the worst sort, and Kovoor spent many years of his life touring throughout India and Ceylon, exposing their claims to miraculous powers.

Kovoor is the author of the book *Begone Godmen!* (667) and of *Selected Works of Dr. Abraham T. Kovoor* (668), as well as of a number of articles in the Indian and Sri Lankan freethought periodicals. He was the editor of the only important Sri Lankan freethought magazine, *The Ceylon Rationalist Ambassador* (666), which was an annual, published from 1966 to 1972 at Colombo. An obituary of Kovoor was published in *The Atheist* of October 1978 (669), and another article about him was in the issue of September 1979. Upon Kovoor's death, Mervyn S. Casie Chetty was elected president of the Sri Lanka Rationalist Association.

REPUBLIC OF SOUTH AFRICA

South Africa (formerly the Union of South Africa) left the British

Commonwealth in 1961. However, it was a British possession from 1795, and a commonwealth member after the Union of South Africa was formed in 1910. Freethought in South Africa was intermittent. Thomas Walker (later of Australia) lived in Capetown for a while in 1881 and published a freethought magazine called *The Reflector* (672) there at that time. In 1889, there was a Freethought Association in Port Elizabeth. From 1888 to 1889, Edward B. Rose, a British/ Australian freethinker, went on an extended freethought lecturing tour of South Africa.

In 1956, the Rationalist Association of Johannesburg began publication of its newsletter, *The Rationalist* (671). In October 1960, the mimeographed newsletter was expanded into a printed monthly magazine called *Die Rasionalis/The Rationalist*. The Afrikaans alternate title and a few articles in that language were added to the former publication. The magazine continued until the May-June 1976 issue. In 1958, the magazine was taken over by the Rationalist Association of South Africa, and not of just Johannesburg. The editor of the magazine was Edward Roux (1903-1966), then his wife Winifred became editor. Roux was the president of the Rationalist Association of South Africa as well. The Association was disbanded in 1978, and merged with the South African Humanist Association, which was formed in early 1979. They publish *The South African Humanist* (674). An article entitled "Rationalism in South Africa," written by Edward Roux (673), appeared in *The Humanist*.

TRINIDAD

The National Secular Society had a branch on Trinidad in the 1890s. The president of the branch society at that time was Edgar Maresse-Smith. There was a Trinidadian freethought magazine called *Progress* (670) published about 1892 and edited by Emanuel dos Santos.

BANGLADESH

There is a Humanist Association in Bangladesh at the present time. It is located in Dacca.

GAMBIA

There is a "Gora Society" in the Gambia. It is an atheist/freethought organization, and was organized recently.

MALAYSIA

There is a Dravidar Association at Kuala Lumpur. This group is modeled upon the Dravidian freethought groups of India.

NIGERIA

There is a rationalist association in Nigeria, but it is still struggling to get completely organized.

BIBLIOGRAPHY

666. *Ceylon Rationalist Ambassador, The*. An annual freethought magazine. It was published at Colombo by Abraham T. Kovoor from 1966 through 1972.

667. Kovoor, Abraham T. *Begone Godmen! Encounters With Spiritual Frauds*. Bombay: Jaico Publishing House, 1976.

668. Kovoor, Abraham T. *Selected Works of Dr. Abraham T. Kovoor*. 2nd ed. Colombo: Siri Sanda Press, 1972. Edited by Susil Wimalaratne. A collection of Kovoor's short magazine and pamphlet pieces.

669. Mythri. "Kovoor: Great Fighter Against Superstition." *The Atheist* (Vijayawada), October 1978, pp. 125-27. There is also an anonymous article, "Dr. Kovoor and His Mission," in *The Atheist*, September 1979, pp. 142-43.

670. *Progress*. A freethought magazine, published in Port of Spain, Trinidad, in about 1892, and edited by Emanuel dos Santos. No copies are known to exist today.

671. *Rationalist, The*. A freethought magazine, published in Johannesburg, South Africa from 1956 until 1976. In October 1960, it became printed rather than mimeographed, and adopted the cotitle *Die Rasionalis*. It was initially published by the Rationalist Association of Johannesburg, but later (1960-1976) published by the Rationalist Association of South Africa. The editors were Edward and then Winifred Roux.

672. *Reflector, The*. A freethought magazine, published in Capetown, South Africa by Thomas Walker in 1881.

673. Roux, Edward. "Rationalism in South Africa." *The Humanist* (London), July 1959, pp. 14-15.

674. *South African Humanist, The*. A quarterly magazine, published at Joubert Park, South Africa by the South African Humanist Association beginning in 1979.

APPENDIX VI

Library Collections on British/Commonwealth Freethought

This Appendix lists library collections, in the United Kingdom, the United States, and elsewhere, that contain large numbers of items relating to British or Commonwealth freethought. Collections concerning freethought in other areas are not considered here, although collections strong in United States freethought are listed in an Appendix to *Freethought in the United States* (140). There are also a number of outstanding private collections that contain a better selection of British/Commonwealth freethought materials than any existing public collection. In the interests of the privacy of these collectors, their names and addresses are not listed here. They are, however, available to serious scholars with specific research needs, by addressing the author in care of the publisher of this book.

THE UNITED STATES:

California: Henry Huntington Library (San Marino): Has the papers of Richard Carlile and much on Robert Taylor.

Connecticut: Yale University (New Haven): Has a strong British freethought periodicals collection.

District of Columbia: Library of Congress: Has perhaps the best collection in the U. S. of bound British freethought periodicals.

Illinois: Northwestern University (Evanston): Has the Kaye Collection of materials on British deism. The University of Chicago: Has a good collection of materials about George Jacob Holyoake.

Indiana: Lilly Library at Indiana University (Bloomington): Has the Gilmour collection of pamphlet materials relating to British freethought in the Victorian era.

New York: Columbia University (New York City): Has the papers of Moncure D. Conway (not complete). Union Theological Seminary

(New York City): Has the McAlpin Collection on early British deism. New York Public Library (New York City): Has the Irving Levy Collection (in the stacks) of hundreds of bound volumes of pamphlets relating to British (and American) freethought.

Pennsylvania: American Philosophical Society (Philadelphia): Has the Gimbel collection of Thomas Paine items.

Wisconsin: University of Wisconsin (Madison): Has the best British freethought pamphlet and book collection; also strong on periodicals.

THE UNITED KINGDOM:

London: Bishopsgate Institute: Has some George Jacob Holyoake papers; also the papers of Charles Bradlaugh. British Library: Has a good collection of books and journals on British freethought; also has the Francis Place papers. National Secular Society: Has a very good collection of British freethought books and periodicals. Rationalist Press Association: Has a good collection of British freethought books and periodicals. South Place Ethical Society: Has a good collection of British freethought books and some periodicals. Theosophical Society in England: Has a good collection of Annie Besant materials.

Manchester: Co-operative Union Institute: Has a large collection of the papers of George Jacob Holyoake and of Robert Owen. Manchester Central Reference Library: Has a good collection of British freethought pamphlet items, especially those relating to Manchester.

Northampton: Northampton Public Library: Has the Ambrose Barker Collection of Charles Bradlaugh material.

Thetford: Thetford Public Library: Has a very good collection of Thomas Paine materials.

AUSTRALIA:

Canberra: National Library of Australia: Has the large Pearce Collection of Australian/New Zealand freethought items.

Melbourne: La Trobe Library: Has a good collection of freethought materials in its Boscher Collection.

Sydney: Mitchell Library: Has a good collection of Australian freethought materials.

NEW ZEALAND:

Auckland: New Zealand Rationalist Society: Has a collection of N. Z. freethought periodicals and some books.

Wellington: Turnbull Library: Has the papers of Robert Stout.

INDIA:

Madras: Theosophical Society: Probably has the best collection of the older Indian freethought journals. Indian Rationalist Association: Has many Indian and British freethought items.

Vijayawada: Atheist Centre: Is replacing the large library which was destroyed in a flood in 1977.

CANADA:

Winnipeg: University of Manitoba Library: Has the Marshall Gauvin Collection of freethought books.

APPENDIX VII
Theses/Dissertations and Works in Progress on British/Commonwealth
——————— Freethought ———————

The first section consists of unpublished theses and dissertations relating to freethought history or biography. If the contents of the thesis or dissertation were subsequently published as a book, the book itself is listed in the appropriate place in the body of this bibliography. There will be no listing of those items in this section unless the unpublished version contained considerably more information than was found in the published version. The second section here consists of books which have been written (or nearly completed), but which have not appeared in print by the time this book was completed.

THESES AND DISSERTATIONS

Bedford, R. D. "The Defence of Truth: Lord Herbert of Cherbury and the Development of Religious Thought in England." Ph.D. dissertation, University of Cambridge, 1969.

Blaszak, Barbara Jean. "George Jacob Holyoake: An Attitudinal Study." Ph.D. dissertation, State University of New York at Buffalo, 1978.

Budd, Susan, "The British Humanist Movement, 1860-1966." D. Phil. dissertation, University of Oxford, 1969. Part of this was published as reference (7).

Campbell, Colin B. "Humanism and the Culture of the Professions: A Study in the Rise of the British Humanist Movement, 1946-1963." Ph.D. dissertation, University of London, 1968.

Course, J. R. "The Rise and Interpretation of Deism." Ph.D. dissertation, Royal Holloway College, 1956.

Daniel, Stephen Hartley. "The Philosophic Methodology of John Toland." Ph.D. dissertation, St. Louis University, 1977.

Eisen, Sidney. "Frederic Harrison: The Life and Thought of an English Positivist." Ph.D. dissertation, Johns Hopkins University, 1957.

Elgin, V. G. "The Eighteenth Century Discussion Concerning the Continuance of Miracles After the Apostolic Age, With Special Reference to the Writings of Conyers Middleton." Ph.D. dissertation, University of Edinburgh, 1959.

Emerson, Roger Lee. "English Deism 1670-1755: An Enlightenment Challenge to Orthodoxy." Ph.D. Dissertation, Brandeis University, 1962.

Francis, Mark. "British Secularism, 1850-85." M. A. thesis, University of Toronto, 1968.

Greene, T. M. "Kant's Religious Theory and Its Relation to English Deism." Ph.D. dissertation, University of Edinburgh, 1924.

Griffin, Janet. "Anticlericalism Among the English Deists." Ph.D. dissertation, St. Louis University, 1969.

Grugel, Lee E. "George Jacob Holyoake: A Study in the Progress of Labor and the British Reform Tradition in the Nineteenth Century." Ph.D. dissertation, The University of Chicago, 1970. Part of this was published as reference (15).

Jones, E. M. "Charles Blount, 8th Lord Mountjoy." M. A. thesis, National University of Ireland, 1946.

Kaczkowski, Conrad J. "John Mackinnon Robertson: Freethinker and Radical." Ph.D. dissertation, St. Louis University, 1964.

Kottich, R. G. "Die Lehre van den angeborenen Ideen seit Herbert von Cherbury." Ph.D. dissertation, University of Berlin, 1917.

Krantz, Charles Krzentowski. "The British Secularist Movement: A Study in Militant Dissent." Ph.D. dissertation, The University of Rochester, 1964.

Luke, Hugh J., Jr. "Drams for the Vulgar: A Study of Some Radical Publishers and Publications of Early Nineteenth Century London." Ph.D. dissertation, The University of Texas, 1963.

Mayo, Thomas Franklin. "Epicurus in England, 1650-1725." Ph.D. dissertation, Columbia University, 1934.

Murphy, J. M. "Positivism in England: The Reception of Comte's Doctrines, 1840-1870." Ph.D. dissertation, Columbia University, 1968.

Nelson, Walter David. "British Rational Secularism: Unbelief from Bradlaugh to the Mid-Twentieth Century." Ph.D. dissertation, University of Washington, 1963.

Nicholl, H. F. "The Life and Work of John Toland." Ph.D. dissertation, Trinity College, Dublin, 1962.

Nott, John William. "The Artisan as Agitator: Richard Carlile, 1816-1843." Ph.D. dissertation, The University of Wisconsin, 1970.

Rajannan, Busnagi, "American Freethinkers and South Indian Free Thought, 1875-1947." Ph.D. dissertation, University of Kansas, 1978.

Royle, Edward. "George Jacob Holyoake and the Secularist Movement in Britain, 1841-1861." Ph.D. dissertation, Christ College, University of Cambridge, 1968. Part of this was published as reference (35).

Smith, F. Barry. "Religion and Freethought in Melbourne, 1870-90." M.A. thesis, University of Melbourne, 1960.

Torrey, Norman L. "The English Critical Deists." Ph.D. dissertation, Harvard University, 1926. Part was published as reference (118).

WORKS IN PROGRESS

Berman, David. *The Repression and Emergence of Atheism in Britain.*

Levy, Leonard W. *Treason Against God: A History of the Offense of Blasphemy.* New York: Schocken, to be published in 1981.

Lloyd-Jones, Michael. (a biography of Joseph McCabe, untitled.)

Page, Martin R. (a biography of J. M. Robertson, untitled.)

Stein, Gordon. (a history of blasphemy prosecutions, untitled.)

Wiener, Joel H. *The Infidel Challenge: A Biography of Richard Carlile.*

ADDITIONAL NOTE: A biography of G. W. Foote, entitled *The Life and Times of G. W. Foote*, was completed in the early 1950s by Herbert Cutner. The manuscript was never published.

ADDENDA

The following books and articles were either published after the numbering had already been given to the section in which they would have appeared, or else they were deemed important enough to include after their section had already been completed and numbered.

A1. Allen, Grant. *The Evolution of the Idea of God*. London: Grant Richards, 1897. A popular work that went through many editions. It could best be called "anthropological."

A2. Bury, John Bagnell. *History of Freedom of Thought*. London: Williams and Norgate, 1913. A well-written and popular book that does not really give a history of *freethought*, but rather a history of *freedom of thought*.

A3. Reade, William Winwood. *The Martyrdom of Man*. London: Trübner and Company, 1872. An influential book that went through many editions on both sides of the Atlantic.

A4. Stein, Gordon. *An Anthology of Atheism and Rationalism*. Buffalo, N.Y.: Prometheus Books, 1980. Reprints, with commentaries and biographies, thirty of the best pieces of British and American freethought writing. Many authors are those mentioned in this book.

A5. Neuburg, Victor E. "The Reading of the Victorian Freethinkers." *The Library* 28 (1973): 191-214. Important bibliographical review.

A6. Bicknell, John W. "The Unbelievers." In *Victorian Prose*. New York: Modern Language Association of America, 1973, David J. DeLaura, ed. pp. 470-495. Important and accurate article on the bibliography of Victorian freethought in England.

A7. *Australian Rationalist Quarterly, The*. A new freethought magazine, first published with the issue of Jan./Feb./March 1980, at Melbourne by the Rationalist Society of Australia. Editors are D. L. Humphries, J. T. Dunn, and P. Crowther.

A8. Grean, Stanley. Shaftesbury's *Philosophy of Religion and Ethics: A Study in Enthusiasm*. Athens, Ohio: Ohio University Press, 1967.

GLOSSARY OF TERMS

Agnosticism The belief that holds that the ultimate cause (God), and the essential nature of things are, by their very nature, unknown and unknowable. The agnostic would say that knowledge about God is impossible for mankind to ever obtain. The term is often misused to refer to people who haven't made up their minds as to whether God exists or not.

Atheism The lack of belief in, or disbelief in, the existence of God. The denial of God's existence, while a form of atheism, is not necessary for an atheistic outlook. Many would say that agnosticism is merely a subclass of atheism.

Deism The belief (based solely upon reason) that God was the creator of the universe, but that He abandoned it and assumed no control over it after setting it in motion. The deist would therefore say that God now has no control over human life, no influence over natural phenomena, and that he gave men no revelation. A deist, therefore, would believe in God's existence, but would not believe in prayer, the Bible, Jesus as Messiah, or in the truth of any organized religion.

Freethinker One who has rejected authority and dogma, especially in his religious thinking, in favor of rational inquiry.

Freethought Thought that is free of the dogmatic assumptions of religion, and that seeks the answers to all questions through rational inquiry. The movement that held that thought should be free of these assumptions, naturally opposed the claims to truth and authority that organized religion put forth.

Humanism The viewpoint that man can produce his own happiness on earth, and that he requires no support from supernatural sources in order to achieve this happiness. It holds that human beings, using their intelligence and cooperation, can bring peace, happiness and beauty to all upon the earth.

Infidel One who has no belief in organized religion. It is sometimes applied to those who do not believe in a particular religion, such as Christianity.

Positivism A school of thought, formulated by Auguste Comte, that attempted to form a religion retaining the ceremonies and trappings of Christianity, but doing away with the supernatural elements of it. Positivism has been described as "Catholicism minus Christianity."

Rationalism (as applied to religious controversy) The doctrine that human reason, unaided by divine revelation, is an adequate guide (or the sole guide) to all attainable religious truth.

Secularism The belief that public education and other matters of civil policy and government should be conducted without the introduction of a religious element. Secularism feels that there may be a place for organized religion, but that that place is not within anything done or supported, by the government of a country.

AUTHOR AND PERSON INDEX

Adams, Robert Chamblett, 138, 140, 141
Adler, Felix, 81
Aldred, Guy, 26, 27, 39, 94
Aldridge, A. O., 6, 14, 24, 39
Alldritt, Charles, 126
Allen, Grant, 165
Amberley, Viscount (John Russell), 76, 84, 106
Anaimuthu, V., 149, 152
Annet, Peter, 8-9, 13, 14, 18, 21, 25, 27, 41, 44
Ares, Richard, 139, 140
Armstrong, R. A., 86
Arnold, Matthew, 79, 95
Arnstein, Walter, 56, 85
Aveling, Edward B., 70, 71-72, 85, 91, 103
Ayearst, M., 139, 140

Bacon, R., 95
Baker, William, 34, 48
Ball, William Platt, 88
Ballance, John, 124, 125, 126
Ballard, Thomas, 8, 14
Barker, Ambrose, xviii, 32, 40, 158
Barker, John Thomas, 35, 40
Barker, Joseph, 35, 38, 40, 46, 53, 54, 65, 76
Bayle, Pierre, 67
Baylen, Joseph, 51
Beadnell, C. M., 111
Beadnell, M., 135
Beauchamp, Philip. See Bentham, Jeremy

Bedford, R. D., 161
Benn, Alfred W., xvi, xvii
Bennett, D. M., 141, 144, 145
Bennett, H. Scott, 134
Bentham, Jeremy [pseud. Philip Beauchamp], 36, 40
Berkeley, George, 100
Berman, David, 7, 15, 18, 21, 40, 163
Bernard, J. -P., 139, 140
Besant, Annie, xv, xix, xxii, 46, 53, 55, 56-58, 67, 75, 76, 77, 78, 79, 81, 84, 85-86, 93, 103, 144, 145, 158
Besant, Frank, 56
Besant, Walter, 56
Besterman, Theodore, xvi, xvii, 58, 86
Bharati, S. L., 148, 149
Bhatta, Jayarasi, 143
Bhattacharya, N., 144, 149
Bicknell, John W., 165
Blackham, H. J., 99, 113, 118
Blaszak, Barbara Jean, 161
Blatchford, Robert, 76, 86
Blavatsky, Helena, 58, 86
Blount, Charles, 4, 5, 15, 116
Boaz, Mr., 138
Bolingbroke, Viscount (Henry St. John), 11, 15
Bonante, Ugo, 4, 15
Bonner, Arthur, 78, 103, 104, 107, 114
Bonner, Charles Bradlaugh, xviii, 99, 104, 107, 108, 114
Bonner, Hypatia Bradlaugh, xv, xvii, 78, 79, 92, 94, 99, 103-4, 107, 112, 114

Bradlaugh, Alice, 55, 103
Bradlaugh, Charles, [pseud. Iconoclast],
    xvii, xxii, 15, 31, 32, 35, 38, 46,
    53-56, 57, 59, 61, 65, 67, 70,
    71, 73, 75, 76, 77, 78, 80, 84,
    85, 86-87, 91, 92, 93, 103, 107,
    108, 111, 112, 130, 131, 138,
    144, 158
Brereton, Lloyd, 140
Brett, R. L., 6, 15
Brhaspati, 143
Bridges, John Henry, 84, 112
Brie, Friedrich, xv, xvii
Bright, Charles, 123, 124, 130, 134
Brown, Marshall G., 40
Buckley, George, xvii
Budd, Susan, xiv, xviii, 161
Buies, Arthur, 139, 140
Burke, Edward, 22, 40
Burns, Cecil Delisle, 113
Burrows, Herbert, 113
Burtis, Mary Elizabeth, 83, 87
Bury, John Bagnell, 165
Butler, Joseph, 12, 15

Cadogan, Peter, 113
Campbell, Alexander, 36, 47
Campbell, Archibald, 14, 21, 123
Campbell, Colin B., 161
Campbell, Patrick, 127
Campbell, Theophilia Carlile, 26, 40
Carlile, Eliza Sharples, 45
Carlile, Jane, 41
Carlile, Richard, 16, 24-26, 27, 34,
    38, 40, 41, 42, 45, 46, 48, 49,
    51, 54, 157
Carlyle, Thomas, 95
Carpenter, William, 49
Carrington, A. E., 125, 127
Casie Chetty, M. S., 153
Cassels, Walter Richard, 76, 87
Cattell, Charles C. [pseud. Christopher
    Charles], 74, 80, 87
Chalmers, George, 42
Charavaka, 143
Charles, Christopher. See Cattell,
    Charles C.
Charlton, Peter, 94
Chattopadhyaya, D., 144, 149
Cheetham, James, 42
Cherbury, Lord (Edward Herbert), 3, 5,
    12, 16

Chilton, William, 28, 33, 34, 47
Chubb, Thomas, 10, 15
Clark, Ronald W., 107, 114
Clifford, W. K., 112
Clodd, Edward, 79, 104, 111, 114
Cobbett, William, 24
Cohen, Chapman, 24, 42, 62, 77, 89,
    93, 99, 100-101, 108, 109, 111,
    113, 114-15
Coit, Stanton, 81, 83, 113
Cole, G. D. H., 26, 36, 42, 112
Coleridge, Justice J., 61
Collins, Anthony, xvi, xxii, 6-8, 15, 16,
    19
Collins, William Whitehouse, 124, 125,
    126, 131, 133, 134
Collis, David, xv, xviii, 89, 99
Comte, Auguste, 83, 168
Congreve, Richard, 84
Conway, Moncure D., 24, 42, 82-83,
    87, 113, 144, 149, 157
Cook, E. V., 141
Cook, W. Glanville, 133
Cooper, Anthony Ashley. See Shaftes-
    bury, Third Earl of
Cooper, Robert, 32-33, 38, 42, 45
Cooper, Thomas, 35, 86
Copernicus, N., 3
Corina, F. J., 99, 108, 112, 116
Course, J. R., 161
Cousins, B. D., 39
Cox, G. W., 96
Crawshay-Williams, Rupert, 107, 115
Crowther, P., 165
Cudworth, Ralph, 4, 15
Curll, Edmund, 10, 15, 16
Curzon, Virginia. See Hawton, Hector
Cutner, Herbert, xviii, 26, 42, 62, 94,
    99, 109, 113, 115, 163

Daniel, S. H., 161
Darlington, C. D., 111
D'Avoine, C. L., 147, 151
D'Holbach, Baron P. H. T. See Hol-
    bach, P. H. T. Baron D'
DeLaura, David J., 165
de Mandeville, Bernard. See Man-
    deville, Bernard de
Denton, William, 130
d'Entremont, John, 83, 87
de Remuset, Charles F., 4, 15
Des Maizeux, Pierre, 5, 16

DesPerriers, Bonnaventure, 3, 16
Dharmalingam, A. M., 149
Dickinson, H. T., 11, 16
dos Santos, Emanuel, 154, 155
Dubuisson, Gabriel, 141
Dunn, J. T., 165

Eaton, Daniel Isaac, 47
Ebury, Len, 99, 108
Edamaruku, Sanal, 147, 150
Edwards, Samuel, 24, 42
Eeramani, K., 150
Eisen, Sidney, 162
Elgin, V. G., 162
Eliot, George, 83
Ellis, J. Spencer, 96, 138, 141
Emerson, R. W., 95
Emerson, Roger Lee, 162
Ernest, G., 64, 90
Evison, Joseph [pseud. Ivo], 124, 126

Fabricius, John Albert, xvi, xviii
Farrah, Frederick, 39, 78
Feinberg, Joel, 12, 16
Finlay, T., 33, 37
Flaws, G. G., 64, 87
Foner, Philip, 24, 42
Foote, G. W., xv, xviii, 55, 61-62, 64,
    65, 72, 73, 75, 77, 80, 84, 87-
    89, 91, 93, 94, 96, 99, 101, 111,
    113, 131, 163
Forder, Robert, 75, 78, 79, 89
Fowler, Thomas, 6, 16
Fox, W. J., 82
Francis, Mark, 162
Francis, Samuel, 41
Franklin, Benjamin, 22
Freret, N., 41

Gandhi, M., 146
Gauvin, Marshall, 92, 138, 159
Gawlick, Günter, 8, 10, 13, 16
Gay, Peter, 13, 16
Ghosh, S., 149
Gibbon, Edward, 12, 21, 42, 95
Gillett, Charles Ripley, xvi, xviii
Gilmour, J. P., 60, 81, 89, 108, 111,
    116
Gilmour, J. S. L., 5, 16, 27, 43, 109,
    116, 157
Gimbel, Richard, xvi, xviii
Gimson, Josiah, 108

Gimson, Sydney Ansell, 108
Glidon, Charles, 4
Goldberg, Isaac, 103, 116
Gora. See Rao, Gopraju Ramachandra
Gorham, Charles Turner, 107, 112,
    116
Goss, C. W. F., xv, xviii, 66
Gossman, Norbert J., 51
Gott, John William, 69, 77, 80, 89,
    97-98, 100
Gottschalk, Herbert, 107, 116
Gould, F. J., xvii, xviii, 24, 43, 79, 80,
    83, 84, 89-90, 93, 99, 105, 112
Grange, John, 69, 80, 97
Grant, Brewin, 65, 71, 90, 97
Grean, Stanley, 165
Greene, T. M., 162
Griffin, Janet, 162
Griffith-Jones, George [pseud. Lara],
    63, 90, 92
Grote, George, 36, 40
Grugel, Lee, xv, xviii, 66, 162
Güttler, Karl, 4, 16

Haeckel, Ernest, 66, 79, 90
Haldane, J. B. S., 112
Haldeman-Julius, E., xiv, 66, 67, 101-
    103
Hammon, William [pseud.], 21, 50
Hanlon, James O., 125, 126
Harrison, A. J., 86
Harrison, Frederic, 84
Harrison, John F. C., 36, 43
Haslam, C. J., 31, 43
Hastings, John, 94
Haviland, E. Cyril, 130, 134
Hawke, David Freeman, 24, 43
Hawton, Hector [pseud. Virginia
    Curzon], 92, 99, 105-106, 111,
    112, 116
Hayward, F. H., 83, 90
Heaford, William, 70, 90
Heath, A. E., 111
Herbert, Edward. See Cherbury, Lord
Herrick, Jim, 89, 99, 110
Hetherington, Henry, 31-32, 39, 42,
    43, 48, 74
Hetherington, Rev. W., 100, 115
Heywood, Abel, 39, 78
Hibbert, Julian, 27, 34, 43, 116
Higgins, Godfrey, 27-28, 44
Hithersay, R. B., 64, 90

Hobbes, Thomas, 4, 17, 95
Hobson, J. A., 113
Holbach, P. H. T. Baron D', 25, 34, 38, 41, 43, 44
Holyoake, Austin, 31, 38, 59, 66, 73-74, 90
Holyoake, George J., xv, xvii, xviii, xix, 25, 27, 29-31, 32, 33, 34, 37, 38, 44, 46, 47, 48, 53, 54, 59, 61, 63, 65-66, 71, 73, 74, 77, 79, 84, 90-91, 94, 96, 102, 104, 111, 157, 158
Hone, William, 24
Hopkins, Kenneth, 107, 116
Hudon, Théophile, 139, 140
Huet, M., 14, 21
Hume, David, 12
Humphries, D. L., 165
Huxley, Thomas, 79
Hyde, Karl, 89

Iconoclast. See Bradlaugh, Charles
Ilive, Jacob, xxii
Ingersoll, Robert G., xvi, xxi, 112, 144, 145
Ivo. See Evison, Joseph

Jacob, T. Evan, 64, 91
Jayagopal, 147, 148, 151
Jesus, 18, 68, 104, 109
Joad, C. E. M., 115
John P. Y., M. D. See Lecount, Peter
Johnson, W. H., 15, 45, 63, 92
Johsi, T. L. S., 151
Jones, E. M., 162
Jones, Lloyd, 36, 45
Joseph, M. C., 152

Kaczkowski, Conrad J., 162
Kafi Viswanatham, V., 150
Kapp, Yvonne, 72, 91
Karve, R. D., 147, 151
Kaye, F. B., 12, 157
Kelly, John E., 130, 135
Kemp, H. A., 61, 73, 75
Kesakambalin, Ajita, 143
Klimkeit, H-J, 148, 150
Knowlton, Charles, 57, 59, 91
Kottich, R. G., 162
Kovoor, Abraham T., 153, 155
Krantz, Charles L., 162
Kurtz, Paul, 148, 150

Lacy, George, 130, 134
Langley, J. S., 132, 133, 134
Lanthenas, François, 22
Lantoine, A., 5, 17
Lara. See Griffith-Jones, George
Laski, Harold J., 111
Lavanam, 148, 149, 150, 151
Lavanam, Hemalata, 150
Law, Edward, 71
Law, Harriet, 60, 71, 73, 77, 91, 94, 96
Lechler, G. V., xv, xviii
Lecount, Peter [pseud. John P. Y., M. D.], 39, 45
Lee, W. T., 62, 89
Leland, John, 12, 17
Leon, Herbert S., 111
Leslie, Charles, 12, 17
Levy, Irving, 158
Levy, Leonard W., 163
Lewes, G. H., 83
Lindsey, Charles, 139, 140
Linton, W. J., 24, 35, 45
Lloyd-Jones, Michael, 103, 163
Locke, John, 5, 17
Lowery, Robert, 36
Luke, Hugh J., Jr., 162

McCabe, Joseph, xv, xvi, xix, 66-67, 79, 80, 83, 90, 92, 99, 101-3, 104, 112, 113, 115, 116-17, 125, 132, 133, 134
McCall, Colin, 89
McCann, James, 62, 88
McGee, John Edwin, xiii, xix, 84, 92
Machiavelli, N., 95
McIlroy, William, 89, 99
Mackay, Charles R., 63, 92
Macknight, Thomas, 11, 17
McLaren, A. D., 88
Macy, Chris, 99, 111
Madison, James, 23
Magee, W. C. (Bishop of Peterborough), 86
Mallet, David, 14, 21
Mandeville, Bernard de, 11-12, 17, 95
Mann, Walter, 113
Maresse-Smith, Edgar, 154
Marke, Ron, 134
Marsh, Emilie Holyoake, xviii
Martin, Emma, 36, 38, 46
Marx, Eleanor, 72

Marx, Karl, 72
Maryat, Miss, 56
Mauthner, Fritz, xiv, xv, xix
Mayo, Thomas F., 162
Merrill, Walter, 11, 17
Micklewright, F. M. Amphlett, 56, 92
Middleton, Conyers, 11, 17
Mill, John Stewart, 83, 95, 106
Mittal, Kewal K., 144, 150
Moore, Charles H., 151
Morey, Chris, 89
Morgan, Thomas, 10, 17
Morley, John, 83
Morrell, Robert W., 109
Mosheim, J. L., 5, 17
Moss, Arthur B., 65, 69-70, 71, 76,
    85, 93, 99
Mouat, Kit, 89, 99, 110, 117
Mudaliar, Murugesa, 145, 151
Muirden, Bruce, 133
Murphy, J. M., 162
Mythri, 150, 155

Narain, Chitra, 147
Narain, Narsingh, 147
Naylor, B. S., 129, 134
Nelson, Walter D., 162
Nethercot, Arthur, xv, xix, 56, 93
Neuburg, Victor E., 75, 93, 165
Nicholl, H. F., 162
Nicholson, William, 21, 41, 46
Noorthouck, John, 9, 14, 21
Nott, John William, 162

O'Dowd, Bernard, 124, 126
O'Higgins, James, 7, 17-18
Olcott, Henry Steel, 144, 145
Oldys, Francis [pseud.] 42
Oliver, Henry, 130, 133
Orr, John, xv, xix
Owen, Robert, xvi, xix, 28, 30, 32, 35,
    38, 47, 74, 158
Owen, Robert Dale, 36, 38, 75, 93

Pack, Ernest, 69, 94
Page, Martin, 69, 94, 163
Paine, Thomas, xvi, 21, 22-24, 38, 39,
    42, 47, 48, 50, 82, 95, 112, 129,
    141, 144, 158
Palmer, Elihu, 24, 25, 34, 38, 41, 47
Paranjpye, R. P., 147
Parvish, Samuel, xxii

Paterson, Thomas, 33, 34, 37, 47, 48
Pearce, Harry Hastings, 29, 48, 125,
    126, 158
Periyar. See Ramaswami, E. V.
Petrie, Charles, A., 11, 18
Pfaff, Christoph M., 13, 18
Phanu, Y., 151
Phatak, N. R., 151
Phelips, Vivian (Philip Vivian), 109, 118
Piddington, Alfred, 137
Pike, Royston, 104, 118
Place, Francis, 36, 158
Podmore, Frank, 36, 48
Pollard, Sidney, 36, 48
Pooley, Samuel, 37
Pooley, Thomas, 31
Powys, Llewelyn, 107, 118
Pradhan, G. P., 151
Pringle, Alan, 138, 141
Pritchard, George, 14
Protonius. See Whyte, Adam Gowans
Pusey, Dr., 57

Racine, Claude, 139, 141
Radde, C. O., 64, 94
Rahakrishnan, S., 144, 151
Rajannan, B., 145, 148, 151, 163
Ramamurti, M. V., 152
Ramanathan, S., 147
Ramaswami, Erode V. [pseud. Periyar],
    145-46, 147, 151, 152
Ramsey, W. J., 61, 73, 75, 94
Rand, Benjamin, 6, 18
Rao, G. S., 151
Rao, Goparaju Ramachandra [pseud.
    Gora], 146-47, 149-50
Ratcliffe, S. K., xvii, xx, 83, 113
Reade, William Winwood, 116, 165
Reddalls, George, 71, 77, 96
Redwood, John, xvii, xx, 5, 18
Renan, Ernest, 79
Reynolds, David, 89
Rickard, Alan, 133
Rickman, Thomas Clio, 23, 49
Ridley, F. A., 89, 99, 109, 111, 113,
    118
Riepe, Dale, 144, 151
Risser, J. A., 138
Ritchie-Calder, Lord, 111
Roalfe, Matilda, 33-34, 37, 38, 48, 49
Robertson, Archibald (Robert Arch),
    94, 113

Robertson, John M., xiii, xiv, xv, xviii,
     xx, xxi, 46, 56, 62, 67-69, 77, 79,
     81, 83, 86, 89, 93, 94-95, 99,
     103, 104, 112, 113, 118
Robertson, Susan Nancy, 139
Robinson, M., 33
Rose, Edward B., 154
Rosetti, Robert Henry, 101, 109, 111
Ross, Robert Samuel, 132, 134
Ross, William Stewart [pseud. Saladin],
     53, 55, 59, 60, 62-64, 77, 78,
     84, 87, 92, 95-96
Roux, Edward, 154, 155
Roux, Winifred, 154, 155
Roy, M. N., 147, 151
Royle, Edward, xiv, xxi, 51, 56, 66,
     96, 163
Ruskin, B., 95
Russell, Bertrand, 76, 106-7, 111,
     118-19
Russell, John. See Amberley, Viscount
Ryall, Maltus Q., 37

St. John, Henry. See Bolingbroke,
     Viscount
Saladin. See Ross, William Stewart
Salt, Henry Stephens, 107-8, 119
Salt, John, 36, 48
Salter, William S., 81
Sanderson, Walter, 34
Sayous, Edward, xv, xxi
Schlegel, Dorothy, 6, 18
Scott, Thomas, 57, 58, 78, 86, 96
Sexton, George, 98
Shaftesbury, Third Earl of (Anthony
     Ashley Cooper), 6, 11, 18, 95
Shah, A. B., 147, 151
Shakespeare, William, 62
Shastri, D. B., 144, 151-52
Shaw, George Bernard, 93
Shepard, Leslie, 28
Sherlock, Thomas, 9, 18
Sherwin, William T., 24, 49
Sichel, Walter, 11, 18
Simon, Walter M., 84, 96
Sinnott, Nigel, 71, 89, 97, 99, 132,
     133, 134
Skinner, E., 130, 134
Smallfield, George, 44
Smith, Adolphe Headingly, 56, 97
Smith, F. Barry, 132, 135, 163

Smith, Henry, 3, 18
Smoker, Barbara, 99, 110, 112
Snell, Lord, 111
Southwell, Charles, 28-29, 30, 37, 38,
     39, 45, 46, 48, 49, 53, 71, 73,
     123, 125
Spencer, Herbert, 79, 95
Spiller, Gustav, xvii, xxi, 83
Spinoza, Benedict, 4, 18, 95
Stackhouse, John, 8, 14
Standring, George, 29, 49, 70, 75-76,
     79, 97
Standring, Sam, 76
Stein, Gordon, xvi, xxi, 40, 163, 165
Stephans, Hildegard, xxi
Stephen, Leslie, xvii, xxi, 95
Stout, Robert, 123, 124, 125, 159
Suryanayana, A., 147, 152
Swinton, W. E., 113
Symes, Joseph, 70-71, 92, 97, 130,
     131-32

Tarkunde, V. M., 151
Taylor, G. H., xiv, xxi, 101, 109, 119
Taylor, Joseph, 96
Taylor, Robert, 26-27, 38, 45, 49, 50,
     51, 157
Taylor, W., 130, 133
Thompson, Clifford, 12, 18
Thomson, James [pseud. B. V.], 54, 97
Thorschmid, Urban, G., xvi, xxi, 6, 10
Thurtle, Ernest, 111
Tindal, Matthew, xvi, xxii, 9-10, 18
Toland, John, xvi, xxii, 5, 6, 18
Torrey, Norman L., 7, 18, 163
Tribe, David, xiv, xv, xxii, 56, 89, 99,
     108, 112, 133, 134
Trinius, J. A., xvi, xxii
Trower, J., 125, 126
Truelove, Edward, xv, xxii, 45, 57,
     74-75, 97
Tucci, Giuseppe, 144, 152
Turner, Jill, 152
Turner, Matthew, 21, 41, 50
Twynam, Ella, 5, 9, 19
Tyerman, John, 129, 134, 135

Vale, Gilbert, 24, 50
Vance, Edith, 76, 98
Van der Wyde, William, 24, 50
Venugopal, B., 152

Vidler, William, 82
Villey, P., 5, 19
Volney, Count (Constantine Chassboef), 34, 50
Voltaire, (F. M. Arouet de), 7, 25, 38, 41
Voysey, Charles, 57

Waddell, W. A., 138
Wakefield, A. B., 98
Walker, Edwin C., 83, 98
Walker, Thomas, 130, 132, 135, 154, 155
Wallas, Graham, 36, 50, 111
Walter, Nicholas, 99, 110, 111, 118
Ward, Percy, 80, 101
Waring, E. Graham, 13, 19
Watson, James, 27, 31, 34-35, 37, 73, 74
Watson, Richard, 23, 50
Watts, Charles, xiv, xxii, 15, 53, 54, 57, 58, 59-60, 63, 72, 74, 76, 77, 78, 79, 81, 84, 85, 86, 87, 90, 93, 96, 98, 137, 138, 141
Watts, Charles A., 60, 77, 78, 84, 92, 99, 105, 111, 119
Watts, Fred C. C., 92, 99, 105, 111
Watts, John, 38, 53, 54, 59, 72-73, 76, 98
Welles, G. [pseud. Geoffrey West], 98

Wesley, J., 12
West, Geoffrey. See Welles, G.
Whale, George, 111
Wheeler, Joseph Mazzini, xvi, xxiii, 64-65, 77, 88, 89, 93, 98
Whiston, William, 10
White, E. M., 83, 90
Whitefield, George, 12
Whitehead, George, 113
Whittle, Mr., 61
Whyte, Adam Gowans [pseud. Protonius], xvii, xxiii, 79, 99, 104, 105, 112, 119
Wickwar, W. H., 26, 51
Wiener, Joel H., 27, 51, 163
Wilke, Agnes Rollo, 70, 93
Williams, David, 13
Williams, Gertrude, 98
Williamson, Audrey, 24, 51
Willis, A. D., 125, 126
Wimalaratne, Susil, 155
Winchester, Elhanan, 82
Wing, Joseph, 130, 134, 135
Woffendale, Z. B., 62, 88
Wollaston, William, 12, 19
Wollstonecraft, M., 95
Wood, Alan, 107, 119
Woolston, Thomas, 6, 8, 13, 19
Wootton, Barbara, 111

TITLE INDEX

Titles of books are in roman. Titles of periodicals are in italics. Titles of articles are in quotation marks.

Abstract of the Life of the Author, The [Toland], 5, 14
"Adam Gowans Whyte: In Tribute," 118
Address to the Men of Science, An, 25, 40, 41
Adelaide Secular and Free Discussion Society's Review, The, 130, 133
Advantages and Disadvantages of Religion, The, 35, 47
Age of Atheism, The, 147, 148
Age of Reason, The, 21, 22, 23, 24, 47, 138, 141, 144
Agnostic, The, 77, 84
Agnostic Annual, 77, 84, 104
Agnostic Journal, The, 63, 77, 84, 96
Agnostic Journal and Secular Review, The, 63, 77, 84, 96
Almost an Autobiography, 100, 114
American Freethinkers and South Indian Free Thought, 1875-1947, 163
Am I an Atheist or an Agnostic?, 119
Anacalypsis, 28, 44
Analogy of Religion . . . , 12, 15
Analysis of Religious Belief, An, 76, 84, 106
Analysis of the Influence of Natural Religion . . . , 36, 40
"Ancient Indian Atheistic Movements," 149
Anima Mundi, 4, 15
Annie Besant: An Autobiography, 58, 85

Answer to Dr. Priestley's Letters to a Philosophical Unbeliever, 21, 50
Answer to the Question, How Did You Become an Infidel, An, 40
Anthology of Atheism and Rationalism, An, 165
"Anthony Collins and the Question of Atheism in the Early Part of the Eighteenth Century," 7, 15
Anthony Collins—The Man and His Works, 7, 17
Anticlericalism Among the English Deists, 162
"Anti-Cléricalisme, Cléricalisme et sens de l'église," 140
"Anti-Cléricalisme dans le Roman Québecois, L', 139, 141
Antient Religion of the Gentiles . . . , The, 4, 16
Anti-religiöse Bewegungen im modern Südindien, 148, 150
Apology for Atheism, An, 29, 49
Apology for the Bible, 23, 50
Apology for the Life of Mohammed, An, 28, 44
Arivu Vazhi, 148, 149
Arrows of Freethought, 61, 87
Artisan as Agitator: Richard Carlile, 1816-1843, 162
Astronomico-Theological Lectures, 50
Atheism in the English Renaissance, xvii
Atheismus und seine Geschichte im Abendland, Der, xiv, xix
Atheist, The, 146, 149, 153
Atheist at Church, An, 76, 97
Atheistic Platform, The, 57, 85

Atheist Journal, The, 132, 133
"Atheist Leader Periyar, EVR," 149
Atheist With Gandhi, An, 146, 149
Auckland Examiner, The, 39, 123
Auguste Comte, 83, 89
Australasian Secular Association
    Lyceum Tutor, The, 124, 126
Australian Atheist, The, 132, 134
Australian Humanist, The, 132, 133
Australian Rationalist, The, 132, 133
Australian Rationalist Quarterly, The,
    165
Autobiographical Sketches (Besant),
    58, 85
Autobiography: Memories and
    Experiences, 82, 87
Autobiography of Bertrand Russell,
    The, 107, 118
Autobiography of Charles Bradlaugh,
    56
Autobiography of Lord Herbert of
    Cherbury, The, 16
Avenir, L', 139, 140

Balak Secundus, 63, 90, 92
Bankruptcy of Religion, The, 102, 116
Baptism, A Pagan Rite, 37, 46
Battle of the Press as Told in the Story
    of Richard Carlile, The, 26, 40
"Beginning and End of the 'Dunedin
    Freethought Association', The,"
    126
Begonne, Godmen!, 153, 155
Bertrand Russell: A Life, 107, 116
Bertrand Russell the Passionate
    Sceptic, 107, 119
Bible and Evolution, 70, 93
Bible Handbook, The, 61, 88
Bible Heroes, 61, 88
Bible: Its Worth, Origin and How to
    Read It, The, 35, 40
Bible No Revelation, The, 37, 46
Bible Romances, 61, 88
Bible Studies, 64, 98
Bible: What It Is, The, 86
Bibliography of Annie Besant, A, xvi,
    xvii, 58
Bibliography of Robert Owen, the
    Socialist, 1771-1858, xix, 36
Biblioteca Antonii Collins Arm., 14
Biographical Dictionary of Ancient,

Medieval and Modern Freethinkers,
    103, 117
Biographical Dictionary of Freethinkers
    of All Ages and Nations, A., xvi,
    xxiii, 64
Biographical Dictionary of Modern
    British Radicals, The, 27
Biographical Dictionary of Modern
    Rationalists, xvi, xix, 102
Biographical Sketch of Arthur B. Moss,
    76, 90, 97
Biography of Charles Bradlaugh, The, 97
Bolingbroke [Dickinson], 16
Bolingbroke [Petrie], 18
Bolingbroke and His Times, 18
Book of "At Random," The, 63, 95
Both Sides, 137, 140
Bradlaugh and Ingersoll, 101, 115
Bradlaugh Case, The, 56, 85
Brhaspati Sutra, 143
Brief Sketch of the Life and Writings of
    the Baron D'Holbach, A, 27, 43
British Humanist Movement, 1860-
    1966, The, 161
British Rational Secularism: Unbelief
    from Bradlaugh to the Mid-Twentieth
    Century, 162
British Secular Almanac, The, 59, 77,
    87
British Secularism, 1850-85, 162
British Secularist Movement: A Study in
    Militant Dissent, The, 162
Building of the Bible, The, 83, 89
Bygones Worth Remembering, 66, 90

Candid History of the Jesuits, A, 102,
    117
Can the Design Argument Be
    Vindicated?, 131, 133
Catalogue of Books from the Library of
    the Late Edward Truelove, xv, xxii
Catalogue of the Library of G. W. Foote,
    xviii
Catalogue of the Library of J. M.
    Robertson, xx
Catalogue of the Library of the Late
    Charles Bradlaugh, xv, xvii
Catalogue of the Library of the Ration-
    alist Press Association, xv, xx
Catalogues 1-10 [of David Collis], xviii
Celtic Druids, The, 28, 44

Ceylon Rationalist Ambassador, The,
    153, 155
Characteristics of Men, Manners,
    Opinions, Times, 6, 11, 18
"Charles Blount (1654-93), Deism and
    English Free Thought," 18
Charles Blount, 8th Lord Mountjoy, 162
Charles Blount: Libertinismo e Deismo
    ne Seicento Inglese, 15
Charles Bradlaugh, 68, 94
Charles Bradlaugh: A Record of His Life
    and Work, xv, 56, 103
"Charles Bradlaugh: Giant of Free-
    thought," 92
"Charles Bradlaugh (1833-1891)
    Breaker and Builder," 93
"Charles Southwell," 49
"Charles Southwell in Australia and
    N.Z.," 29, 48
"Charles Watts," 89, 91
Charvaka, 148, 149
Chats With Pioneers of Modern
    Thought, 83, 89
Cheap Salvation, 32, 43
Christ and Krishna, 67, 95
Christian Doctrine of Hell, 64, 98
Christian Doctrine of Man's Depravity
    Refuted, The, 73, 98
Christian Hell, The, 103, 114
Christianity and Civilization, 107, 116
Christianity and Evolution, 70, 93
Christianity and Mythology, 68, 79, 95
Christianity and Secularism [Holyoake
    and Grant], 90
Christianity and Secularism: Which Is
    True?, 88
Christianity as Old as the Creation,
    9-10, 18
Christianity Not Mysterious, 5, 18
Christianity Proved Idolatry, 29, 49
Christianity Unveiled, 41
Christianity v. Secularism, 88, 97, 100,
    115
Christianizing the Heathen, 103, 114
Christian Warrior, The, 25, 42
Chronology of British Secularism, A,
    xiv, xxi, 101
Church, The, 25, 42
Church Discipline, 102, 117
Churches and Modern Thought, The,
    109, 118
Church of England Catechism

Examined, The, 36, 40
Church of Rome, The, 131, 133
Church Reform, 41
City of Dreadful Night, The, 54, 97
Common Sense, xvi, 22, 47
Company I Have Kept, 108, 119
Complete Catalogue of the Library of
    Anthony Collins, Esq., Deceased,
    8, 14
Complete Writings of Thomas Paine,
    24, 42
Concise History of Religion, A, 83, 89
Confessions of a Freethinker, 29, 49
Confessions of Joseph Barker . . . , 35,
    40
Contribution of Periyar E. V. R. to the
    Progress of Atheism, 146, 149
Controversy, 106, 116
"Conyers Middleton," 14
Courses of Study, xiv, xx, 68
Creed of an Atheist, The, 72, 85
Crimes of Christianity, 61, 64, 88
Crises in the History of the Papacy,
    102, 117
Critical History of the Celtic Religion,
    14
Crusade for Humanity, A, 84, 92
Cultural Heritage of India, The, 151
Cymbalum Mundi, 3, 16

Damnable Opinions, 107, 117
Daniel the Dreamer, 74, 90
Dark Side of Christianity, 74, 87
"Death of Harriet Law," 88, 98
Debate on Christianity, 60, 98
Debate on the Evidences of Christianity
    [Campbell/Owen], 47
Debates in Theology, 56, 86
Decay of Belief, The, 100, 115
Decay of the Church of Rome, The,
    102, 117
Decline and Fall of the Roman Empire,
    The, 21, 43
Defence of Truth: Lord Herbert of
    Cherbury . . . , 161
Deism: An Anthology, 13, 16
Deism and Natural Religion, 13, 19
Deism Fairly Stated and Fully Vin-
    dicated . . . , 9, 14
"Deismus und Atheismus in der
    Englischen Renaissance," xv, xvii
Déistes Anglais, Les, xv, xxi

Deist or Moral Philosopher, The, 25, 40-41

Delectus Argumentorum et Syllabus Scriptorum . . . , xvi, xviii

Demonology and Devil Lore, 82, 87

Descriptive Bibliography of George Jacob Holyoake, A, xv, xviii, 66

Devil's Chaplain: The Story of Rev. Robert Taylor, M. A., MRCS, (1784-1834), The, 39

Devil's Pulpit, The, 26, 49

"Diary of a Pilgrim," 134

Dictionary of Modern Anti-Superstitionists, 27, 43

Diegesis, The, 26, 50

Discourse Delivered to the Society of Theophilanthropists, 47

Discourse of Freethinking, A, 6, 8, 15, 16

Discourse on the Grounds and Reasons of the Christian Religion, A, 7, 15

Discourses on the Miracles of Our Savior, 8, 19

Discussion on Secularism [Holyoake and Grant], 90

"Dr. Kovoor and His Mission," 155

Does Man Survive Death?, 101, 115

Doubts of Infidels, The, 21, 41, 46

Drams for the Vulgar: A Study of Some Radical Publishers, 162

Dynamics of Religion, The, xv, xx, 68

"E. V. Ramaswami: A Great Revolutionary," 149

"Early Dunedin Freethought," 126

"Early New Zealand Freethought," 127

"Early Rationalist Journals," 126

Echo, The, 123, 126

École Confessionelle et la Dissidence, 139, 140

École Laïque, L', 139, 140

Edinburgh Evening News, 67

Eduard, Lord Herbert von Cherbury, 16

Edward Clodd: A Memoir, 104, 117

"Edward Truelove: Bookseller and Publisher," 93

Eighteenth Century Discussion Concerning the Continuance of Miracles . . . , 162

Eighty Years a Rebel, xv, xix, 103

Eleanor Marx, 72, 91

English Critical Deists, The, 163

English Deism 1670-1755 . . . , 162

English Deism: Its Roots and Its Fruits, xv, xix

English Life of Jesus, The, 78, 96

English Review, The, 89

Entwurff der Theologiae Anti-Deisticae, 13

Eipicurus in England, 1650-1725, 162

Essay Concerning Humane Understanding, 5, 17

Essay on the "Essays and Reviews," An, 35, 40

Essay on the Origin of Free-Masonry, 47

Essays in Freethinking, 101, 115

Ethical Movement in Great Britain, The, xvii, xxi, 83

Ethical Record, The, 112, 113, 115

Ethics of William Wollaston, The, 12, 18

European Positivism in the Nineteenth Century, 84, 96

Every Woman's Book, 25, 41

Evolution of the Idea of God, The, 165

Evolution of the Papacy, 109, 118

Examination of the Passages in the New Testament . . . , 23, 47

Examiner, The, 124, 126

Explorations, 95

Exposure of Freemasonry, An, 25, 41

Fable of the Bees, The, 11-12, 17

Facetiae for Freethinkers, 74, 90

Faith of a Rationalist, The, 119

"Famous Freethinkers I Have Known," 70, 93

Few Hundred Bible Contradictions . . . , A, 32, 39, 45

Few Reasons for Renouncing Christianity . . . , A, 37, 46

Few Self-Contradictions fo the Bible, A, 36, 40

Fight for Right, A, 101, 115

First Convention of Indian Rationalists . . . , The, 150

First Easter Dawn, The, 107, 116

First Five Lives of Annie Besant, The, xv, xix, 56, 58

First Two Books of Philostratus, Concerning the Life of Apolonius Tyaneus, 15

Flowers of Freethought, 61, 88

"Foote of the Freethinker," 94

Footsteps of the Past, 64, 98

Fortnightly Review, The, 83

Frederic Harrison: The Life and Thought of an English Positivist, 162

"Frederick Charles Chater Watts," 114

Freedom, 130, 131, 133

Free Enquirer, The, 13, 16, 41

Free Inquiry into the Miraculous Powers . . . , 11, 17

Free Man's Worship, A, 106, 118

Free Mind, 112, 115

Free Review, The, 89

Freethinker, The, 55, 61, 62, 64, 72, 75, 76, 77, 89, 99, 100, 101, 107, 108, 109, 110, 112, 113, 115

Freethinker and New South Wales Reformer, The, 130, 131, 134

Freethinker's Information for the People, The, 32, 38, 42

Freethinker's Library, The, 102, 117

Freethinker's Text Book, The, 56, 57, 85, 86

Freethought [Australia], 130, 132, 134

Freethought [India], 147, 149

Freethought: Its Rise, Progress and Triumph, xiv, xxii

Freethought and Official Propaganda, 106-7, 118

"Freethought Collection and Its Predecessors, A," 116

"Freethought in Australasia," 134

Freethought in the United States, 23, 36, 40, 157

Freethought Journal, 137, 140

Freethought News, 108, 112, 115

Freethought Readings and Secular Songs, 64, 98

Freethought Vindicated, 129-130, 135

Freydenker Lexicon, xvi, xxii

From Statesman to Philosopher, 11, 17

From the Wesleyan Pulpit to the Secularist Platform, 71, 97, 132

Fruits of Philosophy, The, 55, 57, 59, 70, 91, 103

Full Report of the Trial of Henry Hetherington, A, 43

Funeral Sermon Occasioned by the Death of Richard Carlile, A, 46

Gauntlet, The, 25, 38, 42

Genesis: Its Authorship and Authenticity, 56, 86

"Genesis of Avowed Atheism in Britain, The," 40

"Genesis of I.R.A.," 152

George Jacob Holyoake [Grugel], xv, xviii, 66

George Jacob Holyoake [McCabe], 92

George Jacob Holyoake: An Attitudinal Study, 161

George Jacob Holyoake: A Study in the Progress of Labor . . . , 162

George Jacob Holyoake and the Secularist Movement in Britain, 1841-1861, 163

Geschichte der englischen Deismus, xv, xviii

Glory of Life, 107, 118

Glow-Worm, The, 129, 134

God and His Book, 96

God and My Neighbor, 87, 86

Godless Life the Happiest and Most Useful, A, 72, 85

God of the Jews; or Jehovah Unveiled, The, 41

God's Arrow Against Atheists, 3, 18

God Versus Paterson, 33, 48

Good Sense, 41

Good Without God, 138, 140

"Gora," 152

Gora—An Atheist, 147, 151

Gora Vyakti Vyaktitua, 150

Gospel According to Richard Carlile, The, 25, 64

Gospel of Rationalism, The, 116

Grammar of Freethought, A, 101, 115

Grand Old Book, The, 61, 88

Great Is Diana of the Ephesians, 4, 15

Haldeman-Julius Monthly, The, 117

Half-Hours With the Freethinkers, 5, 8, 10, 15, 27, 29, 35, 37

Has Religion Made Useful Contributions to Civilization?, 107, 119

Henry Hetherington (1792-1849), 32, 40

"Hindu Freethought Union: Pioneer of South Indian Free Thought," 151

Historical Account of the Life and Writings of . . . John Toland, An, 5, 15-16

Historical Jesus, The, 68, 95

History and Character of St. Paul, The, 9, 14

History and Growth of Rationalist Movement, The, 148, 150

History and Growth of Rationalist Movement in Tamil Nadu, 148, 149

History of Co-operation, 65, 91

History of English Rationalism in the Nineteenth Century, The, xvi, xvii

History of English Thought in the Eighteenth Century, xvii, xxi, 95

History of Freedom of Thought, 165

History of Freethought, xiv, xxii, 60

History of Freethought . . . to the Period of the French Revolution, xiii, xx, 68, 69

History of Freethought in England, 64

History of Freethought in the Nineteenth Century, A, xiii, xxi, 68

History of the British Secular Movement, A, xiii, xix

History of the Decline and Fall of the Roman Empire, 21, 43

History of the Great French Revolution, 58, 85

History of the Last Trial by Jury for Atheism in England, The, 31, 44

History of the Leicester Secular Society, The, 80, 83, 89

History of the Man After God's Own Heart, The, 8, 14, 21, 41

History of the Popes, A, 102, 117

History of the Rochedale Pioneers, The, 91

Horae Sabbaticae, 28, 44

Hospitals and Dispensaries not of Christian Origin, 71, 97

Hour on Christianity, An, 107, 118

How Did You Become an Infidel?, 35, 40

Humanism and the Culture of the Professions . . . , 61

"Humanism of Bradlaugh, The," 92

Humanist, The, 92, 104, 112, 116, 118, 154

Humanist in Canada, 138, 140

Humanist Outlook, The, 147, 150

Humanist Post, The, 133

Humanist Revolution, The, 106, 116

Humanity's Gain From Unbelief, 56, 86

Hymn Book for the Use of the Spiritualist and Freethought Propagandist Society, 130, 135

Hypatia Bradlaugh Bonner, 104, 114, 116

I Am an Infidel, Why Are You a Christian?, 29

I Learn, 146, 149

Immortality of the Soul, The, 32-33, 42

Impeachment of the House of Brunswick, 56, 86

Important Examination of the Holy Scriptures, The, 41

Impossibility of Atheism Demonstrated, The, 29, 49

Incroyance au Québec, L', 139, 140

Independent India, 151

Indian Atheism: A Marxist Analysis, 144, 149

Indian Atheist, 147, 150

"Indian Iconoclast," 149

Indian Rationalist, The, 147, 150

"Indian Rationalist Convention, The," 148, 149

Infidel Deathbeds, 61, 88

Infidel Challenge: A Biography of Richard Carlile, The, 163

Infidel's Text Book, The, 32, 33, 42

"Influence de Montaigne sur Charles Blount et sur les Déistes Anglais, L'," 19

Ingersoll in Canada, 138, 141

Ingersoll News, The, 132, 134

In Memoriam, Austin Holyoake, 74, 91

"In Memoriam: Edward Clodd (1840-1930)," 118

In Memoriam Saladin, 64, 94

In Prison for Blasphemy, 73, 94

Inquirer's Text Book, The, 33, 42

Insaan, 148, 150

Institut Canadien: An Essay in Cultural History, The, 141

Institut Canadien de Montréal et L'Affaire
    Guibord, L', 140
Introduction to Secular Humanism,
    110, 117
Introductory Discourse to a Larger
    Work, An, 11, 17
Investigator, The, 29, 32, 38, 45
Is Darwinism Atheistic?, 74, 87
Isis, 25, 45
Is Materialism Bankrupt?, 119
Is Spiritualism Based on Fraud?, 102,
    117
Is There a Devil?, 130, 135
Is There a Hell?, 130, 135

"J. P. Gilmour," 114
James Watson: A Memoir, 35, 45
Jesuits, The, 109, 118
Jesus: Man, God or Myth?, 109, 115
Jesus and Judas, 68, 95
Jesus of Nazareth, 104, 114
Jesus Problem, The, 68, 95
Jewish Life of Christ, The, 64, 89
John Mackinnon Robertson: Free-
    thinker and Radical, 162
John Toland, Freethinker, 5, 19
"John Watts," 91
"John William Gott," 91
Joseph McCabe: Fighter for Free-
    thought, 103, 116
Joseph McCabe Magazine, The, 102,
    117
Joseph Skurrie's Freethought
    Reminiscences, 97
Joseph Symes: The "Flower of
    Atheism," 71, 97, 132
"Joseph Symes and the Australasian
    Secular Association," 135
Judging for Ourselves; Or, Free-Thinking
    the Great Duty of Religion, 9, 14
"Julian Hibbert" [Holyoake], 44
"Julian Hibbert" [Wiener], 51
Julian the Apostate, 109, 118
Justice of the Peace, 91

Kant's Religious Theory and Its Relation
    to English Deism, 162
Key to Culture, The, 117
"Kovoor: Great Fighter Against Super-
    stition," 155
Kudi Arasu, 146, 150

Labour and Law, 56, 78, 86
Labour History, 132
Last Four Lives of Annie Besant, The,
    xix, 58, 93
Last Years of a Great Educationist,
    The, 83, 90
Law Breaking Justified, 34, 49
Law of Population, The, 57, 85
Law Times, The, 91
Lecture of Original Sin . . . , 42
Lectures [Annet], 41
Lectures and Essays [Moss], 70, 93
Lehre van den angeborenen Ideen seit
    Herbet von Cherbury, Die, 162
"Len Ebury," 119
Letter Concerning Enthusiasm, A, 6,
    18
Letter From Thrasybulus to Leucippe,
    A, 41
"Letters From W. E. Gladstone to
    Charles Bradlaugh," 92
Letters to Eugenia, 41
Letters to the Clergy, 31, 43, 61, 89
Letter to Sir Samuel Shepherd, Knt., A,
    41
Letter to the Hon. Thomas Erskine, 47
Letter to the Rev. Dr. S. Chandler . . . ,
    41
Lettres sue le Canada, 139, 140
Leviathan, 4, 17
Liberal, The [Australia], 130, 134
Liberal, The [London], 61, 91
Liberator, The, 71, 92, 131, 134
Library of Reason, The, 32, 39, 45
Life and Character of Henry Hethering-
    ton, 32, 44
Life and Character of Richard Carlile,
    The, 25-26, 30, 44
Life and Letters of George Jacob
    Holyoake, xv, xix, 66, 67
Life and Times of G. W. Foote, The,
    163
Life and Work of John Toland, The, 162
Life of Apollonius of Tyana, 4, 15
Life of Bertrand Russell, The, 107, 114
Life of Charles Bradlaugh, M. P., 55,
    63, 76, 90, 92, 97, 103
Life of David, Or History of the Man
    After God's Own Heart, The, 41
Life of Edward, Lord Herbert of
    Cherbury, 4, 16

Life of Francis Place, The, 36, 50
Life of Henry St. John, Vicount Boling-
    broke, 17
Life of James Thomson ("B. V."), The,
    119
Life of Joseph Barker, The, 35, 40
Life of Mr Woolston, With an Impartial
    Account of His Writings, 8, 14
Life of Paine, The [Linton], 45
Life of Robert Owen, 47
Life of Thomas Paine [Carlile], 25, 41
Life of Thomas Paine . . . , The
    [Cheetham], 42
Life of Thomas Paine [Conway], 24,
    42, 82
Life of Thomas Paine, The [Linton], 45
Life of Thomas Paine, The [Oldys], 42
Life of Thomas Paine, The [Rickman],
    49
Life of Thomas Paine, The [Vale], 50
Life of Thomas Paine [Van der Weyde],
    50
Life Pilgrimage of Moncure Daniel
    Conway, The, 83, 95
Life Story of a Humanist, The, 83, 89
Life, Times and Labours of Robert
    Owen, The, 45
Life, Unpublished Letters . . . of
    Anthony, Earl of Shaftesbury, The,
    6, 18
Linee di una Storia del Materialismo
    Indiano, 144, 152
Lion, The, 25, 26, 38, 45
Literary Guide, The, 77, 78, 104, 105,
    106, 107, 108, 112, 116
Logic of Death, The, 30, 44
Logic of Facts, A, 30, 44
Lokayata: A Study in Ancient Indian
    Materialism, 144, 149
London Investigator, The, 32, 45
Lord Chesterfield's Ears, 41
Lord Herbert de Cherbury, sa Vie et ses
    Oeuvres, 16
Ludicrous Aspects of Christianity, 74,
    90
Lyceum Guide, The, 124, 126

McAlpin Collection of British History
    and Theology, The, xvi, xviii
Mail's Theology, The, 138, 141
Man: Whence and How? Religion: What
    and Why?, 86

Man of Reason: The Life of Thomas
    Paine, 39
Manual of Freemasonry, A, 41
Martyrdom of Man, The, 165
Materialism: Has It Been Exploded?,
    101, 115
Materialism in Indian Thought, 144,
    150
"Materialists, Sceptics and Agnostics,"
    151
Matilda, Agnes and Stella Symes, 97
Meaning of Rationalism, The, 60, 98
Memoirs of the Life and Writings of
    Matthew Tindal . . . , 10, 16
Memoirs of the Life of Thomas Paine
    . . . , 49
Memories, 104, 114
Men Without Gods, 106, 116
Metaphysical Parallels, 73, 98
Militant Atheist, The, 102, 117
Mind and Matter in Modern Science,
    119
Miscellaneous Works [Blount], 4, 15
Mock Trial of Richard Carlile, The, 25
Moderator Between an Infidel and an
    Apostate, The, 8, 19
Modern Humanists, 95
Modern Rationalism, 66, 92
Modern Rationalist, The, 147, 150
Modern Skepticism . . . A Life Story, 40
Moncure Conway: 1832-1907, [Burtis],
    83, 87
Moncure Conway: 1832-1907,
    [d'Entremont], 83, 87
Monkanna Unveiled, 63, 90
Moralist, The, 25, 46
Moral Philosopher, The, 10-11, 17
Moral Physiology, 74, 93
Movement, The, 30, 38, 46
Mr. Woolston's Defence of His
    Discourses, 19
Mrs. Annie Besant [Besterman], 58, 86
Mrs. Annie Besant [Welles], 58, 98
My Path to Atheism, 57, 85
My Pilgrimage to the Wise Men of the
    East, 82, 87
Mysticism and Logic, 107, 119
Myth of the Resurrection, The, 85

Nasthika Margam, 148, 150
Nasthika Mitra, 148, 151

Nasthikatvam Adhivruddhi Charita,
    148, 150
Nastikatvamu, 147, 149
Nasthika Yugam, 148, 151
National Reformer, The, 32, 35, 38,
    46, 53, 54, 57, 58, 59, 62, 63,
    65, 67, 68, 70, 72, 73, 75, 76,
    81, 95, 103
National Secular Society Almanac, 69,
    77, 93
Natural History of Evil, The, 104, 119
Naturalistic Tradition in Indian Thought,
    The, 144, 151
Newgate Monthly Magazine, The, 25,
    46
New Humanist, The, 106, 110, 112,
    113, 118
New Testament, The, 83, 90
New View of Society, A, 35-36, 47
New Zealand Humanist, The, 125, 126
New Zealand Rationalist, The, 125,
    126, 127
New Zealand Rationalist and Humanist,
    125, 126
North American Review, The, 86
Now That the Gods are Dead, 107, 118

"Obituary" [George Standring], 98
"Obituary: Hector Hawton," 114
"Occasional Notes," 91
On the Value of Scepticism, 119
100 Years of Freethought, xiv, xxii,
    108, 112
Oracle of Reason, The, 28-29, 30, 33,
    34, 38, 46
Oracles of Reason, 4, 15
Orthodoxy Unmasked, 130, 135
Our Corner, 58, 77, 93
Outline of Evolutionary Ethics, An, 100,
    115
Outline of Intellectual Rubbish, An, 119

Pagan Christs, 68, 95
Paganism in Christian Festivals, 98
Paine, 43
Pakutharivu, 146, 151
Paley Refuted in His Own Words, 30,
    45
Pamphlets for the People, 101, 115
Papers of Charles Bradlaugh, The, 96

"Paradoxical 'Genius' of J. M.
    Robertson, The," 94
"Parti Rouge and the Clergy, The," 140
"Passage Through India, A," 148, 150
Passionate Pilgrim, The, 58, 98
Pathetic Fallacy, The, 107, 118
Pays, Le, 139, 141
Penalties Upon Opinion, 103, 114
Pennsylvania Magazine, 22, 48
"Periyar and Gora: Outstanding
    Atheists of Modern India," 149
"Periyar E. V. Ramaswami: A Saga of
    Indomitable Courage," 149
Personal Pie, 104, 119
Peter Annet (1693-1769), 9, 19
Philalethean, The, 27, 38, 50
Philosophical Atheism, 71, 97
Philosophical Inquirer, The, 145, 151
"Philosophic Consequences of Ancient
    Indian Atheistic Movements," 149
Philosophic Methodology of John
    Toland, The, 161
Pioneer Humanists, 68, 95
Pioneer Pith, 138, 140
"Pioneers of Freethought in India," 148
Pioneers of Johnson's Court, The, xvii,
    xviii, 79, 83, 104
Plain Man's Plea for Rationalism, A,
    107, 116
Plain View, The, 118
Plea for Atheism, A, 56, 87
Plebeian, The, 34, 48
Political Essays [Bradlaugh], 87
Poor Man's Guardian, The, 31, 35, 48
Positive Atheism, 149
"Positive Atheist," 152
"Positivism in England: The Reception
    of Comte's Doctrines . . . , 162
Powys Brothers: A Biographical
    Appreciation, The, 116
Practical Grammar, 45
Précursor de la Francmaçonnerie: John
    Toland, Un, 5, 17
Present Day, The, 65, 94
President Charles Bradlaugh, M.P., xv,
    xxii, 56, 108, 112
Principles of Nature, 24, 25, 34, 38,
    41, 47
"Problem de l'Anti-Cléricalisme au
    Cananda Française, Le," 140
Progress [London], 61, 77, 94
Progress [Trinidad], 154, 155

Progressive Spiritualist and Freethought Advocate, The, 129, 134
Prompter, The, 25, 38, 48

Queensland Humanist, The, 133
Queen vs. Edward Truelove, The, 97
Quest For the New Moral World, 36, 43
Question, 106, 112, 118
Question: If a Man Die, shall He Live Again?, The, 104, 114

R.P.A. Annual, The, 77, 79, 94, 104, 112
Radical Humanist, The, 147, 151
Radicals, Secularists and Republicans, xiv, xxi
Raison, Le, 139, 141
Rasionalis, Die, 154, 155
Rationalism, 68, 95
"Rationalism in Auckland—Struggles and Achievements," 127
"Rationalism in South Africa," 155
Rationalist, The [Australia], 132, 133, 134
Rationalist, The [Canada], 138, 141
Rationalist, The [N.Z.], 124
Rationalist, The [South Africa], 154, 155
Rationalist Annual, The, 77, 79, 94, 104, 106, 112
Rationalist Encyclopedia, A, xvi, xix
Rationalist News, 132, 134
Rationalists of Maharashtra, 148, 151
"Reading of the Victorian Freethinkers, The," 165
Reason, 147, 151
Rason, Ridicule and Religion, xvii, xx
Reasoner, The, 27, 31, 38, 48, 65, 73
Rebel! A Biography of Tom Paine, 42
"Recollections of a Rationalist," 126
Reflections on the French Revolution, 22, 40
Reflector, The, 154, 155
Reformer, The [London], 68, 77, 94, 103
Reformer, The [Australia], 130, 134
Relations, 140
Religion and Freethought in Melbourne, 1870-90, 163
Religion and Science, 107, 119

Religion and Sex, 101, 115
Religion of Nature Delineated, The, 12, 19
Religion of the Open Mind, The, 104, 119
Religion of the Twentieth Century, The, 67, 79, 92
"Remembering Hector Hawton," 114
Reply to the Bishop of Llandaff, 23, 47
Report of the Trial of Humphrey Boyle . . . , 41
Report of the Trial of Mary-Anne Carlile . . . , 41
Report of the Trial of Mrs. Carlile, 41
Report of the Trial of Mrs. Suzannah Wright . . . , 41
Reports . . . Being the Mock Trials of Richard Carlile . . . , 41
Repression and Emergence of Atheism in Britain, The, 163
Republican, The, 24, 25, 34, 38, 49
Resurrection of Jesus Considered . . . , The, 9, 14
Review of a Controversy Between the Rev. Brewin Grant and G. J. Holyoake, 29, 49
Rib Ticklers, Or Questions for Parsons, 69, 89
"Richard and the Georges," 94
Richard Carlile [Cole], 42
Richard Carlile [Standring], 76, 97
Richard Carlile, Agitator, 26, 39
Riddle of the Universe, The, 66, 79, 90, 102
Rights of Man, 22, 24, 47
Rise and Interpretation of Deism, The, 161
"Robert Forder," 85
Robert G. Ingersoll: A Checklist, xvi, xxi
Robert Owen [Cole], 42
Robert Owen: A Biography, 48
Robert Owen: Prophet of the Poor, 48
Robert Owen and the Owenites in Britain and America, 43
Robert Taylor, 42
Rome in Canada, 140
Roses and Rue, 63, 96
Ross' Magazine, 132, 134
Rouges, Liberalisme, Nationalisme et Anti-Cléricalisme . . . , 139, 140

Ruins of Empires, 34, 38, 50
Russell Remembered, 107, 115

Sacred Anthology, The, 144, 149
Saladin the Little, 64, 91
Sangam, 148, 151
Satan, Witchcraft and the Bible, 64, 98
Satirist, The, 130, 135
Sceptical Essays, 106, 119
Scourge, The, 25, 48
Search for a Soul, A, 131, 133
Second Supplement to the Moderator
    Between an Infidel and an
    Apostate, 19
Secret Doctrine, The, 58, 86
Secular Chronicle, The, 71, 77, 96
Secularism, Skepticism and Atheism,
    91
Secularism: What It Is, 74, 87
Secularist, The [London], 61, 65, 77,
    96
Secularist, The [India], 147, 151
Secularist's Guide, A, 130, 134
Secularist's Manual of Songs and
    Ceremonies, The, 74, 90
Secular Review, 59, 61, 63, 65, 77,
    84, 96
Secular Thought, 60, 96, 137, 138,
    141
Selected Works of Dr. Abraham T.
    Kovoor, 153, 155
Selection of the Political Pamphlets of
    Charles Bradlaugh, A, 56, 87
Selection of the Social and Political
    Pamphlets of Annie Besant, A, 58,
    86
Self-Help by the People: A History of
    Co-operation in Rochdale, 31, 45,
    65
Sepher Toldoth Jeschu, 64, 89
Shaftesbury and Hutcheson, 6, 16
"Shaftesbury and the Deist Manifesto,"
    6, 14
Shaftesbury and the French Deists, 6,
    18
Shaftesbury's Philosophy of Religion
    and Ethics, 165
Shakespeare and Other Literary
    Essays, 87
Sherwin's Political Register, 24, 49

Short and Easy Method With the Deists,
    A, 12, 17
Short and Easy Method With the Saints,
    A, 30, 45
Short History of Christianity, A, 68, 95
Short History of Freethought, A, xxi
Short History of Indian Materialism,
    Sensationalism and Hedonism,
    144, 152
Siècle de la Raison, La, 22, 47
Sinthanayaian, 148, 152
Sixty Years of an Agitator's Life, 66, 91
Sketch and Appreciation of Moncure
    Daniel Conway, A, 83, 98
Sketch of the Life and Character of C.
    Watts, 96
Sketch of the Life and Character of
    Saladin (W. Stewart Ross), 63, 87,
    90
Sketch of the Life of Saladin (W.
    Stewart Ross), 64
Socialist, The, 134
Some Memoirs of the Life and Writings
    of John Toland, 5, 16
"Some Reminiscences of No. 17
    Johnson's Court," 119
"Some Uncollected Authors: XVII:
    Charles Blount," 16
"Some Uncollected Authors: XXVI:
    Julian Hibbert," 43
Source Book of Indian Philosophy,
    144, 151
Sources of the Morality of the Gospels,
    The, 102, 117
South African Humanist, The, 154, 155
Speeches [Bradlaugh], 56, 87
Spiritual Inquirer, The, 130, 135
Spoken Essays, 68, 95
Spur, The, 94
Sri Gora, 147, 150
Stockwhip, The, 130, 135
Stockwhip and Satirist, The, 130, 135
Story of Religious Controversy, The,
    102, 117
Story of South Place, The, xvii, xx, 83
Story of the RPA (1899-1949), xviii,
    xxiii, 79, 104, 105
Story of the Soudan, The, 85
Struggle for Freedom of the Press,
    1819-1832, The, 26, 51
Student's Darwin, The, 72, 85

Studies in Religious Fallacy, 68, 79, 95
Supernatural Religion, 76, 87
Superstition Unveiled, 29, 49
Supplement to the Moderator Between
   an Infidel and an Apostate, A, 19
Syntagma of the Evidences
   of the Christian Religion,
   26, 50
System of Nature, The, 34, 43, 44

Tattvopaplavasimha, 143
Teachings of Experience, Or Lessons
   I Have Learned . . . , 40
Testament of Christian Civilization, The,
   102, 117
Theism or Atheism, 101, 115
Theism or Atheism: Which Is the More
   Reasonable?, 89
Theological Essays [Bradlaugh], 56, 87
Theological Essays and Debates
   [Besant], 58, 86
Theological-Political Treatise, 4, 18
Theological Works [Paine], 24, 47
There Was a War in Heaven, 75, 89
Thinker's Handbook, The, 106, 116
Third Earl of Shaftesbury, The, 6, 15
Thomas Paine (1737-1809), 43
Thomas Paine: A Bibliographical
   Checklist of Common Sense, xii,
   xviii
Thomas Paine: An Investigation, 68, 95
Thomas Paine: His Life, Work and
   Times, 51
Thomas Paine: Pioneer of Two Worlds,
   42
Thomas Paine Collection of Richard
   Gimbel . . . , The, xvi, xxi
Thomas Paine Society Bulletin, 112,
   119
Thoughts of Periyar EVR, 151
Times Literary Supplement, 110
Tirukkuval, 146
Travels in Faith From Tradition to
   Reason, 138, 140
Treason Against God, 163
Trial and Imprisonment of J. W. Gott for
   Blasphemy, The, 69, 94
Trial of Charles Southwell for Blasphemy,
   The, 29, 49
Trial of Theism, The, 45

Trial of the Reverend Robert Taylor
   . . . Upon a Charge of Blasphemy,
   50
Trial of Thomas Paterson for Blasphemy,
   The, 34, 48

Tribune, The, 124, 126
"Tribute to Joseph Symes, A," 134
True Gospel of Jesus Christ Asserted,
   The, 10, 15
True Intellectual System of the Universe,
   The, 4, 15
True Story of the Roman Catholic
   Church, The, 102, 117
Truthseeker, The [England], 69, 77,
   97, 100
Truthseeker, The [N.Z.], 125
Truth Seeker, The [New York], 69, 98,
   138, 141
Tryal of the Twelve Witnesses, The, 9,
   18
Twelve Years in a Monastery, 66, 92
"Twilight Thoughts," 119
"Two Contemporaries, The," 115

"Unbelievers, The," 165
Universal Despair, 71, 97
University Magazine and Free Review,
   89
Upanisads, 143

Value of Free Thought, The, 119
Varieties of Unbelief, xiv, xviii
Veritate, De, 3, 4, 16
Versuch einer Vollständingen
   engelländischen freydenker-
   bibliothek, xvi, xxii
Victoria Humanist, The [Australia], 133,
   135
Victorian Humanist, The [Canada], 138,
   141
Victorian Infidels, xiv, xxi, 66
Victorian Prose, 165
Viduthalai, 146, 152
View of the Principal Deistic Writers,
   A, 12, 17
Viewpoints, 133
Vikasam, 148, 152
Vita, Fatis et Scriptis Joannis Tolandi,
   De, 5, 17
Voltaire and the English Deists, 7, 19

Was Jesus an Imposter?, 70, 93
Watson Refuted, 41
Watts' Literary Guide, 92, 104
We Become Atheists, 146, 150
Westminster Review, The, 14
Westralian Secularist, The, 132, 135
What Humanism Is About, 110, 117
What Is the Use of Prayer?, 85
Why I am an Agnostic, 63, 96
Why I am a Socialist, 85
Why I am Not a Christian, 107, 119
Why I Dare Not Be a Christian, 72, 85

Why Should Atheists Be Persecuted?, 85
"Wollaston and His Critics," 16
Woman: Her Glory, Her Shame and Her God, 63, 96
Works of Lord Bolingbroke, With a Life, The, 11, 15
Writings of Thomas Paine, 42, 82

Yukthivadi, 147-48, 152
Yukthi Vicharanam, 148, 152

SUBJECT INDEX

Addenda, 165
Aeropagus, 38
Agnosticism: definition of, 167
Agnostics, xiii
American Philosophical Society, 158
Anticlericalism, 129, 139
Antideist works, 5, 12-13
Anti-Persecution Union, 37
Anti-Priestcraft Association, 147
Association Rationaliste du Québec,
    139
Atheism: definition of, 167
Atheist Centre (India), 146, 147, 159
Atheist Society of Australia, 132, 133
Atheist Society of India, 148
Auckland Rationalist Association, 124,
    125
Auckland Secular Society, 123
Austin and Company, 38
Australasian Secular Association, 130,
    131
Australia, 29, 70-71, 129-35

Bangladesh, 154
Barbados, 121
Barhaspatya, 143
Bermuda, 121
Bibliographies, xv, xvi
Biographical Dictionaries, xvi
Bishopsgate Institute, 158
Blasphemy, 24, 26, 28-29, 30, 33,
    34, 37, 61, 69, 73, 114
Bowman Case, 62, 101
Bradlaugh Bonner, A & H (publishers),
    107

Brahmins, 145
Brhaspati Sutra, 143
British Humanist Association, 113, 114
British Library, 158
British Secular League, 69, 80
British Secular Union, 59, 81

Canada, 60, 137-41
Canadian Secular Union, 138
Canterbury Freethought Association,
    124
Ceylon/Sri Landa, 153
Ceylon Rationalist Association, 153
Charvaka, 143
Cheap Reprints (RPA), 79
Columbia University, 157
Conway Hall, 94, 112, 113
Co-operative Movement, 31, 65
Co-operative Union Institute, 158
Cyprus, 121

Deism, xiii, xv, xvi, 5-19; definition of,
    167
Deist Clubs, 13
Dravidian Federation, 146
Dunedin Mutual Improvement
    Association, 123

Edinburgh Secular Society, 81
Elek Publishing Company, 112
Encyclopedias, xvi
Ethical Culture, xiii, 81-83

Fleet Street House, 37
Forder, R. (publisher), 78

Freethinkers: definition of, 167
Freethinkers, xiii
Freethought: definition of, 167
Freethought Association (N.Z.), 123
Freethought Association (S. Africa),
    154
Freethought Publishing Company, 59,
    77

Gambia, 154
General Freethought Association, 137
Ghana, 121
Glasgow Eclectic Institution, 81
Glossary, 167
Gora Society, 154

Halls of Science, 37, 80
Hetherington, H. (publisher), 32, 39
Hindu Freethought Union, 145
Holyoake & Company (publishers), 38,
    74
Hong Kong, 121
House of Lords, 101
Humanism: in Australia, 132; in Canada,
    138; definition of, 167; in N.Z.,
    125; in United Kingdom, 113
Humanist Association (Bangladesh),
    154
Humanist Society of New Zealand,
    125, 126
Huntington Library, 157

India, 143-52
Indian Humanist Union, 150
Indian Rationalist Association, 147,
    150, 152, 159
Indian Rationalist Convention, 148
Indian Renaissance Institute, 147
Indian Secular Forum, 147
Indian Secular Society, 147
Infidel: definition of, 167
Institut Canadien, 139
Ireland, 81

Jamaica, 121
John Street Institution, 37
Justice Party, 146

Kenya, 121
Knowlton Trial, 55, 57, 59, 62, 70

La Trobe Library, 158
Leicester Secular Society, 66, 80, 83
Liberal Association of New South
    Wales, 130
Library of Congress, 157
Lilly Library (Indiana University), 157
Lokayata, 143
London Atheistical Society, 37
London Secular Society, 37

Malaysia, 155
Malta, 121
Manchester Central Reference Library,
    158
Manitoba, University of, 159
Materialistic Thought, 143
Missionaries, 144
Mitchell Library, 158
Mouvement Laïque, 139
Myth Theory of Jesus, 68, 109

Nastika-mata, 143
National Library of Australia, 158
National Library of Wales, xix
National Secular Society (NSS), 46, 59,
    72, 75, 79, 80, 99, 100, 108,
    111, 154, 158
Newcastle Secular Society, 129
New York Public Library, 158
New Zealand, 29, 123-27
New Zealand Freethought Federal
    Union, 124
New Zealand Rationalist Society, 159
Nigeria, 155
Northampton Public Library, 158
North of England Secular Federation,
    80
Northwestern University, 157

Paragon Hall, 38
Parti Liberal, 139
Parti Rouge, 139
Pemberton Publishing Company, 106,
    112
Pioneer Freethought Club, 138
Pioneer Press, 111, 112
Pitman Publishing Group, 106, 110
Positivism, xiii, 83, 84; definition of,
    168
Progressive Publishing Company, 77

Radical Humanist Movement, 147
Rationalism: definition of, 168
Rationalist Association of India, 147
Rationalist Association of Johannesburg,
    154, 155
Rationalist Association of South Africa,
    154, 155
Rationalist Press Association (RPA),
    xvii, xx, 77, 78, 83, 99, 104, 110,
    118
Rationalist Society of Australia, 132,
    133
Rationalist Society of New South Wales,
    132, 134
Revolution Tranquile, 139
Rotunda, The, 38

Scottish Secular Union, 81
Secularism, xiii, 31, 65; definition of,
    168
Secular Publishing Company, 138
Secular Society of Victoria, 132
Self-Respect Movement, 145
Self-Respect Propaganda Institution,
    147
South Africa, 153
South African Humanist Association,
    154, 155
South Place Ethical Society, xvii, 83,
    113, 114, 158
South Place Religious Society, 81
Spiritualist and Freethought Pro-
    pagandist Association, 129

Sri Lanka. See Ceylon
Stewart, W. & Company (publishers),
    63, 78

Theosophical Society, 145, 158, 159
Theosophy, 58, 144
Theses and Dissertations, 161
Thetford Public Library, 158
Thinker's Library, 105, 111, 112
Thomas Paine Society, 112
Toronto Association of Freethinkers,
    137
Toronto Secular Society, 60, 137
Trinidad, 154
Truelove, E. (publisher), 74-75
Turnbull Library, 159

Union Theological Seminary, 157
Unitarians, xiii, 81, 82

Watson, J. (publisher), 34, 38
Watts & Company, 59, 78, 92, 102,
    110
Winnipeg Rationalist Society, 138
Wisconsin, University of, 158
World Atheist Conference, 148
World Union of Freethinkers, 107, 112

Yale University, 157

Zetetic Societies, 37, 81
Zimbabwe-Rhodesia, 121

ABOUT THE AUTHOR

GORDON STEIN is a physiologist and editor. His interest in freethought extends over fifteen years, and has resulted in one of the largest collections of freethought books in private hands. His earlier works include *Freethought in the United States* (with Marshall G. Brown, Greenwood Press, 1978), *An Anthology of Atheism and Rationalism*, and *Robert G. Ingersoll: A Checklist*.